THE ORDER OF MELCHIZEDEK TRILOGY: VOL I

The Order of Melchizedek

REDISCOVERING THE ETERNAL ROYAL PRIESTHOOD OF JESUS CHRIST AND HOW IT AFFECTS THE CHURCH AND MARKETPLACE!

The LORD hath sworn ... Thou art a priest for ever after the order of Melchizedek (Psalm 110:4 KJV).

DR. FRANCIS MYLES

Published by
Francis Myles International
P.O. Box 2467
Scottsdale, AZ 85252

For Worldwide Distribution
Printed in the USA

ISBN 978-0-61587-931-4

1 2 3 4 5 6 7 8 9 10 / 12 11 10 09

Acknowledgments

W HAT WE BECOME IN GOD is a sum total of the divine encounters we have had, the people we have met, our experiences, and the books we have read. The saying "No man is an island" is certainly true in the context of authoring this book. I want to acknowledge the impact that the following men and women of God have had on my life: Dr. Jonathan David (my father in the faith), Apostle Harrison Chileshe (my pastor), Apostle John Eckhardt (who introduced me to the apostolic), Dr. John P. Kelly (who commissioned me as an apostle), Dr Tim Johns, Apostle Robert Ricciardelli, Prophet Kevin Leal (my big brother), Pastor Frank Rosenstein (my business partner), Dr. G.E. Bradshaw (my covenant brother), Danny Seay (who has become a living example of this book's message) Larry Favalora (for being a true Joseph), Bishop Robert Smith (who introduced me to the message on the One New Man), Dr Jay Simms, Dr. Paula Price, Apostles Greg Howse, Trevor Banks, Pam Vinnett and Cheryl Fortson—their teachings and personal conversations with me over the years have added to the richness of this book.

While the material in this book is original, there are a few quotes throughout that have been taken from the published works of other notable Christian authors, which add depth to the topic or focus. Each is documented in the Endnote section.

Hall of Appreciation

"The Lord gave the word: great was the company of those that published it" (Psalm 68:11 KJV).

I T HAS BEEN SAID that great projects are never the work of one man, but the collective effort of a *team that shares a common destiny*. I want to give a heartfelt "God bless you" to the following brothers and sisters for making the publishing of this book a reality. May God give you a tremendous harvest for every person who will be transformed by the truths contained within.

My parents, Daniel and Ester Mbepa, for raising me in the fear of the Lord

Dr. Jesse Bielby

Pastor David Brace

Carmela Real Myles for being the love of my life and an amazing glue and connector for God's Kingdom

Morris and Blanch Hershbeger, Harrisonville, Missouri

Larry Scott, Castries, St. Lucia

Danny and Diane Seay, Lenexa, Kansas

Jack and Anna Hersma, Kansas City, Missouri

Breakthrough City School of the Prophets

Joe Frazier, Little Rock, Arkansas

Kyle Newton, Rob Moss, Robert Sproat, Jeff McHarton, Jeff Arias and all my K-300 brothers

Members of Full Gospel Foundation Building Ministries, Bloomfield, Connecticut

Endorsements

I enjoyed the Melchizedek blessing because it is so practical first of all. I love things that are practical and work. This truly works. And yet Pastor Myles has a way of introducing this material that makes it interesting. Its really heavy material but he brings it down in a way I can understand it and be inspired by it. Not just be inspired but to implement it in my life. In realizing the role that we all have as prophets, priests and kings unto God. That we are all in that Melchizedek Order, it's not exclusive, and obviously there is a price to walk in it. But It's not just a matter of exclusivism, its open to everybody. Isn't that wonderful? I can have that Melchizedek blessing and I do everyday. I pray for it. It is at the top of my prayer list everyday, I say, "Lord let me be like Melchizedek! Let me have that anointing and all the good things that go with it." The most incredible thing that I have ever witnessed is this teaching on the DNA and spiritual heritage, because it is really the answer to about what many people are having questions about. And you really have come into the plane of practicality about this issue. Concerning the healing of the DNA and deliverance from Generational Curses, that Francis teaches in his book, "Breaking Generational Curses Under the Order of Melchizedek" is really the most incredible thing I have ever heard relating to this subject.

—Dr. Ralph and Eileen Wilkerson
Founders of Melodyland Christian Center
Anaheim, California

Jesus asked a very penetrating question to His disciples saying, "Who do men say that I am?" Their answer reflected the common points of view and philosophies of the day, "Some say John the Baptist, some Elijah and others Jeremiah or one of the prophets."

As then so today our need to know who Jesus is must be addressed directly—Jesus asked "Who do you say that I am?" This is not a matter of debate nor philosophy but of revelation. Simon Peter answered and said, "You are the Christ, the Son of the Living God." Through the revelation given to Dr. Francis Myles in "The Order of Melchizedek" our eyes, like Simon Peter are opened to who Melchizedek is and how his life interfaces with ours nearly three thousand years after he walked the earth. For any who are seeking God, "The Order of Melchizedek" is compelling reading. Dr. Myles book is practical in addressing issues in ones individual life, marriage, the church, the marketplace and yes even in our society. The age old truths spoken of from the pages of the Bible and brought to life by Dr. Myles' straight forward writing style are sure to cause you to want to answer the question Jesus posed for your own life. I highly recommend this book to believer and seeker alike.

—Pastor Tom Deuschle
Founder and Senior Pastor,
Celebration Ministries International

Run, don't walk, to buy this book, and do it now. The last chapter alone is worth the price of the entire book. I devoured it in one weekend, despite it being full of meat throughout. *The Order of Melchizidek* is full of fresh revelation and nuggets of truth. This is a seminal work from a seasoned apostle and, depending on your perspective, either the missing piece or the capstone of the marketplace canon. I sense we have found the headwaters of a new river...Deep calls unto deep.

—Dr. Bruce Cook
Founder, K.E.Y.S. Summit, Leander, TX

Each of us is called to live as a son or daughter of our Father. Dr Francis Myles helps us understand why living under The Order of Melchizedek allows us to fulfill this destiny for each of us. This book will help you understand and apply the power of this truth.

Os Hillman
President, Marketplace Leaders;
Author, *The 9 to 5 Window* and *TGIF Today God Is First*

Dr. Myles has given us permission to step into our greatness by uncovering the truth about the priestly order of Melchizedek. He shows us how we as Christians are both kings and priests in the mission or purpose in our lives and he shows us how to walk in that purpose with our Royalty as a king and our relationship with Father God as a priest. I thoroughly enjoyed this book and have applied it in my life, in my business and in my purpose. "Awaken the Sleeper"!

—Nick Castellano,
President, Business Mentorship International, Mesa, AZ

This book unfolds a strategic revelation for this hour. Understanding that every believer is a part of the Order of Melchizedek provides a solid biblical basis for all Christians to function in both kingly and priestly roles. This is not about ancient history; it is about future marketplace and societal engagement. A must read for those who desire to advance the cause of Christ!

—Dr. Berin Gilfillan
CEO, International School of Ministry
San Bernardino/Redlands, CA

This subject of Melchizedek is so relevent to an understanding of the marketplace, kings and priests, and the last days that it was just a matter of time till someone wrote the book. I am glad Francis answered the call! He has an incredibily fresh and profound grasp of the matter and presents it in a way that is easy to grasp without forfeiting any of the depth surrounding the mystery of this ancient priest and his order.

—Dr. Lance Wallnau
President, Lance Learning

Table of Contents

Foreword

Many followers of Christ are experiencing a divinely inspired restless agitation directed at institutional Christianity. The Holy Spirit is motivating a high level of discomfort to prod believers out of the seducing influences of the Christian religion. Unfortunately, most of us have deficient coaching on what to do and where to go next. We know what we don't want, tempting us to live in reaction to what is bad. We are prone to harshly judge the Christian religious system, but then we become judged as we have judged and find ourselves being religiously irreligious. Now, due to our pride, we are in even graver danger. What we need is a positive description of what we want and need—Christ and the Kingdom of God. We need teaching and coaching on the prophetic promises of God that describe who we are as "kings and priests" in the order of Melchizedek. Dr. Myles does a wonderful job illuminating this amazing capacity we have to be priests, prophets, and kings who reign with Christ, bringing His Kingdom on earth as it is in Heaven. I highly commend this exciting book to all who want to appropriate all the promises of God that have been purchased through Christ's shed blood. The profound implications of this teaching will revolutionize your life!

—Dr. Timothy M. Johns
Founder & Apostolic Leader of the
Rock International "Tribe"
Kansas City, Missouri

Apostle Paul, one of God's greatest custodians of divine truth, wrote these words in the book of Hebrews 5:10-11 KJV concerning Jesus Christ, "Called of God an high priest after the order of Melchisedec. Of whom we have many things to say, and hard to be uttered, seeing ye are dull of hearing."

Paul also wrote these intriguing words in Hebrews 7:11-12 KJV, "If therefore perfection were by the Levitical priesthood, (for under it the people received the law,) what further need was there that another priest should rise after the order of Melchisedec, and not be called after the order of Aaron? For the priesthood being changed, there is made of necessity a change also of the law."

Why was this information so vital? Why was it so relevant to the church? Why did God fashion the ministry of Jesus Christ after the order of Melchizedek? These questions can best be answered by the facts presented in Hebrews 7:11-12. There was "of necessity a change also of the law," because God had developed a newer and greater "technology" by which to execute this great mandate of divine relationship between Himself and His people. A *priesthood* of greater and more expanded dimensions and diversity had to appear. This priesthood carried the "quantum dynamics" of supernatural power! The dynamics of this truth would carry God's people further than ever before...once it is revealed!

My covenant brother, Apostle Dr. Francis Myles, has become one of God's present-day custodians of the divine and supernatural truth of *The Order of Melchizedek–Rediscovering the Eternal Priesthood of Jesus Christ and How It Affects Us Today*. I believe that the global Church is about to get the awakening that it has never had before concerning this great spiritual pattern. The tremendous grace and blessing that will cover entire congregations and networks because of this technology cannot be emphasized enough!

Dr. Myles has dissected this great truth with the precision of a neurosurgeon. He has inspected the "psychology" of this truth like a master analyst, and has inspected the flow and the details of this subject with forensic aptitude! He has left no stone unturned in the explanation of this illuminating truth.

I highly suggest every believer read this book—it is definitely recommended rhema!

—Dr. G.E. Bradshaw
Presiding Apostle
Global Effect Ministries Network
Dolton, Illinois

Dr. Francis Myles has written a wonderful new book entitled *The Order of Melchizedek*. I found it to be a very challenging book to our own religious mindset. We live in a day when the Holy Spirit is bringing fresh insight and revelation to the Body of Christ.

When I began reading this book, I was challenged in every chapter to deal with old wineskin thinking. Dr. Myles' teaching on King David certainly brought a freshness of David's life to me. On reading the chapter on Melchizedek, I realized that many of us are operating under law instead of grace.

In these days of Kingdom advancement, *The Order of Melchizedek* is a book that will bring the Body of Christ into the new day. I believe this book needs to be in the hands of every minister who is willing to go to the next level. I highly recommend you read *The Order of Melchizedek* with an open heart and mind.

—Dr. Bob Lemon

Harvest Fire International, Inc.

Canton, MI

"I believe one of the next great moves of God is going to be through the believers in the workplace." —Dr. Billy Graham

I can say I wholeheartedly agree with Dr. Graham's statement. Having served as a youth pastor and then associate pastor for several years and now serving the Lord full-time through my entrepreneurial endeavors, I'm seeing the division between the sacred and the secular finally dissolve.

In Germany it took decades for the wall that divided East Berlin and West Berlin to come down, so too, was it a long-fought and often painful journey for me and my family to find peace as we tried to make sense of the division between Church and the Marketplace and finally to bring unity between both vital parts of our lives.

In the early days of our experience of the "wall of separation" we, like those who snuck over, under and around the wall as they escaped to West Berlin, would make "trips" into the Entrepreneurial World while carrying with us a nagging fear that we were somehow forfeiting a higher, more sacred calling and also positioning ourselves at least for Divine displeasure and at worst, Kingdom deportation.

We had been "indoctrinated" by Institutional Christianity that the five-fold ministry gifts were the supreme calling and everything else was second class. Even worse, story after story would be recounted to us that those who had "jumped the wall" and crossed over to the secular world of the marketplace had lost their faith, family and even at times, their lives. It is thus, no wonder, as we made our journey to full-time Marketplace Ministry we did so with much fear and trembling.

It has been over a decade now that we made our initial journey and we have lived and not died. Not only have we lived but we have prospered, even as our souls and spirits have prospered as we have potentially impacted more lives for the Gospel of the Kingdom than possibly we could have ever touched in our previous calling.

Yet, this new land of "Marketplace Ministry" is still somewhat undefined and as of yet not fully explored. As more people awaken to the concept of Business as a Mission and Marketplace Ministry our numbers are growing but so too is the need for a clarion call of order, guidance and direction for this rediscovered expression of His Body.

I praise God on a regular basis that Dr. Myles has rediscovered and encapsulated in this work the technology of the Order of Melchizedek. For me, *The Order of Melchizedek* is the clarion call that I was searching for and is one of those books you leave on your desk as a hand book and resource for defining and executing your calling as a marketplace leader and minister.

This message has clarified for me in crystal clear language that God is not just the Father of the Church but also the Father of the Marketplace and the King-Priests who serve there each day in their jobs or entrepreneurial endeavors.

Since being introduced to this book and this Order, my life, businesses and passions have accelerated at a supernatural pace. At one end of the spectrum we have the Father's love for us that is so great that He sent his only Son to us to make a way for us. He is always pressing in to seek and save that which is lost and desiring that none should perish and that all would come into the fullness of the Gospel of the Kingdom. On the other end of the spectrum is the heart of man that, whether he knows it or not, has a vacuum that desires to draw God in and fill the void with His love and grace. *The Order of Melchizedek* is literally a spiritual technology and conduit connecting the God of Heaven with the heart of man on Earth.

Be prepared that when you read this book and embrace the Order, you are stepping into a supernatural channel that connects Heaven and Earth and within it flows a mighty wind that will help propel you into abundant Kingdom living!

After reading this book and embracing the Order, I want to encourage you to join me and thousands of other Melchizedeks around the world in the phenomenal Kingdom Community (www.MyKCMPortal.com) that Dr. Myles has provided for you to continue your journey in the Order..

—Kyle Newton
Founder of Tribus
www.iTribus.com

Preface

If it's at all possible for God to think thoughts, then we must assume that whenever God thought His first thought, He thought all thoughts in the "One thought," since He has always been all knowing!

—Saint Pregorias, an early church father

THE GREAT KING DAVID is a biblical character who never ceases to amaze me. His heart of an uninhibited passion for God both fascinates and challenges me. His ability to repent quickly whenever God convicted him of any sin in his life has also challenged me on many occasions. The life of this great king of Israel underscores what is possible in our walk with God, when we provide the necessary ingredients for establishing an intimate walk with the Lord. David's intimate walk with the Lord turned him into what Bishop Tudor Bismark calls a "dimensionalist." According to Bishop Bismark, a dimensionalist is a person who has a keen prophetic insight to perceive what God has already done in the heavenly realms who also has the grace to allow what God is showing them to alter their present spiritual experience.[1]

Unfortunately the ongoing dilemma of being a dimensionalist is that you are constantly living between "two worlds or two time frames." As a dimensionalist, you are usually caught between the present order of things and what God has in store for His people in the future. The dilemma of being a dimensionalist is further compounded by the fact that God has no measurable past or future. God exists in an *eternal state of NOW!* Everything with God is *NOW!*

For those of us who are trapped in *time,* the past, present, or future is always separated into different and separate time frames. We must remember that God is the One who created the cylinder of *time* but He exists outside it. God is not bound to time, either.

Since God exists in an *eternal state of NOW,* it therefore follows that His eternal work of creation, restoration, and renovation was *finished* before the fall of Lucifer and the fall of humankind. The Bible even goes further to suggest that Christ was the Lamb of God who was *slain before the foundation of the world.* This means that *time* is a spiritual instrument God uses to systematically and progressively manifest in *time* His finished *work.*

> *Declaring the end from the beginning, and from ancient times*
> *the things that are not yet done, saying, My counsel shall stand,*
> *and I will do all my pleasure* (Isaiah 46:10 KJV).

Based on our comprehension of this divine principle, it therefore follows that if we are able to prophetically see the finished work of God in a future time frame and are able to draw the grace of that particular time frame into our present, we can begin to experience the *future in the NOW.* The power and benefits of what God intends to do in the future for His people *who are trapped in time* will be made readily available to us. It is quite obvious as to why many dimensionalists like King David are so misunderstood and persecuted during their lifetime. Many people cannot handle those who are able to *touch the future in the NOW.* Jesus Christ was also very misunderstood. He was persecuted viciously by the religious leaders of His day because He was the Master Dimensionalist.

> *At about that time Jesus was walking through some grainfields*
> *on the Sabbath. His disciples were hungry, so they began break-*
> *ing off some heads of grain and eating them. But some Pharisees*
> *saw them do it and protested, "Look, your disciples are breaking*
> *the law by harvesting grain on the Sabbath." Jesus said to them,*
> *"Haven't you read in the Scriptures what David did when he*
> *and his companions were hungry? He went into the house of*
> *God, and he and his companions broke the law by eating the*
> *sacred loaves of bread that only the priests are allowed to eat.*
> *And haven't you read in the law of Moses that the priests on*

duty in the Temple may work on the Sabbath? I tell you, there is one here who is even greater than the Temple! But you would not have condemned my innocent disciples if you knew the meaning of this Scripture: 'I want you to show mercy, not offer sacrifices'" (Matthew 12:1-7).

Jesus did and also allowed His disciples to do things on the Sabbath that the disciples of the Pharisees and Sadducees were not allowed to do under the Old Testament Levitical priestly order. For instance, Jesus healed people on the Sabbath but the religious order of His era believed that no one should be healed on the Sabbath. Being a prophet of God and a dimensionalist, King David peeped into God's *eternal state of NOW* and overheard a very exciting conversation within the Godhead. In this conversation, the heavenly Father was making a pledge to His begotten Son, even our Lord Jesus Christ. The heavenly Father was bequeathing a priestly mantle upon his begotten Son that was not functional in the nation of Israel during King David's era.

King David, like most Jewish people of his era, was living under the priestly Order of Aaron, or what is commonly known as the Levitical priesthood. To his utter amazement, the conversation he overheard within the Godhead made no mention of the Levitical priesthood. To the contrary, King David heard the heavenly Father make a decree that His Son Jesus Christ was an eternal High Priest after the Order of Melchizedek. Under this eternal priestly order, King David realized that the High Priest was operating from a sanctuary not *"made with human hands."* David also saw that under this priestly Order of Melchizedek there was no veil of flesh or clothing that stood between the presence of God and His covenant people.

The LORD hath sworn ... thou art a priest for ever after the order of Melchizedek (Psalm 110:4 KJV).

This revelation radically affected King David, so much that he reorganized the structure of the Tabernacle of Moses. In the Tabernacle of Moses there was a thick veil of clothing that separated the holy place from the Holy of Holies and only once a year could the high priest enter the Holy of Holies. The general public's access to the presence of God was restricted to the outer court. The penalty for overstepping these boundaries of restriction was instant death. *These restrictions caused many worshippers under the Levitical priesthood to go into a state of panic whenever they felt like they were getting too close to the presence of God.*

But when King David discovered the priestly Order of Melchizedek through the spirit of revelation, what he saw in the heavens completely changed His life and his perception of the person of God. David discovered by the spirit of illumination that in this higher and eternal priestly order, God does not want any boundaries of restriction between His presence and His covenant people. Based upon this powerful revelation, King David created a new prophetic structure of worship that was not patterned after the Levitical priestly order. King David's new structure of prophetic worship came to be known as the *Tabernacle of David.*

Under the Tabernacle of David, King David placed the Ark of the Covenant under one tent, but removed all man-made barriers between the Ark of God's presence and the people who came to worship God. Under the Tabernacle of David there was an atmosphere of *ongoing worship and intercession* and there was absolutely no barrier between the worshippers and the Ark of God's presence. What's more, nobody died under the Tabernacle of David for coming too close to the presence of God Almighty. This was nothing short of spectacular.

I am very sure that King David's new structure of worship must have bothered many of the Levitical priests and frightened many worshippers who had been raised in a priestly system that made approaching the presence of God a frightening experience. Nevertheless, the Tabernacle of David was a stunning success. It transformed *distant worshippers* who were terrified of intimate contact with the glory of God's presence, into *intimate worshippers.* By revelation, King David had managed to bring His people into a new day under a new Order of Priesthood. God used King David's ability as a dimensionalist to give the people of the Old Testament era a taste of the heavenly priestly Order of Melchizedek that was yet to come in its fullness with the advent of our Lord Jesus Christ.

This book will reintroduce many in the global Church to the present day reality of the priestly Order of Melchizedek. The underlying intent is to show and demonstrate the superiority of the priestly Order of Melchizedek over the Old Testament Levitical priesthood and how this royal priesthood affects us today. *The objective of this writing is to help the Body of Christ rediscover the eternal priesthood of Jesus Christ and how this revelation impacts our ability to advance God's Kingdom here on earth.*

Explained is how the sacrament of Holy Communion demonstrates the spiritual power of the sacred bread and wine that are the eternal emblems of the priestly Order of Melchizedek. We will trace the sacrament of Holy Communion back to Abraham's first encounter with Melchizedek, the king of Salem and High Priest of God Most High. There is also a very surgical attempt to show how rediscovering the priestly Order of Melchizedek impacts the technology of tithing in the Body of Christ. Also revealed is how the Order of Melchizedek affects the future of the Jewish nation—the natural descendants of Abraham, plus much more!

Yours for Kingdom advancement,

—Dr. Francis Myles
Founder and Chairman of the Board: Kingdom Marketplace Coalition Inc.
Founder and Chairman of the Board: The Order of Melchizedek
Leadership University
Senior Pastor, Breakthrough City Kingdom Embassy, McKinney, Texas

CHAPTER ONE

The Death of Institutional Christianity

I F YOU ARE EVER IN KANSAS CITY, please do yourself a favor and go to Jack Stack Barbeque restaurant—loosen your belt buckle and just eat! I promise that you will feel like you have died and gone to heaven. Awhile back a dear friend, Danny Seay, invited my wife and me to meet with his spiritual mentor at Jack Stack Barbeque. Those ribs were heavenly! But as much as I enjoyed the food, my prophetic conversation with Dr. Tim Johns about the Kingdom of God and the Order of Melchizedek kept me completely captivated. The more we talked and shared notes about the Kingdom of God, the more we felt like we were being airlifted into God's glory zone.

The heavenly Father continued to flood us with revelation about issues related to the Kingdom of God, when we noticed that the restaurant was about to close. We decided to continue our passionate discussion outside. As soon as we stepped out of the restaurant, we walked into a portal of God's glory that was almost overwhelming. Dr. Tim Johns began to prophesy over me and Danny Seay. While he was prophesying, the Lord dropped a very explosive impression in my spirit.

I heard the words *the death of Institutional Christianity;* they rose powerfully in my spirit. I said, "Lord what are You trying to tell me?" The Lord replied quickly, "I am killing the Christian religion so that I can move My people into the Kingdom. You must include a chapter in your book on the Order of Melchizedek titled 'The Death of Institutional Christianity'!" As you can see, I obeyed the Lord, but it was no easy task because the religion of Christianity has done much good in our world and is the largest and fastest growing religion on our troubled planet. I dare not awaken the wrath of those who worship the Christian religion! It is NOT my intent to either diminish or demonize the Christian religion; but the Lord wants to circumcise that aspect of Christianity that has become institutional and completely counter productive to the advancement of the Kingdom of God. Christianity itself was NEVER meant to become a mere religion; so in essence this chapter will save "Christianity" itself from man made and demonically engineered "Trojan Horses" that have invaded its corporate expression. Christ and His Kingdom MUST take center stage again in the global and corporate expression of the Christian Faith!

Compared to many world religions, Christianity is one of the most peaceful religions even though its past history is marred with periods of religious intolerance and violence, which is explored in a later chapter. Christianity's deep belief in the Bible as the infallible Word of God makes it the best religion for those who have not yet been awakened to the message of the Kingdom. I have no personal negative feelings toward Christianity as a whole, except to say that like every religion, it fails to bring men and women into a genuine Kingdom experience and lifestyle.

My Time in the Christian Religion

Before you accuse me of sacrilege or undermining Christianity, I will explain why I lost confidence in the Christian religion and how I discovered the message of the Kingdom and the powerful spiritual dynamics that are imbedded in the joy of Kingdom living.

I was born in Central Africa to parents who were staunch and committed Roman Catholic Christians. I was told daily that I was a Roman Catholic Christian. My father told me that the Catholic Church was the only true church. He told me that all other Christian churches were simply in rebellion to the true church. I was convinced that I was a Christian because I never missed mass, even though I lived like the devil's first cousin most of the time. This was before I knew that I needed to be born again in order to enter into the Kingdom of God.

When I came to the saving knowledge of Jesus Christ, I was told by those who led me to the Lord that I was still a Christian, but now I was a "born-again Christian." After a few months I joined a church in Zambia (Africa), where I was told that I was now a "born-again-Pentecostal Christian." I was warned against fellowshipping with "Baptist Christians" because they did not speak in tongues like we did. Even more serious and sinister, I was told never to talk to the idol-worshipping Roman Catholic Christians. I was advised to avoid them like a plague.

A few months later I became part of a church that believed in and practiced the nine gifts of the Spirit. I was told almost instantaneously that I was now a "Charismatic Christian." I was also told that I really had to be careful not to fellowship too much with the "Pentecostal Christians" because the power of God was upon the Charismatic Christians. After awhile I became part of another Christian organization who identified themselves as "Prophetic Christians" because they believed in the operation of the gift of prophecy. This group was even more reclusive and exclusive. They exhibited an air of superiority over the other "uninformed" Christian churches who did not function in the prophetic.

For me, these spiritual transitions were quite unsettling because they made me increasingly aware of just how deeply divided the Christian religion really is. I couldn't understand why so many Christian groups who believed in the same Lord (Jesus Christ) could be so deeply divided. This created a holy frustration in my spirit that forced me to look for a "more excellent way" of living and expressing my new found faith in Christ Jesus. Unknown to me at the time was the fact that these divisive chasms between different Christian denominations are typical of all religions.

TWO CLASSES OF CHRISTIANS

Within the Christian religion there seems to be two main classes of Christian groups:

1. nominal Christians
2. committed or born-again Christians

There are several categories within the nominal Christian group. In the New Testament there were Gentile Christians who wanted to integrate their pagan sinful activities into the Christian life, and there were Jewish Christians who demanded Christians follow the Law of Moses and be circumcised in addition to believing in Christ for salvation. There was also the Epicurean type of Christian who believed that the flesh was naturally evil and uncontrollable and therefore allowed no restrictions to the fulfillment of their fleshly desires. The Ascetic type of Christian concluded that the physical body was inherently evil with all of its physical desires, and so they overly restricted themselves and others. Generally, nominal Christians believe in Christ but are not really born again. For most of these nominal Christians, salvation is always in the future and never in the present. Roman Catholic and Christian Science Christians are classic examples of this group. However, there are many Roman Catholic Christians who would take serious offense to being labeled as nominal Christians.

The second group of Christians consists of committed or born-again believers. As the name suggests, this second group of Christians pride themselves in having a more committed personal relationship with Christ. This second group of Christians believes in the born-again experience. They believe that the eternal salvation of the soul takes place the moment a person confesses Christ as their personal Lord and Savior. This group believes that they receive eternal life the moment they receive Christ into their heart. But this second group of Christians is as divided as the first group. This group of committed Christians consists of mostly Evangelicals, Pentecostals, Charismatics, Prophetic, Apostolic, and Fundamentalists, just to name a few. The doctrinal divides between these groups are deep and far reaching. Many behave more like corporate competitors rather than brothers and sisters in Christ.

> But when the Pharisees heard this, they said, "It is only by Beelzebub, the prince of demons, that this fellow drives out demons." Jesus knew their thoughts and said to them, "Every kingdom divided against itself will be ruined, and every city or household divided against itself will not stand. If Satan drives out Satan, he is divided against himself. How then can his kingdom stand? And if I drive out demons by Beelzebub, by whom do your people drive them out? So then, they will be your judges.

*But if I drive out demons by the Spirit of God, then the kingdom
of God has come upon you"* (Matthew 12:24-28 NIV).

In this passage, Jesus Christ made it very clear that the Kingdom of God is
not divided, just like the devil's kingdom is also not divided. In the Kingdom
of God, God does not have two classes or groups of Kingdom citizens. You are
either in the Kingdom of God and under its sovereign government or you are
not. *The Kingdom is not as divided as Christianity is.* This is why the unity of the
Spirit will return to the New Testament Church as more and more born-again
believers walk out of the Christian religion and into the Kingdom. The global
Church will soon become more concerned about *seeking God's Kingdom and
all of His righteousness* than debating who is more doctrinally sound. These are
the days of the *Kingdom age.* God is supernaturally awakening the passion for
His Kingdom in the spirits of all of His children.

Jesus said something profound in *Luke 11:17 KJV...*

*"...every kingdom divided against itself is brought to desolation;
and a house divided against a house falleth."*

In order to truly understand the application of this text we must define
the term *"divided."* It comes from the Greek word *Diamerizo,* meaning: *To
partition thoroughly.* In other words, when a kingdom is divided or *partitioned
thoroughly* against itself, it has developed a series of separate identities which
eventually *war* against the concept of the whole identity of the kingdom or
house. The example of both a "kingdom" and a "house" were used in this illustration because they both share the same spiritual architecture or *DNA* as far
as how they reproduce and survive. Kingdoms and family lineages or "houses"
thrive through the continuity of their proper identities, cultures, governmental
strengths and vision. When a kingdom or house is divided, the main culture
by which the house or lineage is to function is fragmented into many different
sub-cultures that distract from the energy of the main culture (Kingdom culture) and its proper identity.

It is easy for spiritual sub-cultures to develop within the body of Christ that
can eventually overpower the main culture (Kingdom culture) and purpose of
God. It happens all of the time. Groups of believers are always subject to the
enemy called "division." This enemy seeks to develop a sub-culture within the
mainstream group by creating differences of priorities and vision. This is why

God is initiating the death of institutional Christianity, which has become a powerful machinery for producing spiritual subcultures that are competing with the establishment of the culture of the Kingdom in His Church. These spiritual sub-cultures must give way to Kingdom culture before they become the "Trojan Horse" that destroys the work of the Kingdom from the inside out!

ALL RELIGIONS ARE THE SAME

All religions are the same in the sense that they attempt to answer the questions of power and meaning. They all promise power to control life and circumstances and to explain life and death. They all claim to have the truth. They all claim superiority over each other. They all compare and compete with each other. They all demand adherence to their particular belief system while denying others. They all are motivated by contention and usually thrive in an isolated culture that excludes other segments of humanity. In fact, all religions seem to glory in a spirit of segregation and separatism. Rather than uniting humanity with common power and knowledge of purpose, religion has proven itself instead to be the great divider of mankind.[1]

For ye are yet carnal: for whereas there is among you envying, and strife, and divisions, are ye not carnal, and walk as men? For while one saith, I am of Paul; and another, I am of Apollos; are ye not carnal? Who then is Paul, and who is Apollos, but ministers by whom ye believed, even as the Lord gave to every man? (1 Corinthians 3:3-5 KJV)

In the transitions that I made from one group of the Christian faith to the other, I discovered that these divisive chasms between different Christian denominations were rooted in matters of doctrine. The side of the divide you find yourself on is predicated by the doctrine(s) that you are willing to believe. Consequentially, *these doctrinal divides become extremely powerful "chambers of containment"* that aid the clergy (the power brokers) in making sure that their followers do not cross over to the other side and fellowship with "those other Christians" who do not believe what they believe! Never mind that these born-again believers who are *trapped* in these *doctrinal chambers of containment* erected by the clergy are all Kingdom citizens who belong to one Lord and King—Jesus Christ!

The more I studied the spiritual dynamics of these doctrinal chambers of containment within the Christian religion, the more I discovered a very disturbing trend. Doctrinal chambers of containment ultimately lead to the formation of very strong spiritual subcultures. *These spiritual subcultures ultimately rob Kingdom citizens of their real God-given spiritual identity and quarantine the proper expression of the Kingdom in their lives.* Spiritual subcultures brainwash and reprogram Kingdom citizens into thinking and behaving more like Baptist, Pentecostal, Charismatic, or Fundamentalist Christians rather than citizens of the Kingdom of Heaven! The Lord Jesus Christ is putting an end to this foolishness and *pre-empting* the power of these doctrines of containment by killing the Christian religion worldwide!

WHY IS CHRISTIANITY DYING IN EUROPE?

"Christianity is nearly dead in Europe, where only 1-3 percent of the population identifies themselves as Christian. The Christian religion is being replaced by another more aggressive religion— Islam. What does Europe, the United States, and the rest of the world need? Do we need more religion, even if it's the Christian religion? Absolutely not! The earth needs the Lordship of Christ, His powerful, compassionate kingly rule over all of life—a paradigm shift from religion into the Kingdom of God. We need the reclaiming of Christ's Kingdom all over the world."[2]

For many who worship the Christian religion, the death of Institutional Christianity in Europe is a frightening fact. I thought so too until the Lord corrected my perspective. The Lord showed me that Institutional Christianity has become the *biggest obstacle* to the advancement and spreading of the gospel of the Kingdom. The spiritual subcultures that have mushroomed within the Christian religion are keeping many Kingdom citizens from *coming together* around our *common destiny and spiritual ancestry.*

It is interesting to note that the Lord has allowed Institutional Christianity to die in Europe of all places. Students of history know that Europe is the birthplace of modern-day Christianity. God wants to kill the Christian religion at the source so He can reintroduce Europe and the rest of the world to the gospel of the Kingdom. *The death of the Christian religion does not mean that Christianity as a religion will cease to exist.* It simply means that the influence of the Christian religion over the affairs of nations will continue to slide downhill, *while the influence of the Kingdom of God will continue to explode.* The Prophet Daniel's vision of a *"stone cut without hands"* growing all over Europe is about to come to pass. *The fire of the gospel of the Kingdom shall replace the dying embers of the Christian religion in Europe! Transitioning from institutional Christianity to the Kingdom is the greatest spiritual transition of our time.*

Historically, politics has played more of a role in the formation of world religions than the voice of God has. People developed religious systems based upon the opportunity that religion provides to control the lives and lands of others. Christianity in Europe and elsewhere was no different.

The organized Christian religion began to develop strongholds over territories and people. Monarchies, dictatorships, and other forces began to develop their own belief systems and denominations were born. Thirteen major theological systems formed over the years to influence how Christianity and the Bible were to be interpreted.

The thirteen religious systems are as follows:

1. Traditional Roman Catholic Theology

2. Natural Theology

3. Lutheran Theology

4. Anabaptist Theology

5. Reformed Theology

6. Arminian Theology

7. Wesleyan Theology

8. Liberal Theology

9. Existential Theology

10. Neo-orthodox Theology

11. Liberation Theology

12. Black Theology

13. Feminist Theology[3]

With the influence of so many cultural and geographic dynamics, it is almost impossible for the origins of God to remain untainted by the conglomerate mix of human ideologies and opinions. Needless to say, these theological formats have influenced the original doctrinal system of Christianity in ways that have both tainted and twisted the plan of God for His Church, whether intentionally or not. Various interpretations on matters of faith, which are based more on the intellectual assessment of the leaders of the faith than on revelation knowledge and the inspiration of the Holy Spirit, have contributed to a difficult scenario when it comes to the necessities of what is truly required to satisfy the heart of God.

CHRISTIANITY IN THE LIGHT OF HISTORY

Then Barnabas went to Tarsus to look for Saul, and when he found him, he brought him to Antioch. So for a whole year, Barnabas and Saul met with the church and taught great numbers of people. The disciples were called Christians first at Antioch. During this time some prophets came down from Jerusalem to Antioch (Acts 11:25-27 NIV).

What and who is a Christian? Let's examine the first and only biblical account in Acts 11:25-26 where this title was born. According to Unger's Bible Handbook, the term *Christiani (partisans of Christ)* was probably an official name for Jesus' disciples given by Roman officials at Antioch. Certain historical accounts imply that the title was meant to be derogatory, a mockery of Christ and His followers. The term *Christians* means "little Christs." It is no wonder the Church has remained small and marginalized in the eyes of the world with a name that we chose to identify ourselves with since the Roman Emperor Constantine made Christianity the official religion of Rome.

God desires His Church—the Body of Christ—to come into the "full stature of the Son of God" (see Ephesians 4:12), but the Church keeps

canceling this powerful process of ascension into complete Kingdom dominion by calling ourselves *little Christs* (Christians). There is no biblical account
of any command from God through any of the prophets or apostles that would
suggest that born-again believers should be called Christians. Therefore the
term *Christian* has no direct sovereign mandate. Paul the apostle, who is the
primary custodian of New Testament doctrine, never used the term once (in
the original Hebrew version of the Bible), even though he constantly used the
word "saints" to describe born-again believers. Furthermore, of all the names
the Bible uses to describe born-again believers in the New Testament, the
name "Christians" is the only one that was coined by the world.

What was intended by God to be a lifestyle of divine relationships and
interactions with humankind (Kingdom living) soon became a point of leverage and control for the power brokers of the world system and the kingdoms
they served. Emperor Constantine was one of the first politicians to realize how
his political aspirations could be well-served by aligning himself with the disciples of Christ, while neutralizing their godly influence by making Christianity
the official religion of the Roman Empire. By making Christianity the national
religion, Constantine killed two birds with one stone. He brought the growing
influence of the disciples of Christ under his political control and also annexed
many of the pagan religions of Rome into the new Christian religion. This
would explain why some Christian traditions or rituals are rooted in ancient
pagan practices. Rituals like the popular "Easter Egg" hunt on Easter can be
traced all the way to back to the "worshipping of ancient Babylonian fertility
gods." So every Easter (I prefer to call it Resurrection Sunday) the Lord Jesus
Christ has to share the news about his glorious resurrection with an "Easter
Egg" demonic god. But most Christians disagree even though there is more
than ample historical evidence to the contrary.

NAMES ARE IMPORTANT

*When the baby was eight days old, they all came for the circum-
cision ceremony. They wanted to name him Zechariah, after his
father. But Elizabeth said, "No! His **name** is John!"*

*"What?" they exclaimed. "There is no one in all your family by that name." So they used gestures to ask the baby's father what he wanted to **name** him. He motioned for a writing tablet, and to everyone's surprise he wrote, "His **name** is John"* (Luke 1:59-63).

*And he said, Thy **name** shall be called no more Jacob, but **Israel**: for as a prince hast thou power with God and with men, and hast prevailed* (Genesis 32:28 KJV).

These two Scripture passages strongly suggest that names play a critical role in determining the nature of a thing and how it ultimately functions. Before Isaac was born, God called out his name. Before King Josiah was born, God called out his name and announced his destiny as a reformer. Before the birth of the prophet John the Baptist, the angel Gabriel appeared to his father Zachariah and gave him explicit instructions to name his firstborn son John.

The angel Gabriel appears one final time in the New Testament to announce the birth of the world's promised Messiah—Jesus. When the angel Gabriel appeared to Joseph in a dream, he told him to call the child who was going to be born out of Mary's womb, Jesus! *Jesus* means "Savior." These incidences clearly showcase the importance of names in the spirit realm. An incorrect name can give birth to an inaccurate expression of a person or an entity's intended purpose.

*And out of the ground the LORD God formed every beast of the field, and every fowl of the air; and brought them unto Adam to see what he would call them: and whatsoever Adam called every living creature, that was the **name** thereof* (Genesis 2:19 KJV).

I am afraid that many members of the Body of Christ do not really respect the "technology of names" as much as God does. But the truth is that this ancient spiritual technology is the method that God uses to *determine the capacity, function, and nature of a thing.* God imparted this technology of names to Adam. The Bible says that God brought all the animals on earth to Adam to see what he would call or name them. The Bible tells us that whatever name Adam gave to any animal, the name would enshrine that particular animal's purpose, potential, and nature.

The technology of names also shows us that whoever names a person, a product, or an organization has inherent power over what they name. This is why I am not particularly impressed when people identify me as a Christian because the name *Christian* was a name that was imposed on the New Creation by officials of the Roman Empire at Antioch. How did the world choose a name for God's royal priesthood? What kind of spirit inspired these worldly officials to come up with the name Christians, or "little Christs"? I am not suggesting that those who identify themselves as Christians are sinning against God; by no means! But I will not identify myself as such anymore, knowing what I know. I prefer to indentify myself as a Kingdom citizen, disciple of Christ, child of God or ambassador of Christ, just to name a few!

The following are some of the names that Jesus Christ and the Holy Spirit use to describe the corporate Body of New Testament born-again believers:

- Kingdom Citizens (Ephesians 2:19, Philippians 3:20)
- The New Creation (2 Corinthians 5:17)
- The One New Man (Ephesians 2:15)
- Children of God (John 1:12)
- The Church (Matthew 16:19)
- The Body of Christ (1 Corinthians 12:27)
- Ambassadors of Christ (2 Corinthians 5:20)
- The Royal Priesthood (1 Peter 2:9)
- Disciples of the Lord (Acts 9:1)

I always wonder what will happen when New Testament born-again believers begin to identify with the names that God gave them. I guess we will soon find out because there is a growing company of born-again believers who are stepping out of the Christian religion right into the Kingdom. Dr. Myles Munroe says that they are *"rediscovering the Kingdom."* The God-given names listed in the previous paragraph crystallize who we really are—they collectively describe the spiritual DNA that God has invested in His covenant people. These names contain the true *nomenclature* of Kingdom citizens on earth.

CHRISTIANITY'S ATROCITIES IN THE NAME OF CHRIST

Christians who are trying to convert Jews from Judaism to the so-called Christian faith are terrible students of history. Jews have suffered heinous torture and humiliation in the name of Christianity. Adolph Hitler, who tortured and killed six million Jews in gas chambers, was a devout Catholic. His hatred for the Jews was fueled by the anti-Semitic teachings of both the Roman Catholic church, as well as those of Protestant Christian churches. These churches taught that Jews were bloody murderers who had crucified the Savior (Jesus). In addition to torture and humiliation, many Jews lost their property to Christian leaders who confiscated their belongings and property. This is why the name *Christian* triggers serious emotional and psychological mechanisms for many Jewish people. I cannot say that I blame them.

> The Crusades, for instance, were military expeditions undertaken by Western European Christians between 1095 and 1270, usually at the behest of the papacy, to recover Jerusalem and other Palestinian places of pilgrimage from Muslim control. The word "crusade" (from Latin translated "cross," the official emblem of the Crusaders) was also applied, especially in the 13th century, to wars against pagan nations, Christians accused of heresy, as well as political foes of the papacy.[4]

As though these atrocities were not horrendous enough in themselves, the greatest blight on the Christian religion is the period of the infamous Inquisitions. The victims of these bloody inquisitions performed under the banner of Christ were Jews, Muslims, and Protestants. Many of the victims who were declared guilty were burned alive while tied to stakes. Their desperate screams could be heard miles away, while men and women carrying crosses looked on religiously. This is why I believe that only the true Church can reach Jews and Muslims for Christ with the gospel of the Kingdom. Jewish people are not waiting to become Christians: to the contrary they are anxiously waiting to inherit the Kingdom. Let us examine one of the questions that Jewish apostles asked Jesus Christ when He rose from the dead. This question shows us that the quickest way to convert Jews to Christ is to present them with the gospel of the Kingdom and not force Christianity down their throat.

*When they therefore were come together, they asked of him, say-ing, Lord, wilt thou at this time restore again the **kingdom** to Israel?* (Acts 1:6 KJV Emphasis added by author)

Christianity and Politics

Before you accuse me of completely discarding the value and important contributions of the Christian religion to the general welfare of men and women worldwide, I want to state emphatically that I appreciate the contributions Christianity has made to the fight for basic human rights. History shows us that more often than not the Christian religion has helped to liberate more men and women from political tyranny, slavery, poverty, human trafficking, prostitution, and genocide than any other religion.

At the beginning of this chapter I made mention that the Christian religion is one of the best religions in the world today, in the same way that democratic ideology trumps communism. One of the areas where the Christian religion has made great inroads is in the area of political activism. Christian political activism has really become a force to reckon with; but Christian political activism can also become quite divisive even among Christians who politic with good intentions.

The presidential campaign between Barack Obama and John McCain caused a great rift within the body of Christianity in the United States. Many African American Christians voted for Barack Obama, while many Caucasian and Hispanic Christians voted for John McCain. I witnessed heated, demoni-cally engineered, and mean-spirited debates between pro-Obama Christians and pro-McCain Christians that were quite embarrassing to say the least. This is why it is dangerous for church leaders to mistake the sacred work of advancing the Kingdom of God with Christian political activism. Sometimes Christian political activism can be a force for change, but in some cases its good intentions have been hijacked by ambitious politicians who want to fulfill their own political agenda. Many politicians seem to "find Christ" whenever they are campaigning for a coveted political position.

This is why I am neither Democrat nor Republican by obligation; I am an ambassador of the Kingdom of God. When my wife and I vote, we vote accord-ing to the "issues" and not necessarily along party lines. I am so excited when

I can simply operate by Kingdom principles! I have nothing against Kingdom citizens who are involved in Christian political activism, in their desire to influence government to enact righteous laws in the land. I agree with the unshakable testimony of Scripture which says, *"when the righteous are in authority, the people rejoice"* (Proverbs 29:2 KJV).

Christian political activism is an important platform for rallying Christians (part of this group includes Kingdom citizens) and conservatives around issues of morality. Christian political activism is a natural and fallible instrument for effecting political and social changes, but the advancement of the Kingdom of God through transformed hearts is God's sure method for transforming nations. Kingdom citizens who sense a strong calling toward the Mountain of Law (politics) must read my book *The Kingdom of God and the 7 Mountains of Babylon* to gain a deeper understanding of Christian political activism in light of the gospel of the Kingdom.

THE KINGDOM AND POLITICS

One of the greatest dangers of Christian political activism is that many born again believers confuse it with the work of the Kingdom. This is a toxic error, in need of a careful and surgical course correction. The confusion between the work of the Kingdom and Christian political activism is rooted in the fact that many well meaning born-again believers do not understand the dynamics of their dual citizenship. Understanding how this dual citizenship affects Kingdom citizens in the political process is the key to effecting the needed course correction.

Saint Paul makes it very clear that every born again believer is a citizen of the Kingdom of heaven. (Philippians 3:20.) *As Kingdom citizens, our primary responsibility is to preach the gospel of the Kingdom so that the hearts of sinners can be transformed by the saving knowledge of Jesus Christ.* This is how the Kingdom of God is advanced in the earth, heart-to-heart, spirit-to-spirit. The Kingdom of God can never be advanced through a political process; to the contrary, trying to advance the Kingdom through a political process diminishes the complete sovereignty of the Kingdom of God in the affairs of men. God never asked for a vote when He decided to temporarily remove King

Nebuchadnezzar from the Babylonian throne. The Kingdom of God is too powerful to quarantine in a man-made political process. Since the Kingdom of God cannot be advanced through a political process, how then is it advanced? It is forcefully advanced through transformed hearts displaying the power, signs and wonders of the Kingdom in the marketplace. This is how Joseph, Daniel and the apostle Paul advanced the Kingdom of God. (Romans 15:18-19.)

Jesus Christ, who is the head of our Order, made it very clear that the Kingdom of God is not of this world and as such it can never be advanced through the ballot boxes. He had this press conference on the Kingdom and politics in front of Pontius Pilate. He told Pontius Pilate that had His Kingdom been of this world, He would have attempted to deliver Himself through a political process or military campaign. He even rebuked Peter during His arrest in the garden of Gethsemane for using violence to advance His Kingdom.

> *When Pilate heard this, he was more frightened than ever. He took Jesus back into the headquarters again and asked him, "Where are you from?" But Jesus gave no answer. "Why don't you talk to me?" Pilate demanded. "Don't you realize that I have the power to release you or crucify you?" Then Jesus said, "You would have no power over me at all unless it were given to you from above. So the one who handed me over to you has the greater sin"* (John 19:8-11).

"Francis, are you suggesting that Kingdom citizens are not supposed to be involved in the politics of their nation?" The answer is an emphatic "NO!" This is not what I am suggesting. This is where the "dual citizenship" of Kingdom citizens comes into play. As naturalized citizens of their countries of residence, Kingdom citizens have a civic duty and moral obligation to politic for the election of political candidates who are most friendly to the core values of the Kingdom. *Better still, the Church needs to become the breeding ground for politicians who are already in the Kingdom.* But such politicking must never be confused with the work of the Kingdom, even though such politicking is largely influenced by the moral values and worldview of the Kingdom citizen so engaged. Such politicking must be seen for what it is: the civic duty of all good and moral citizens. (Romans 13.)

Politicking for the Republican or the Democratic Party, for instance, must never be confused with Kingdom work. The Kingdom of God can work in both parties and yet it transcends both of them. The Kingdom of God must never be compromised by its citizens to the degree that it is brought under the jurisdiction of unsaved politicians with questionable political agendas. I have seen vicious slander take place between Kingdom citizens (brothers and sisters in Christ) who were politicking for opposing sides. Kingdom citizens must never treat each other like enemies, in order to advance any political agenda. But I dare conclude by saying that Kingdom citizens need to have an *unshakable Bible-based theology* behind their politics which is shaped by the *counsel of God and the core values* of the Kingdom. For instance if God and His Kingdom stand for "LIFE" then all true Kingdom citizens must follow suit, without any reservations, even when they are personally enchanted by a charismatic politician who does not believe in the values of the Kingdom. There can be no "grey areas" when it comes to the issue of Kingdom citizens agreeing with the core values that Christ has set for His Kingdom. This is why Jesus Christ said *"So why do you keep calling me 'Lord, Lord!' when you don't do what I say?* (paraphrase of Luke 6:46). This is what I call the theology of politics.

Religion Versus the Kingdom

Dr. Myles Munroe says the following, "The power of religion lies in its ability to serve as a substitute for the Kingdom and thus hinder humankind from pursuing the genuine answer to the dilemma. My study of the nature of religion and how it impacts the process of man's search for the Kingdom uncovered several significant truths:

- *Religion preoccupies man until he finds the Kingdom.*

- *Religion is what man does until he finds the Kingdom.*

- *Religion prepares man to leave earth; the Kingdom empowers man to dominate the earth.*

- *Religion is reaching up to God; the Kingdom is God coming down to man.*

- *Religion wants to escape the earth; the Kingdom impacts, influences and changes earth.*

- *Religion seeks to take earth to Heaven; the Kingdom seeks to bring Heaven to earth.*"[5]

Perhaps this is why Jesus Christ never came to the earth to restore a lost religion; He came to restore a Kingdom that was lost. Jesus Christ never died on the cross to give birth to a religion. He shed His blood on the cross to secure our spiritual inheritance in the Kingdom of God. As one writer stated:

> One version of Christianity is a religion invented by people. It is much different from the Kingdom of God, led by Christ the King. Religion is an attempt to reach God and improve our lives now and for eternity by obtaining some state of heaven through human ideas, efforts, and strategies. Religions are designed so that we can remain in power while attempting to get God and others to do what we want, in the way we want it. Religion is a clever enterprise to stay in control, so we can function as our own god. At the same time we try to manipulate the One True God into serving us by using religious language, rituals and sacrifices. But the Kingdom of God is initiated by God, for God's own glory, and involves His will, done His way, by His Spirit, all the time, and in every area of life. He is a living King, who rules another dominion or realm of reality. He has every intention of fully bringing His rule and realm onto Planet Earth through His sons and daughters by His Holy Spirit.[6]

GOD'S PATTERN SON

God, who at various times and in various ways spoke in time past to the fathers by the prophets, has in these last days spoken to us by His Son, whom He has appointed heir of all things, through whom also He made the worlds; who being the brightness of His glory and the express image of His person, and upholding all things by the word of His power, when He had by Himself purged our sins, sat down at the right hand of the Majesty on high (Hebrews 1:1-3 NKJV).

And a voice from heaven said, "This is my dearly loved Son, who brings me great joy" (Matthew 3:17).

There is no well-versed post-Calvary preacher of the gospel or theologian who can deny the fact that the Lord Jesus Christ preached on the message of the Kingdom more than any other spiritual leader in recorded human history. Jesus Christ talked about the Kingdom of God and Kingdom living much more often than the prophets Moses, David, and Daniel combined.

In Christ's eternal perspective, everything that He came to do on earth was centered on uncovering and restoring the Kingdom of God to our troubled planet. As the Creator incarnate, Jesus Christ knew that Adam and Eve did not lose a religion in the Garden of Eden—they lost their place in the Kingdom that God had given them here on earth. Jesus knew that only the restoration of the Kingdom of God in the hearts of sinful men could turn the tide of humankind's self-engineered spiritual suicide. Since Jesus Christ is God's pattern Son, His life and ministry style are the blueprints for real Kingdom living here on earth. Understanding the Order of Melchizedek will help us advance and spread the message of the gospel of the Kingdom to every sphere of human endeavor.

A Stone Cut Not by Hands

As you watched, a rock was cut from a mountain, but not by human hands. It struck the feet of iron and clay, smashing them to bits. The whole statue was crushed into small pieces of iron, clay, bronze, silver, and gold. Then the wind blew them away without a trace, like chaff on a threshing floor. But the rock that knocked the statue down became a great mountain that covered the whole earth (Daniel 2:34-35).

I believe that Daniel 2:34-35 is one of the strongest spiritual manifestos on the colonization of our troubled planet by the Kingdom of God. What is significant is that Daniel was interpreting a prophetic dream that God had given to the king of one of the most powerful Babylonian kingdoms in recorded history. King Nebuchadnezzar's Babylonian kingdom had spread to almost every part of the known world. Conquered lands and the inhabitants thereof had already been annexed into the Babylonian kingdom.

The people groups whom the Babylonians had conquered and assimilated into their kingdom were put through a very thorough re-education program. They were taught the manners and customs of the Babylonians. They were forbidden to speak openly in their native tongues. The Chaldean language became their primary language. These conquered people groups then adopted the culture of the Babylonians. This process of indoctrination and assimilation was sealed by the official act of giving each conquered person a suitable Babylonian name.

It follows, therefore, that fewer kings in the ancient world could have appreciated the power and concept of "Kingdom" like King Nebuchadnezzar. When Daniel was interpreting King Nebuchadnezzar's dream, he made it very clear that the God of all creation was going to set up His Kingdom over the colony called earth. The prophet Daniel saw a stone cut without human hands which grew rapidly until it had covered the whole of the earth. Prophetically the phrase a "stone cut without human hands" refers to the birth of our Lord Jesus Christ through the virgin birth and the advancement of Christ's Kingdom to every corner of human enterprise. Daniel's vision is another clear confirmation that Jesus Christ never came to the earth to restore a religion. He came to establish an everlasting Kingdom.

The Kingdom Now, and It Is Coming

The Son of Man will send his angels, and they will remove from his Kingdom everything that causes sin and all who do evil (Matthew 13:41).

"Mark my words—I will not drink wine again until the day I drink it new with you in my Father's Kingdom" (Matthew 26:29).

The law and the prophets were until John: since that time the kingdom of God is preached, and every man presseth into it (Luke 16:16 KJV).

There are Bible scholars who believe that the Kingdom age has not yet arrived. They believe that the Kingdom of God will come to the earth at the second coming of Christ. There are also prophetic teachers who believe that the Kingdom age is *now!* They believe that the Kingdom of God is active in the earth today. Both of these camps have an important piece of a whole truth.

Both belief systems pieced together equal the whole truth. The *Kingdom Now* is true because Jesus Himself said that the Kingdom of God is "within you." The Kingdom "within us" refers to Christ's millennial Kingdom which is continuously increasing in government and spiritual jurisdiction until all of Christ's enemies are placed under His footstool. Christ's Kingdom is the "stone cut without human hands" that Daniel said would increase until it had covered all of the earth.

As a matter of Bible study, Christ's Kingdom here on earth started with the preaching of John the Baptist and will last until the end of Christ's millennial reign. During this millennial reign, Christ will rule His Kingdom from Jerusalem, where He will rule all nations with a rod of iron. During Christ's millennial reign, God will bring all of Christ's enemies under His footstool. Said simply, Christ's Kingdom will last until the end of time as we know it. Christ's Kingdom is the complete restoration of the Kingdom of God on earth that Adam and Eve lost to the devil when they sinned in the Garden of Eden. This is why we cannot allow ourselves to get trapped in the Christian religion when God has given us a front row seat in advancing Christ's Kingdom!

> *Then cometh the end, when he shall have delivered up the kingdom to God, even the Father; when he shall have put down all rule and all authority and power. For he must reign, till he hath put all enemies under his feet* (1 Corinthians 15:24-25 KJV).

But the *Kingdom is also coming!* The Kingdom is "coming" refers to the Father's Kingdom, which God Himself prepared for His people from before the foundation of the world. The Father's Kingdom does not go into full manifestation here on earth until the end of Christ's millennial Kingdom. The twentieth chapter of the book of Revelation takes us to the end of Christ's millennial Kingdom. The final two chapters in the book of Revelation point to the establishment of the Father's everlasting Kingdom here on earth, which is foreshadowed by the descending of the New Jerusalem.

> *And I [John] saw the holy city, the new Jerusalem, coming down from God out of heaven like a bride beautifully dressed for her husband. I heard a loud shout from the throne, saying, "Look,*

*God's home is now among his people! He will live with them,
and they will be his people. God himself will be with them. He
will wipe every tear from their eyes, and there will be no more
death or sorrow or crying or pain. All these things are gone forever"* (Revelation 21:2-4).

The Scriptures tell us that when Christ has put down all rule, authority, and
power under His footstool, then He will take His Kingdom and deliver it up to
His Father. When Christ deliverers up His Kingdom to the Father, then God
will become all and in all! When this happens, the Father's Kingdom will be stationed on earth, forever. At this point the Kingdom age, as it relates to measur-
ing the Kingdom in time frames, will come to an end. The Father's Kingdom is
the Kingdom dimension we will all live in for all eternity after time as we know
it has ceased to exist. The Father's Kingdom here on earth starts immediately
after the Great White Throne Judgment and the eternal banishment of the
devil and his angels to the lake of fire. (See Revelation 19:20.)

The Emerging Kingdom Culture

*Seek the Kingdom of God above all else, and he will give you every-
thing you need. "So don't be afraid, little flock. For it gives your
Father great happiness to give you the Kingdom"* (Luke 12:31-32).

*For the Kingdom of God is not a matter of what we eat or drink,
but of living a life of goodness and peace and joy in the Holy
Spirit* (Romans 14:17).

Beloved, we are living in the days of the fulfillment of the Prophet Daniel's
prophetic vision. The stone cut without human hands (Christ's Kingdom) is
spreading and advancing rapidly across the nations of the world. The gospel of
the Kingdom is repositioning the Church of Jesus Christ into a place of national
influence and prominence. Many born-again believers are becoming awakened
to the message of the Kingdom. They are stepping out of the chambers of doctrinal confinement that the Christian religion imposed upon them, and they are
entering into a dynamic Kingdom lifestyle befitting of Kingdom citizens.

Worldwide, God's children are discovering the true culture of the Kingdom of heaven. They are discovering that the Kingdom of God is not in meat or drink but in righteousness (right thinking), peace, and joy in the Holy Ghost. This emerging Kingdom culture is superimposing itself over the many spiritual subcultures that were formed by the Church's obsession with the Christian religion. Under this emerging Kingdom culture, there are no Baptist, Pentecostal, Charismatic, or Fundamentalist Christians—just Kingdom citizens. *Under this emerging Kingdom culture, our common citizenry and spiritual ancestry are more important than our doctrinal differences.*

THE ORDER OF MELCHIZEDEK

The religious leaders replied, "He will put the wicked men to a horrible death and lease the vineyard to others who will give him his share of the crop after each harvest." Then Jesus asked them, "Didn't you ever read this in the Scriptures? 'The stone that the builders rejected has now become the cornerstone. This is the LORD's doing, and it is wonderful to see.' I tell you, the Kingdom of God will be taken away from you and given to a nation that will produce the proper fruit (Matthew 21:41-43).

But you are not like that, for you are a chosen people. You are royal priests, a holy nation, God's very own possession. As a result, you can show others the goodness of God, for he called you out of the darkness into his wonderful light (1 Peter 2:9).

In this day and time, systems must die to make way for greater things. As a religious system, Institutional Christianity and its edicts of formality and overly structured human activity must die in order to produce *"a new and life-giving way through the curtain into the Most Holy Place. And since we have a great High Priest who rules over God's house, let us go right into the presence of God with sincere hearts fully trusting him. For our guilty consciences have been sprinkled with Christ's blood to make us clean, and our bodies have been washed with pure water"* (Hebrews 10:20-22).

This high priestly order is none other than the **Order of Melchizedek** that brings us into the maturity and posture by which we can exercise our governmental authority as kings and priests in the earth. Those who truly understand the concept of resurrection will understand that God wants everything that He does to reflect life in His blood-washed people. To many, the Christianity of today only reflects the death of Jesus, not the everlasting power and priesthood of an eternal order. The ministry of Christ is full of life and hope, the kind of *zoe*-life and hope that should be reflected through the reality of how His Kingdom citizens live now on earth. Many of the systems of the Christian religion produce a death that must, itself, be put to death.

Jesus said, *"He is not the God of the dead, but the God of the living: ye therefore do greatly err"* (Mark 12:27 KJV).

It becomes increasingly clear that Institutional Christianity must die for us to evolve into the fullness of the next level of Kingdom living and lifestyle! Let's bury the old system (the Christian religion) so that we may truly live in the new—the Order of Melchizedek (The Royal Priesthood of Jesus Christ)!

Sitting across the table from Dr. Tim Johns at Jack Stack Barbeque restaurant, he asked me a profound question that made me think: "Francis, in a nutshell, what is the Order of Melchizedek?" I gave him a detailed explanation of what the Lord has shown me from His Word about the Order of Melchizedek. But when I left the restaurant, Dr. Johns' question came back to my spirit. I turned to the Lord and directed the question to Him.

The answer that the Lord gave me got me really excited. He said, "The Order of Melchizedek is an eternal spiritual order of kings and priests who have both covenantal and custodial rights to advance and teach the gospel of the Kingdom; until the kingdoms of this world have become the kingdoms of God and of His Christ." After the Lord gave me this definition, I realized that God had placed in a capsule what will take me this entire book to properly explain to you. The answer the Lord gave me to Dr. Johns' question also showed me one of the primary reasons why the Christian religion must die. God wants to take His blood-washed people out of Institutional Christianity and into the Order of Melchizedek—the divine agency responsible for advancing and spreading the gospel of the Kingdom here on earth.

This book is my humble attempt to introduce you to the Order of Melchizedek and your role in this powerful Kingdom agency. This might come as a shock to those who worship the Christian religion, but Abraham was not a member of Judaism and neither was he a Christian, even though both of these great religions have their roots and origins in Abraham. The truth of the matter is that Abraham was a prophet of God and a Kingdom businessman, who engaged an extraordinary God in the spirit of total obedience. It was this same extraordinary God who introduced Abraham to the Order of Melchizedek. Since we are the seed of Abraham, it would be prudent of us to understand the Order of Melchizedek and how it affects us today.

THE GREAT TRANSITION: FROM CHRISTIANITY TO THE KINGDOM

Without a doubt the greatest transition of our time is the transition from Christianity to the Kingdom. This spiritual and mental transition will be as difficult for many Christians as transitioning from Judaism to the Kingdom was for the Jewish people. This great and difficult transition is also compounded by the fact that in order to make this transition successfully, there must also be a transition in language. Indentifying ourselves as Kingdom citizens, followers of Christ or Ambassadors of Christ will be quite difficult for those of us who are so used to identifying ourselves simply as "Christians." *Many will misconstrue this transition as assault on Christianity or Christians in general. Nothing could be further from the truth.* But for those who have already made this transition, the immeasurable joy and freedom of Kingdom living that we have discovered after making this transition is worth all the persecution. Historically, many Christians have made fun of the Jews for their failure to embrace the Kingdom as Christ preached it, while He was on earth. But many Christians get angry and defensive when I tell them that Jesus Christ never came to our troubled planet to establish a religion called Christianity. He came to establish an absolute order called the unshakable Kingdom. (Hebrews 10:31.) Adam and Eve did NOT lose a religion in the Garden of Eden; they lost a Kingdom and their place in it. So it's the Kingdom that must be restored to man to satisfying his deep yearning for spiritual significance, not another religion, even if that religion is the Christian religion.

Imagine how deeply offended many Orthodox Jews must have been when Jesus and the apostle Paul made it clear that the religious system of worship and sacrifices that they had lived under for over 3000 years was being abolished in favor of the unchanging Person (Christ) and His unshakable Kingdom. Before Jesus Christ came to our troubled planet, Judaism was the best religion that anyone could belong to, in the same way that Christianity is presently one of the best religions that you could ever belong to. But like Judaism before it, Christianity is not the Kingdom even though it has many trace elements of the Kingdom in many of its body of teachings that are in some cases mingled with the doctrines of men.

God wants His Church to step out of many of the seducing influences of the Christian religion and step into its true inheritance-the unshakable Kingdom. *Even among Christians it is becoming increasingly difficult to accurately define the term "Christian" because it means so many different things to so many people.* If you asked a group of Christians from different denominations what they think qualifies one to be a Christian, you would be shocked by the divisive nature of the answers you would get. This is why the transition from Institutional Christianity to the Kingdom of God is an absolute must, because Christ is determined to establish His Kingdom rule on the earth and unite His people around their common ancestry as citizens of the Kingdom. God will not allow any religion, even if that religion is the "Christian religion," to compete with the establishment of Christ's unshakable Kingdom here on earth. This transition does not mean that we must be ashamed of our "Christian Heritage" in the same way that Jews should never be ashamed of celebrating their "Judaic Heritage." *But the Lord Jesus Christ never excused the Jews from their need to transition from Judaism to the Kingdom, just because they had a rich "Judaic Heritage."* The same principle applies to Christians. When it comes to the Kingdom, God will not accept any substitutes.

LIFE APPLICATION SECTION

MEMORY VERSE

The religious leaders replied, "He will put the wicked men to a horrible death and lease the vineyard to others who will give him his share of the crop after each harvest." Then Jesus asked them, "Didn't you ever read this in the Scriptures? 'The stone that the builders rejected has now become the cornerstone. This is the LORD's doing, and it is wonderful to see.' I tell you, the Kingdom of God will be taken away from you and given to a nation that will produce the proper fruit (Matthew 21:41-43).

REFLECTIONS

What is the difference between the Kingdom of God and the Christian religion?

Write eight of the names that God's Word uses to describe the corporate Body of New Testament born-again believers.

What is the Technology of Names?

How does the dual citizenship of Kingdom citizens affect them in the political process?

JOURNAL YOUR PERSONAL NOTES ON THIS CHAPTER

CHAPTER TWO

The Tabernacle
of David

Afterward I will return and restore the fallen house of David. I
will rebuild its ruins and restore it (Acts 15:16).

T HE STORY OF KING DAVID, the young and bashful shepherd boy
who became the greatest and most beloved of the kings of Israel, has
inspired God-seekers for thousands of years. When we consider the
cradle of his humble beginnings, we are left with the feeling that with God all
things are truly possible. (Matthew 19:26.) David's life story is a living monu-
ment and testament to what is possible in the lives of ordinary men who engage
an extraordinary God.

GOD'S BLACK SHEEP

Many of us who have suffered and felt the bitter sting of being singled out
as the black sheep of our family can easily relate to the story of David. David,
the despised and uncelebrated shepherd boy from an unpretentious Jewish
family, became one of the most celebrated and divinely favored kings of Israel.
This young and huskily handsome boy who won no accolades of glamour in his
own family, ends up as the "apple of God's eye." Whosoever said that God is
not romantic at heart, has not read the story of this beloved psalmist and king
of Israel.

When they arrived, Samuel took one look at Eliab and thought, "Surely this is the LORD's anointed!" But the LORD said to Samuel, "Don't judge by his appearance or height, for I have rejected him. The LORD doesn't see things the way you see them. People judge by outward appearance, but the LORD looks at the heart." Then Jesse told his son Abinadab to step forward and walk in front of Samuel. But Samuel said, "This is not the one the LORD has chosen." Next Jesse summoned Shimea, but Samuel said, "Neither is this the one the LORD has chosen." In the same way all seven of Jesse's sons were presented to Samuel. But Samuel said to Jesse, "The LORD has not chosen any of these." Then Samuel asked, "Are these all the sons you have?" "There is still the youngest," Jesse replied. "But he's out in the fields watching the sheep and goats." "Send for him at once," Samuel said. "We will not sit down to eat until he arrives." So Jesse sent for him. He was dark and handsome, with beautiful eyes. And the LORD said, "This is the one; anoint him" (1 Samuel 16:6-12).

David was so marginalized and lightly esteemed in his own family's eyes that when the Prophet Samuel invited Jesse (David's father) to bring his sons to a very important family meeting, David was not even invited. While David's seven brothers made strenuous and meticulous preparations for what they considered to be the most important meeting of their lifetime, David trailed away into the wilderness, leading his father's sheep to greener pastures. Perhaps it was constantly fighting off the bitter sting of being the rejected one in his own family that drove this psalmist into the hands of a loving God. God was more than happy to oblige and became David's constant source of unconditional love and acceptance.

David was the forgotten shepherd boy. Jewish historians tell us that many of the Psalms of David were written during this season of marginalization as he tended to his father's sheep. During these times of God encounters, an unquenchable thirst and hunger for God was forged in the inner chambers of David's love-starved soul. God became the greatest pursuit of David's life. *The time David spent with the great Prophet Samuel at Ramah served to intensify the longing for the Ark of God's presence in David's heart.* David did not know that this journey of desire would providentially lead him into one of the greatest spiritual discoveries of his lifetime. David would eventually stumble upon the knowledge of an ancient heavenly priesthood, called the Order of Melchizedek. What David would discover about this kingly-priestly order would change his life forever and his personal perception of God.

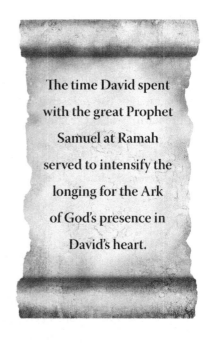

The time David spent with the great Prophet Samuel at Ramah served to intensify the longing for the Ark of God's presence in David's heart.

> *Remember, dear brothers and sisters, that few of you were wise in the world's eyes or powerful or wealthy when God called you. Instead, God chose things the world considers foolish in order to shame those who think they are wise. And he chose things that are powerless to shame those who are powerful. God chose things despised by the world, things counted as nothing at all, and used them to bring to nothing what the world considers important. As a result, no one can ever boast in the presence of God* (1 Corinthians 1:26-29).

In First Corinthians, the apostle Paul echoes the sentiments that must have been self-evident in the life of King David. Saint Paul's sentiments concerning the subject of divine election seem to suggest that God never considers our education, nobility, pedigree, or race when He selects us for greatness in His Kingdom as part of His royal priesthood. Maybe that would explain why many of us are so captivated by the story of King David. Who doesn't enjoy rooting for the underdog? Perhaps it is because many of us feel like underdogs compared to the giants that stand in the way to our destiny.

You may be wondering why I am spending so much time writing about David in a book titled *The Order of Melchizedek*. The answer is simple but has far-reaching spiritual ramifications. Much of what we know scripturally about the eternal priestly Order of Melchizedek was revealed to only three men. Two of the men are in the Old Testament and the other is in the New Testament. Abraham and David are two of the Old Testament prophets who were given a firsthand revelation of the priestly Order of Melchizedek. The bulk of this incredible revelation about this powerful heavenly priesthood, which is headed by the Lord Jesus Christ, was later given to the apostle Paul.

There is simply no way we can come to appreciate the power and ultimate importance of the priestly Order of Melchizedek without canvassing the lives and teachings of these three historical figures. The lives and teachings of these men provide us with many important clues about the nature and inner workings of this eternal kingly-priestly order. These important clues show us how the Order of Melchizedek affects us today, as New Testament believers.

The Birth of a Psalmist

Now the Spirit of the LORD had left Saul, and the LORD sent a tormenting spirit that filled him with depression and fear. Some of Saul's servants said to him, "A tormenting spirit from God is troubling you. Let us find a good musician to play the harp whenever the tormenting spirit troubles you. He will play soothing music, and you will soon be well again." "All right," Saul said. "Find me someone who plays well, and bring him here." One of the servants said to Saul, "One of Jesse's sons from Bethlehem is a talented harp player. Not only that—he is a brave warrior, a man of war, and has good judgment. He is also a fine-looking young man, and the LORD is with him" (1 Samuel 16:14-18).

One of the most obvious clues about the nature and power of the kingly-priestly Order of Melchizedek comes in the form of the order of worship that is made available to Kingdom citizens under this order of priesthood. The order of worship in this highest kingly-priestly dimension creates waves of supernatural power that challenge demonic powers in the atmosphere (heavenly realms). Examining David's life offers us a better glimpse at the uniqueness of the order of worship that God has made available to His people under the Order of Melchizedek.

While David was tending to his father's flock, his journey of desire stirred the gift of prophetic worship that had been lying dormant in his spirit man. From this moment onward, David composed many inspirational psalms, most of which he sang back to the Lord. David's new style of worship was revolutionary because it was very different from the liturgical and structured worship of the Levitical priesthood. David's new style of worship was very prophetic (Spirit-led), spontaneous, and inspirational. David's new style of worship was based upon a new order of priesthood. David's new style of worship was also very *governmental in expression,* such that it created fresh waves of God's power and glory in the atmosphere.

Some of the servants of King Saul, the rejected king of Israel, must have experienced firsthand the dazzling music skills of this young shepherd boy and his revolutionary style of worship. When the Spirit of God left King Saul and a tormenting evil spirit took its place, Saul's servants knew by experience that David's new style of prophetic worship would bring spiritual relief to the troubled king.

When the servants of King Saul saw how depressed and troubled he was when the tormenting spirit came upon him, they suggested that the king solicit the services of a young talented psalmist—David. Saul wasted no time in securing the services of David. Whenever the evil spirit came upon Saul to torment him, David would play the prophetic songs and sounds that he had received from heaven during his times of worship in the wilderness. Within moments, the governmental energy of these prophetic songs and sounds filled the atmosphere and began to dislodge demonic activity. Whenever this happened, the evil spirit would run out of the king's head and palace, *like a mouse in a house full of cats!*

Any New Testament worship leader must be able to operate in the same spiritual order of worship that David was operating in while he ministered to King Saul because there are many evil spirits in the earth's atmosphere who are tormenting the souls of many of the people who come through the doors of our churches every Sunday morning. Why should these troubled souls leave our worship services the same way they came in? Sadly, this last observation seems to be the norm for many New Testament Christ-professing churches. People come to church services tormented in the soul and leave highly entertained by many of our flesh-driven worship performances. They leave our church services entertained but largely unchanged. This sad state of affairs in the global Church is indicative of the fact that very few New

Testament worship leaders are operating under the Order of Melchizedek like David did. This explains why the order of worship in many churches is so shallow and powerless.

THE BIRTH OF A WORSHIPPING WARRIOR

One of the servants said to Saul, "One of Jesse's sons from Bethlehem is a talented harp player. Not only that—he is a brave warrior, a man of war, and has good judgment. He is also a fine-looking young man, and the LORD is with him" (1 Samuel 16:18).

When the servants of King Saul were going through David's resume, they told the king that besides being a very gifted minstrel, David was also a brave warrior and a man of war. During his journey of desire in the wilderness, David had found a way to merge his prophetic worship with his ability to wage war on the battlefield. Said simply, David was a prophetic prototype of a new kind of "worshipping warrior." Under the Levitical priestly order, members of the priesthood were not allowed to enlist in the military. Such an act would have disqualified them from leading worship in the temple of God. But God was using the canvas of David's life to showcase a new order of priesthood where it is possible to be a man of war as well as lead worship in the temple of God.

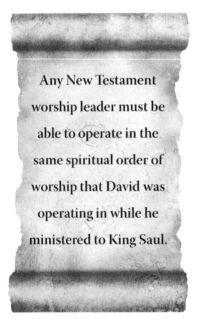

Any New Testament worship leader must be able to operate in the same spiritual order of worship that David was operating in while he ministered to King Saul.

As Goliath moved closer to attack, David quickly ran out to meet him. Reaching into his shepherd's bag and taking out a stone, he hurled it with his sling and hit the Philistine in the forehead. The stone sank in, and Goliath stumbled and fell face down on the ground. So David triumphed over the Philistine with only a sling and a stone, for he had no sword. Then David ran over and pulled Goliath's sword from its sheath. David used it to kill him and cut off his head (1 Samuel 17:48-51).

David's "hybrid matrix" as a worshipping warrior came to the forefront when the armies of Israel were faced with their biggest nemesis—Goliath, the Philistine giant. For 40 days Goliath tormented the armies of Israel with a challenge that they were afraid to answer. Goliath challenged Israel to send one of their men of war to battle against him in a fight-to-the-death, winner-takes-all confrontation.

David happened to stroll into the army's campgrounds, and he overheard the menacing giant shout out his unmet challenge. Unbeknown to the taunting giant, David had stumbled upon a very powerful technology of worship that belonged to a different order of priesthood. This new technology of worship had so infused him with *dunamis* (power) from on High to such a degree that David killed a bear and a lion with his bare hands. It does not take a rocket scientist to figure out that any human being who can kill a full grown bear or a lion with his bare hands must be endued with supernatural strength, like Samson. (See Judges 14:5-6.)

David took one look at the taunting giant and all he could see in his mind's eye were the pictures of a bear and a lion shredded to pieces by his bare hands. Armed with a sling shot and five smooth stones, David moved in the direction of the baffled giant. The armies of Philistia looked on and sneered in undisguised contempt for the choice of a warrior that the armies of Israel had settled on. Only God and the devil knew that the Philistine giant was going to be the devil's special guest that day in the portals of hell. Hell beneath was getting ready to accommodate the menacing giant. The Philistine giant had seen his last day on earth. He had arrogantly challenged a man who belonged to the highest order of priesthood known to human-kind. Goliath had picked a fight with a man whose life was patterned after the Order of Melchizedek.

David threw one of the stones in his pouch using his sling shot. The stone, energized by God, entered the skull of the stunned giant who fell to the ground like a flying dragon that had lost the favor of gravity. To the amazement of the armies of Philistia, David cut off the head of the fallen giant using Goliath's own sword. Panic spread like a malignant cancer throughout the armies of Philistia, who feared and fled for their lives. God gave the armies of Israel a great victory that day through David, His worshipping warrior.

Looking at the life of King David we quickly come to terms with the order of ministry that is available to every believer under the kingly-priestly Order of Melchizedek. This powerful "order of ministry" is driven by a prophetic process. It is also very governmental and passionately militant in its corporate expression. The closer we get to the millennial reign of Christ, the more we are going to see an abundance of kingdom-minded churches and ministers that are patterned after the Order of Melchizedek. These Davidic type of governing churches and ministers will be very governmental and militant in their approach to the subject of advancing the Kingdom of God. These governing churches and Kingdom businesses will rise in *governmental-apostolic authority* to challenge and *dethrone the strongman of their cities.*

Like King David of old, these new breed of churches and kingdom-minded believers will not be afraid to challenge the Goliath in their cities who has been hindering the advancement of the gospel of the Kingdom. Many of these people-friendly and seeker-sensitive churches that are focused on catering to man's needs rather than safeguarding God's inheritance in the saints, will become spiritual dinosaurs and objects of divine rejection in the light of God's burning passion to transform His blood-washed people into a functional royal priesthood. God never intended for His Church to become a spiritual greenhouse.

A greenhouse provides a safe and man-controlled environment for growing delicate plants like flowers and vegetables. The only problem with vegetables is that they have a very weak spine (stem). You cannot place anything of weight on a vegetable growing in a greenhouse and expect it not to break. In like manner, many of these seeker-sensitive greenhouse churches produce Kingdom citizens who look very glamorous on the outside but break easily under the weight of spiritual warfare to advance God's Kingdom here on earth.

A Man after the Heart of God

Now the LORD said to Samuel, "You have mourned long enough for Saul. I have rejected him as king of Israel, so fill your flask with olive oil and go to Bethlehem. Find a man named Jesse who lives there, for I have selected one of his sons to be my king" (1 Samuel 16:1).

On the human level, a person can never have the succession rights to the throne of any kingdom, unless they were born into the royal family of the said kingdom. The only other way a person who was not born of royal blood can gain succession rights to the throne of a kingdom is to be adopted into the royal family by the reigning king. Nevertheless, the more excellent way of becoming a king or a person of royal blood is to be adopted into God's divine family of kings. The latter is what happens each time a sinner repents and is adopted into God's family through the finished work of Christ.

But now your kingdom must end, for the LORD has sought out a man after his own heart. The LORD has already appointed him to be the leader of his people, because you have not kept the LORD's command" (1 Samuel 13:14).

Even though David, the beloved psalmist and black sheep of his own family, was not born of royal blood, God declared that He was going to make a king out of this uncelebrated shepherd boy. God is the only true King by virtue of His supreme authority over heaven and earth. Since God is also the creator of everything, He is also the supreme King because He has creative rights to everything and everyone on earth. In layman's terms, if anyone is truly qualified to make a king out of anybody, it is God.

So Jesse sent for him. He was dark and handsome, with beautiful eyes. And the LORD said, "This is the one; anoint him." So as David stood there among his brothers, Samuel took the flask of olive oil he had brought and anointed David with the oil. And the Spirit of the LORD came powerfully upon David from that day on. Then Samuel returned to Ramah (1 Samuel 16:12-13).

In a matter that was a foregone conclusion, God sent the prophet Samuel to the house of Jesse (David's father) and invited him with his sons to the sacrificial ceremony. Jesse showed up with seven of his highly prized sons, even though he had eight sons. After God had rejected all seven sons of Jesse, the frustrated prophet asked Jesse if he had any other sons. At this inquiry, Jesse told Samuel that he had an eighth son who was tending sheep in the fields of Judah. Without mincing words, the prophet Samuel told Jesse that the anointing service would not go on until David arrived.

Jesse quickly sent for David, who came in a hurry. As soon as the prophet's eyes locked with those of David, the prophet knew intuitively that this hand-some, husky-looking lad was the chosen one of God. The prophet Samuel remembered what God had told him in his time of private communion. *"I have found Me a man after My own heart!"* God had boasted to Samuel. Samuel looked at David and realized that this young man was the man after the heart of God.

This leads me to the sobering and exciting conclusion that when many members of the Body of Christ gain a better functional understanding of the spiritual dynamics of living under the Order of Melchizedek, there will be a rise of Davidic-type believers who have a heart after God's own heart. The Order of Melchizedek produces a royal priesthood of believers who can oper-ate within the Kingdom of God, with a heart of extravagant devotion to God just like the Lord Jesus.

Oops! Uzzah Is Dead

> *"It is time to bring back the Ark of our God, for we neglected it during the reign of Saul." The whole assembly agreed to this, for the people could see it was the right thing to do. So David summoned all Israel, from the Shihor Brook of Egypt in the south all the way to the town of Lebo-hamath in the north, to join in bringing the Ark of God from Kiriath-jearim* (1 Chronicles 13:3-5).

It is difficult to appreciate why David was God's favorite king among all the kings of Israel without understanding David's deepest desire. Without looking at David through the lens of his one driving passion, we will miss the main rea-son God was so in love with David. Not even the richest and wisest king who ever lived, King Solomon, occupied the same special spot in the heart of God that David did. Why is this so? In David's own words:

> As the deer longs for streams of water, so I long for you, O God. I thirst for God, the living God. When can I go and stand before him? Day and night I have only tears for food, while my enemies continually taunt me, saying, "Where is this God of yours?" (Psalm 42:1-3)

> One thing have I desired of the LORD; that will I seek: that I may dwell in the house of the LORD, all the days of my life, to behold the beauty of the LORD, to inquire in His temple (Psalm 27:4 NKJV).

These two passages of Scripture from the book of Psalms both capture and crystallize the driving passion of David's life. David had no driving ambition to become the greatest king in the ancient world, even though he became such a king. He had no driving ambition to become the most famous musician in the ancient world. David's spiritual life was very deep in its spiritual reach but very simple in its driving motivation. The greatest longing of David's life was to live in the manifest presence of God! Everything else in his life paled compared to this one desire.

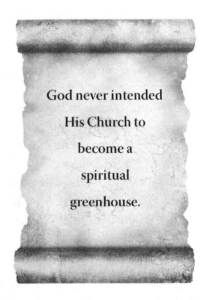

God never intended His Church to become a spiritual greenhouse.

What David discovered about...

* Prophetic worship
* Prophetic ministry and prophecy
* Governmental prayer
* Spiritual warfare
* The coming Messiah
* The Order of Melchizedek

...was accidental and providential. He stumbled upon these important truths that changed his life during his journey of desire. Loving God with extreme devotion and abandonment led him into these amazing spiritual discoveries. When King Saul was told by the prophet Samuel that God had rejected him and taken the kingdom out of his hands, King Saul started a ferocious demonically-engineered campaign to retain his kingdom. To the contrary, when King David was confronted by the prophet Nathan concerning his sin with Uriah's wife, David never once campaigned to retain his throne.

The cry of King David that is recorded in the famous fifty-first psalm shows us the true priorities of a man after God's own heart. In this famous and heart-wrenching psalm, David did not ask God to preserve his throne or his kingdom. To the contrary, David's cry is driven by the one desire that was at the core of everything David did and wanted in life. David pleaded with God not to take His holy Spirit from him. King David also begged God not to cast him away from His presence. These are not the cries of a man who is drunk with political ambition. If the central message of Psalm 51 does not challenge you in your own journey of desire, then you are spiritually dead.

> *They placed the Ark of God on a new cart and brought it from Abinadab's house. Uzzah and Ahio were guiding the cart. David and all Israel were celebrating before God with all their might, singing songs and playing all kinds of musical instruments— lyres, harps, tambourines, cymbals, and trumpets. But when they arrived at the threshing floor of Nacon, the oxen stumbled, and Uzzah reached out his hand to steady the Ark. Then the LORD's anger was aroused against Uzzah, and he struck him dead because he had laid his hand on the Ark. So Uzzah died there in the presence of God. David was angry because the LORD's anger had burst out against Uzzah. He named that place Perez-uzzah (which means "to burst out against Uzzah"), as it is still called today* (1 Chronicles 13:7-11).

Central to David's one desire was the desire to see the restoration of the Ark of the Covenant to the nation of Israel. The Ark of the Covenant, which symbolized the fact that God was with His people, had been captured by the Philistines during the days of Eli's priesthood. When King Saul became Israel's first king, he made no attempt to retrieve the Ark of God's presence. Living in the favor of God's presence was not as important to King Saul as retaining his political power over the nation of Israel. Unfortunately, the spirit of King Saul is upon many church leaders who preside over today's spiritually dry churches; they have no meaningful desire to see their churches flooded with the presence of God. These spiritual Sauls are intoxicated with the religious and political power that they wield over their unsuspecting churches.

But when David became king over Israel, his first duty was to retrieve the Ark of the Covenant from the land of the Philistines. David gathered an army and Levites from the land of Israel to get the Ark of the Covenant. After they obtained it, they began the long procession home. David could hardly contain his excitement. He danced like a little kid.

Their tumultuous celebration was brought to a sudden and sorrowful end. At the threshing floor, the new cart carrying the Ark of the Covenant stumbled and the Ark of the Covenant was about to fall to the ground, but Uzzah reached out to steady it. As Uzzah touched the Ark of the Covenant, he was smote by the hand of God almost immediately. The sudden death of Uzzah silenced everyone's praise and brought somberness over the parade. David was very angry with God for killing a man who was only trying to steady the Ark from falling. In any case, the procession stopped and the mission of bringing the Ark of the Covenant back to Israel was suspended. The Ark of God's presence was left in the care of Obed-edom of Gath.

A SEASON OF HOLY FRUSTRATION

David was angry because the LORD's anger had burst out against Uzzah. He named that place Perez-uzzah (which means "to burst out against Uzzah"), as it is still called today (1 Chronicles 13:11).

Imagine how the trip back to Israel must have felt for King David and the rest of his procession after the death of Uzzah. What had started out as a day of tremendous joy and national celebration ended in an unexpected funeral. Place yourself for a moment in David's shoes. All David wanted was to get as close as possible to the God he loved dearly. The Ark of the Covenant was the ultimate symbol of proximity to the presence of the living God. But Uzzah's sudden death had reminded King David and his entire procession just how dangerous it was to get close to the presence of the living God under the Levitical priestly Order.

> *David was now afraid of God, and he asked, "How can I ever bring the Ark of God back into my care?" So David did not move the Ark into the City of David. Instead, he took it to the house of Obed-edom of Gath. The Ark of God remained there in Obed-edom's house for three months, and the LORD blessed the household of Obed-edom and everything he owned* (1 Chronicles 13:12-14).

It is said that God allows seasons of divine frustration to patronize the lives of those who truly seek after Him, so He can show them a "more excellent way." I agree with wise sages who have said that *frustration with the present creates the future.* I imagine that King David went into his bed chambers after the failed attempt to bring back the Ark of the Covenant and probably cried himself to sleep. David's question sums up his state of mind at the time, "How can I ever bring the Ark of God back into my care?"

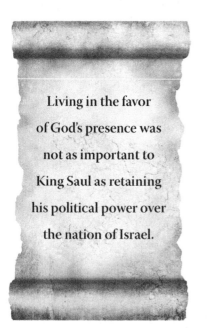

Living in the favor of God's presence was not as important to King Saul as retaining his political power over the nation of Israel.

King David may also have asked himself these questions:

- God, why did You kill Uzzah for touching Your presence?

- Why is it that only the Levites get to have a closer look at Your presence?

- Lord, is there a priestly Order under which everyone can touch and live in the favor of Your presence?

I am convinced many of these questions were lodged in David's mind as he searched for a permanent solution to his predicament. David was simply tired of having other men go before God on his behalf. He wanted to taste the goodness of God's presence for himself. I really believe that it was during this season of holy frustration that David stumbled upon one of the greatest spiritual discoveries of his lifetime.

DAVID DISCOVERS THE ORDER OF MELCHIZEDEK

The LORD said to my Lord, "Sit at My right hand, till I make Your enemies Your footstool." The LORD shall send the rod of Your strength out of Zion. Rule in the midst of Your enemies! Your people shall be volunteers in the day of Your power; In the beauties of holiness, from the womb of the morning, You have the dew of Your youth. The LORD has sworn and will not relent, "You are a priest forever, According to the order of Melchizedek" (Psalm 110:1-4 NKJV).

As King David continued looking for a more excellent way of approaching the presence of God, something supernatural happened. During one of his "devotions of desire," God opened a portal through the heavens for David to access. David found himself in the heavenly realms in the midst of a very important conversation between the Godhead. This divine conversation was between God the Father and God the Son. This revelation was going to answer David's deepest desire to get close to God's presence without the fear of divine retribution.

David could clearly see that under this priestly Order of Melchizedek, Christ was the everlasting High Priest and that there was no veil of restriction between God and His people.

In summary, this is what King David heard during this divine encounter. "The LORD said to my Lord, 'Sit at My right hand, till I make Your enemies Your footstool. The LORD has sworn and will not relent, You *are* a priest forever, according to the order of Melchizedek. (Psalm 110:1,4)." As God's flashlight of revelation flooded David's soul, the far-reaching spiritual implications of what God had shown him began to sink in.

To David's complete surprise, the divine conversation within the Godhead was centered on a heavenly priesthood which was not functioning in its official capacity within the nation of Israel. Since the day of his birth, David had lived under the spiritual influence of the Levitical priestly Order. David also knew that since he was not born a Levite, he was excluded from the Covenant of Levi. He knew that no matter how much he loved God, he could never have the close proximity of the presence of God that he so desperately desired. He knew that under the Levitical priesthood the penalty for touching the Ark of God for a non-Levite was instant death. This rule did not sit well with David, whose only desire was to touch God in a very meaningful way.

The more David listened to the divine conversation the more excited he became. He realized that God also had a driving desire to be touched by His people and to live among them. David realized that he had discovered the most powerful priestly Order that operates from within the realms of eternity. David could clearly see that under this priestly Order of Melchizedek, Christ was the everlasting High Priest and that there was no veil of restriction between God and His people. David also realized that under this priestly Order every one of God's holy children can hear the voice of God and walk in His divine power in the beauty of holiness.

THE TABERNACLE OF DAVID

After this I will return, and will rebuild the tabernacle of David, which has fallen down; I will rebuild its ruins, and I will set it up (Acts 15:16 NKJV).

The heavenly vision that King David received about the Order of Melchizedek completely altered his life. All the spiritual hang ups that he had from the sudden death of Uzzah and his initial failure to bring back the Ark of God disappeared. With renewed vigor, King David made a second attempt to retrieve the Ark of God's presence from the house of Obed-edom of Gath. This time David made sure that the Ark of the Covenant was carried on the shoulders of the Levites as they journeyed back to Israel. But David couldn't wait for the Ark of the Covenant to get to the City of David so he could test the power of his latest spiritual discovery. *I am not suggesting that this was the actual chronological order of how David stumbled upon the revelation concerning the priestly Order of Melchizedek; but what is of critical importance is that David made this very important discovery during his journey of desire or divine pursuit.* Somewhere between 1 Samuel 30 and 1 Chronicles 15, David made this amazing discovery and came to appreciate the practical ramifications of being under Christ's Order of Melchizedek priesthood.

> *David built houses for himself in the City of David; and he pre-*
> *pared a place for the ark of God, and pitched a tent for it. Then*
> *David said, "No one may carry the ark of God but the Levites, for*
> *the LORD has chosen them to carry the ark of God and to min-*
> *ister before Him forever." And David gathered all Israel together*
> *at Jerusalem, to bring up the ark of the LORD to its place, which*
> *he had prepared for it* (1 Chronicles 15:1-3 NKJV).

When the Ark of God got to the City of David, King David did not place the Ark of the Covenant in the Tabernacle at Shiloh, were it had originally been before it was captured by the Philistines. David does something very unusual. He created a new tabernacle to house the Ark of the Covenant that was based upon a new structure of worship. It was quite clear to those who were familiar with the Tabernacle of Moses, that David's new temple structure was very different from the blueprints that the Levitical priesthood had.

In the Levitical Tabernacle, only the high priest could look upon the Ark of God inside the Holy of Holies once a year. But under the Tabernacle of David, the Ark of God was placed under a simple tent, in plain sight of everyone who desired to catch a glimpse of the Ark of God's presence. David then invited all the people of Israel to come and worship the Lord in plain sight of the Ark of God.

No doubt there were many common people in Israel who were initially terrified of David's new structure of worship because they thought God would kill them if they looked upon or came too close to the Ark of God. After news spread that no one was dying for being close to the Ark of God under King David's new structure of worship, droves of people came to worship God.

Some of the people and Levites who had experienced the death of Uzzah first-hand could not understand why non-Levites were not dying.

The answer: King David was not operating under the Levitical priestly Order when he established this new structure of worship. He was operating under the priestly Order of Melchizedek, which is an infinitely higher priestly Order than the Levitical priesthood. King David came to realize that Uzzah had died because he had touched the Ark of the Covenant while operating under the Levitical priestly system. Under this Levitical priestly system, any non-Levite who was guilty of touching the Ark of God was killed instantly. The principal truth is that God always deals with His people on the basis of the revelation that they have of Him. God can never operate outside the amount of light that we are walking in. When we increase our level of light we exponentially increase the activity of God in our lives.

> *After this I will return and will rebuild the tabernacle of David,*
> *which has fallen down; I will rebuild its ruins, and I will set it*
> *up* (Acts 15:16 NKJV).

King David was operating under the premise of a new and highly superior priestly Order and he brought the people who came to the Tabernacle of David to worship God under the same covering of grace. *King David's revelation had fast-forwarded him past the crucifixion, past the resurrection, and right into the post-Calvary priestly ministry of Jesus Christ.* Wherever the priestly ministry of Jesus Christ is fully functional, it removes the veil of restriction between God and His people. This is exactly what happened under the Tabernacle of David because of King David's revelation concerning the Order of Melchizedek. This explains why God singled out the Tabernacle of David in the book of Acts and promised to rebuild it. (See Acts 15:16.)

God could have promised to rebuild the Tabernacle of Moses or the highly expensive and glamorous gold-plated Solomon's Temple, but He didn't. To the contrary, God promised to restore and rebuild the Tabernacle of David that has fallen into ruins. Why would God say that? The answer is dazzlingly simple but deeply profound. The Tabernacle of David is the only Old Testament tabernacle that was structured after the priestly Order of Melchizedek. All the other Old Testament tabernacles, all the way to Zerubbabel's Temple, were patterned after the Levitical Order of priesthood. All these tabernacles erected a veil of restriction between God and His people.

The fact that the promise to rebuild the Tabernacle of David was made to New Testament apostles is a clear indication that the order of worship under the Tabernacle of David aligns itself with the finished work of Christ. This divine promise made to New Testament apostles also indicates that one of the primary assignments of New Testament apostles is to help rebuild and set up the Tabernacle of David in their church or city. The Tabernacle of David is the house of prayer for all nations that Jesus called "My House"! This is why I am saddened by preachers of the gospel who make light of the New Testament importance of the Order of Melchizedek.

DAVID'S THREE MINISTERIAL OFFICES

1. David Functioned as a *King*

    *So there at Hebron, David made a covenant before the LORD with all the elders of Israel. And they **anointed him king** of Israel, just as the LORD had promised through Samuel* (1 Chronicles 11:3).

1. David Functioned as a *Priest*

    *Three days later, when David and his men arrived home at their town of Ziklag, they found that the Amalekites had made a raid into the Negev and Ziklag; they had crushed Ziklag and burned it to the ground. David was now in great danger because all his men were very bitter about losing their sons and daughters, and they began to talk of stoning him. **But David found strength in the LORD** his God. Then he said to Abiathar the priest, **"Bring me the ephod!"** So Abiathar brought it. Then David asked the LORD, "Should I chase after this band of raiders? Will I catch them?" **And the LORD told him,** "Yes, go after them. You will surely recover everything that was taken from you!"* (1 Samuel 30:1,6-8).

1. David Functioned as a *Prophet*

*Dear brothers, think about this! You can be sure that the patri-arch David wasn't referring to himself, for he died and was bur-ied, and his tomb is still here among us. But he was a prophet, and he knew God had promised with an oath that one of David's own descendants would sit on his throne. **David was looking into the future** and speaking of the Messiah's resurrection. He was saying that God would not leave him among the dead or allow his body to rot in the grave (Acts 2:29-31).*

King David is the only one of the kings of Israel who understood by rev-elation that there was an eternal heavenly priesthood that he could belong to that would release him from the many restrictions of the Levitical priesthood. This would certainly explain why King David is also the only king of Israel who functioned as a priest.

King David functioned under what many scholars call the "Messiah's anointing." David functioned as a king-priest with a powerful prophetic anointing, the same as Jesus Christ did during His earthly ministry. Some of King David's messianic prophecies are unri-valed in their spiritual depth and histori-cal accuracy. When David and his men got to Ziklag, they discovered that an invading horde had burned the city to the ground and captured all of their families. Many of David's men were so distraught they spoke of killing him. But instead of panick-ing, David asked one of the priests to give him the priestly ephod. Only priests were allowed to wear the priestly ephod when they were inquiring from God.

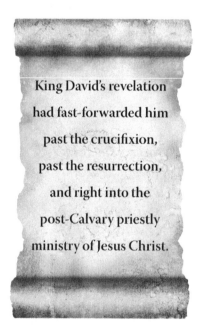

King David's revelation had fast-forwarded him past the crucifixion, past the resurrection, and right into the post-Calvary priestly ministry of Jesus Christ.

God spoke to David and told him to pursue the enemy. God told him that he would overtake the enemy and recover all. So here is the million dollar question:

If King David was a priest, what priestly Order was he from since he was from the tribe of Judah? Moses never spoke anything concerning the priesthood regarding the tribe of Judah. So how could David function as a priest under the Old Testament? The answer to this crucial question can only be answered in understanding the nature, scope, and spiritual dynamics of the Order of Melchizedek. Comprehensively answering that important question is what this entire book is all about.

It is my deepest prayer that God will give you the power to finish reading the remainder of this life-changing and Spirit-filled work I am sharing with you.

LIFE APPLICATION SECTION

MEMORY VERSES

This Melchizedek was king of the city of Salem and also a priest of God Most High. When Abraham was returning home after winning a great battle against the kings, Melchizedek met him and blessed him. Then Abraham took a tenth of all he had captured in battle and gave it to Melchizedek. The name Melchizedek means "king of justice," and king of Salem means "king of peace" (Hebrews 7:1-2).

REFLECTIONS

What is the Tabernacle of David?

_____

_____

_____

_____

What comes to mind when you read the expression, "David the Worshipping Warrior?"

_____

_____

_____

_____

_____

What kind of Goliath are you up against right now?

What is the connection between the presence of God and profitability in the Marketplace?

JOURNAL YOUR PERSONAL NOTES ON THIS CHAPTER

CHAPTER THREE

Abram Meets Melchizedek

W HEN ABRAM ANSWERED the call of God and left the land of his nativity for the Promised Land, he did not know that his choice to obey the voice of God had placed him on a collision course with one of the most powerful spiritual Orders in all of creation. I have served God long enough to know that when we obey God and make choices that set us on a course toward our God-given destiny, God will supernaturally weave Himself into the matrix of our lives.

> The LORD had said to Abram, "Leave your native country, your relatives, and your father's family, and go to the land that I will show you. I will make you into a great nation. I will bless you and make you famous, and you will be a blessing to others. I will bless those who bless you and curse those who treat you with contempt. All the families on earth will be blessed through you" (Genesis 12:1-3).

When God becomes involved with the affairs of our lives, the devil will also try to intercept the course of our lives to derail us from pursuing our spiritual destinies. The devil knows that from the moment the proceeding Word of God enters our airspace, we enter into a period of transition until the Word of the Lord concerning us has been fulfilled. The devil knows that more often than not the negative impact of emotional upheaval, mental and financial stress, combined with our human fragility, can force us to renegotiate our spiritual destiny. Many of God's people abort and abdicate their Kingdom assignments during periods of such transitions. Immediately after God gave Abram a powerful prophetic promise to migrate to the Promised Land, the devil tried to set him up for a fall using the vehicle of circumstance.

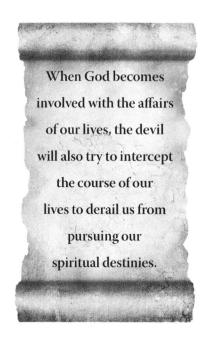

When God becomes involved with the affairs of our lives, the devil will also try to intercept the course of our lives to derail us from pursuing our spiritual destinies.

At that time a severe famine struck the land of Canaan, forcing Abram to go down to Egypt, where he lived as a foreigner. As he was approaching the border of Egypt, Abram said to his wife, Sarai, "Look, you are a very beautiful woman. When the Egyptians see you, they will say, 'This is his wife. Let's kill him; then we can have her!'" (Genesis 12:10-12).

Without any obvious warning, demonic agencies from the second heaven (Satan's headquarters) began to manipulate the spiritual atmosphere and natural climate around Abram's habitat. These demonic powers stopped the chambers of the first heaven from pouring their rain on the land Abram was living on! This resulted in a serious famine, which dried every well and water source around Abram. The ensuing drought caused Abram to panic and forced him to reconsider his position. He made a hasty decision out of his own sense of panic and insecurity and headed toward the godless nation of Egypt. *This decision would haunt Abram for a very long time.*

When we know that there is a higher calling of God upon our lives, we must train ourselves to run to God during times of painful transition. If we fail to do so, we will make hasty decisions, which serve to strengthen the demonic technology and agenda against us. Abram made a hasty decision and "ran to Egypt" because he was not firmly grounded in his relationship with God. Abram did not know the awesome power of the spiritual Order that he had been called to serve under.

Broken Covenants

When Abram and his household approached the borders of Egypt, Abram turned to his wife Sarai and had a conversation with her that would be every married woman's nightmare. Instead of risking his life for her, Abram asked his wife to lie about the true nature of their relationship. Abram was afraid of the Egyptians discovering that he was the husband of such a beautiful woman, and believed that they would kill him so they could present her to Pharaoh. Sarai, being a submissive wife, agreed to Abram's flawed proposal and the covenant of marriage between them was broken!

Covenants are made and broken with words. This is why our words are very important and carry tremendous weight in the spirit realm. When demonic agencies saw that the spiritual boundaries around Abram's marriage had been breached, evil spirits rushed in like a pack of African hyenas to the slaughter. Pharaoh's officers wasted no time telling their lustful king that a beautiful Hebrew woman had just come into the land of Egypt.

When the palace officials saw her, they sang her praises to Pharaoh, their king, and Sarai was taken into his palace. Then Pharaoh gave Abram many gifts because of her—sheep, goats, cattle, male and female donkeys, male and female servants, and camels. But the LORD sent terrible plagues upon Pharaoh and his household because of Sarai, Abram's wife (Genesis 12:15-17).

Pharaoh wasted no time bringing Sarai into his bedchamber. In exchange for anticipated sexual escapades with Sarai, Pharaoh treated Abram with great kindness because he thought Abram was Sarai's brother. The king of Egypt gave Abram a great company of sheep, oxen, camels, and

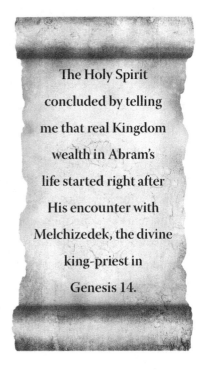

The Holy Spirit concluded by telling me that real Kingdom wealth in Abram's life started right after His encounter with Melchizedek, the divine king-priest in Genesis 14.

donkeys. He also gave Abram many male and female servants. *Abram became a very rich man overnight by lying and selling his wife to a demonic system!* Kingdom business men and women must be careful that they do not adopt deceptive business practices that guarantee quick profits but violate principles of common decency.

I imagine that Abram was horrified by the prospect of having his wife raped by a lustful Egyptian king. Using Sarai as a sexual toy was definitely what the king of Egypt had in mind when he chauffeured her into his bedroom. Fortunately, God intervened and terrorized the house of Pharaoh with grievous plagues. God warned Pharaoh against sexually exploiting Sarai because she was the wife of a prophet. Pharaoh restored her to Abram in great haste and instructed his servants to drive Abram and his household out of the land of Egypt.

MIXED BLESSINGS

When Abram and Sarai left Egypt, they had more material possessions than they had come with. The king of Egypt had given them a generous bounty before he realized that Abram had deceived him. When Pharaoh threw them out of his country he did not take back the riches that he had given them. But the possessions that the king of Egypt gave to Abram turned out to be more of a curse than a blessing.

Among the many possessions that the king of Egypt had given to Abram was a young Egyptian maid named Haggar. The demonic entrapment was already set. Many people do not realize that the devil is not stupid. He knows that most people would never pick up a venomous snake with their bare hands. But the devil also knows that if you hide a venomous snake inside a bag filled with gold and diamonds, most people would take it in a hurry. This is why our spiritual technology for unlocking financial resources for our ministries and businesses must be very accurate or we will set ourselves for a fall in our future destiny when the *snakes in our moneybags begin to manifest.*

STRIFE IN THE HOUSE

Finally Abram said to Lot, "Let's not allow this conflict to come between us or our herdsmen. After all, we are close relatives! The whole countryside is open to you. Take your choice of any section of the land you want, and we will separate. If you want the land to the left, then I'll take the land on the right. If you prefer the land on the right, then I'll go to the left." Lot took a long look at the fertile plains of the Jordan Valley in the direction of Zoar. The whole area was well watered everywhere, like the garden of the LORD or the beautiful land of Egypt. (This was before the LORD destroyed Sodom and Gomorrah) (Genesis 13:8-10).

Immediately after Abram returned from the land of Egypt, serious infighting broke out between Abram's herdsmen and those of Lot. The demonic snakes that were buried in the money bags that they had taken from the king of Egypt were already beginning to manifest themselves in the form of strife and division in Abram's house! The only thing that saved the day was Abram's attitude of humility and his ability to choose the high road. The memory of how God's power had rescued his wife from the jaws of a dangerous demonic system in the land of Egypt had left an indelible mark on Abram's impressionable spirit. Abram was slowly beginning to understand the power of the spiritual order that he had brought himself under when he answered the call of God.

Instead of fighting with Lot, Abram told his nephew that they needed to separate. Furthermore, Abram told Lot that he was free to choose whatever land space he needed to sustain his livestock. Abram chose to take whatever was left over. Lot, who was already infected by the spirit of the king of Egypt, chose the rich portion of land which was next to Sodom. Sodom was the most wicked nation of the ancient world. Sodom was also the birthplace of every form of sexual perversion, including homosexuality. Lot's carnal decision had set the stage for the chain of events that would soon set Abram on a collision course with the king of Sodom and the priestly Order of Melchizedek.

ABRAM'S GREATEST EMBARRASSMENT

So Abram left Egypt and traveled north into the Negev, along with his wife and Lot and all that they owned. (Abram was very rich in livestock, silver, and gold) (Genesis 13:1-2).

During the course of writing this book, the Holy Spirit gave me a revelation that shook me at the core of my being. This is what the Holy Spirit told me, *"Son, for as long as the Church thinks that Genesis 13:1-2 is an example of supernatural prosperity, it is never going to experience real kingdom wealth."* This statement shook me because I have used Genesis 13:1-2 many times in my teachings on Kingdom prosperity. The Holy Spirit continued, *"Son, Genesis 13:1-2 is not the basis for real Kingdom wealth because Genesis 13:1-2 describes Abram's tainted wealth that He obtained by selling his wife to a demonic system."* The Holy Spirit told me that "tainted wealth" can never form the basis of real Kingdom wealth. The Holy Spirit then said something to me that placed the icing on the cake, *"Many preachers and businessmen in the Body of Christ are doing the same thing that Abram did to his wife while he was in Egypt. They are prostituting the Body (bride) of Christ or their business for money and then calling their resulting prosperity real Kingdom wealth."* When the Holy Spirit said this to me I had to repent, because I discovered that I was also found wanting.

Abram replied to the king of Sodom, "I solemnly swear to the LORD, God Most High, Creator of heaven and earth, that I will not take so much as a single thread or sandal thong from what belongs to you. Otherwise you might say, 'I am the one who made Abram rich'" (Genesis 14:22-23).

After Abram and Sarai left Egypt with an abundance of material possessions that Abram had obtained by deceiving the king of Egypt, the king told everyone who had an ear that he was the one who had made Abram rich. These malicious rumors followed Abram wherever he went. It was quite embarrassing to say the least. *When Abram met Melchizedek (the priest of God Most High) he received a revelation on how he could sanctify his tainted wealth.* Abram gave Melchizedek a tithe of all he had. *This divinely inspired tithe not only destroyed the spirit of greed in Abram's life, it also became the supernatural purifying element which sanctified everything that Abram owned!* Abram's tithes into this eternal king-priest brought everything that he owned into divine alignment. Abram's tithes into the Order of Melchizedek rolled away the reproach of Egypt from his life. This is why it is so important for the global Church to rediscover the Abrahamic tithing model.

When the king of Sodom offered Abram gold and silver from the treasuries of Sodom, Abram knew that he could not afford to make the same mistake twice. Abraham knew that if he took the money, the king of Sodom was going to join the king of Egypt in declaring that he was the one who had made Abram rich. Abram's refusal of the king of Sodom's generous offer underscores the power of tithing into the Order of Melchizedek.

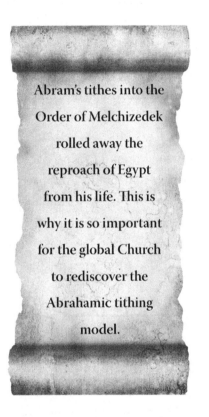

Abram's tithes into the Order of Melchizedek rolled away the reproach of Egypt from his life. This is why it is so important for the global Church to rediscover the Abrahamic tithing model.

Then the Holy Spirit concluded by telling me that real Kingdom wealth in Abram's life started right after His encounter with Melchizedek, the divine king-priest in Genesis 14. Melchizedek the king-priest brought Abraham into a living covenant with God. It follows then that the global Church will never experience real Kingdom wealth until it understands what Christ has made available for it through His Order of Melchizedek priesthood.

The Power to Prevail

Long after Lot's migration to the wicked nation of Sodom, five powerful kings from the East came against the king of Sodom and ravaged his country. In their victory, these foreign kings took men, women, and children as prisoners of war. They also emptied the treasuries of Sodom of most of its gold and silver. Lot, Abram's nephew, was among the prisoners of war who were taken captive by the invading horde. A man who had escaped the rampage ran to the house of Abram the Hebrew and told him that Lot had been captured by the armies of the kings from the East.

> *The victorious invaders then plundered Sodom and Gomorrah and headed for home, taking with them all the spoils of war and the food supplies. They also captured Lot—Abram's nephew who lived in Sodom—and carried off everything he owned* (Genesis 14:11-12).

Abram rose in haste and dressed himself for war. He assembled an army of about 318 men who were born and trained in his own house. He was also joined by a few of his allies. With the determination of an Olympic sprinter, Abram pursued the kings who had captured his nephew and his family. In less than twenty-four hours, Abram and his men overtook the foreign armies. Abram slaughtered these formidable enemy combatants with his homegrown force of men! Abram rescued all of his family members, including all the people of Sodom who had been taken captive. Abram also brought back all the gold and silver that these foreign kings had taken from the treasuries of Sodom.

KING OF JERUSALEM AND PRIEST OF GOD MOST HIGH

While Abram was returning from the slaughter of the foreign kings, a man who was set to alter the course of Abram's life intercepted him. When Abram met this majestic man, he began to realize by revelation that meeting this heavenly man was what every road in his life had been leading up to. Abram had by divine orchestration entered into the moment of moments. The mystery of God was about to be revealed. *Time and eternity were fixing to embrace. The promise-bearer was about to meet the promise-giver.*

There was a divine aura and deep sense of dignity upon this heavenly man that Abram had never seen or felt before. From his feet to the hair on his head this heavenly man exhibited a degree of divinity and righteousness that was simply overpowering. Abram realized that this man was the greatest and most important man that he would ever meet here on earth.

Who Was this Heavenly Man?

There are several schools of thought regarding the identity of this mysterious high priest who appeared to Abram in the valley of Shaveh. We will quickly examine some of these schools of thought and then I will tell you what I believe is the most logical answer as to the identity of this mysterious man. Some think Melchizedek was:

- the first Adam.

- Shem, the son of Noah.

- the priest-king of ancient Salem.

- the pre-incarnation appearance of Christ.

There are those who believe that *Melchizedek was the first Adam* returning in his glory because Adam was the only man in Scripture who had no earthly genealogy. But this belief stands on slippery ice because:

- Even though Adam had no earthly genealogy, he nevertheless had a spiritual genesis. The Bible clearly tells us when he was created, which means that Adam had a clear and traceable "beginning." This is in direct contrast to what the apostle Paul tells us in Hebrews chapter 7 about the Melchizedek, who met Abram in Genesis chapter 14. Paul says that this particular Melchizedek was "without beginning of days or end of life." Adam's life on the other hand had a beginning and a sure ending.

- Second, Adam became a slave to sin and its insidious powers after he fell from grace in the Garden of Eden. This means that in his fallen sinful condition there is simply no way Adam could be referred to as the king of righteousness. The name Melchizedek literally means "king of righteousness." Adam was anything but the king of righteousness. Even before they fell short of God's glory, Adam and Eve were both innocent but not righteous. They were as innocent as a newborn baby is innocent, but not righteous; so there is no way Adam could be the Melchizedek that appeared to Abraham.

- Third, the first Adam died without ever having broken the sentence of death over his own life. This in itself disqualifies him from being the prophetic representation of an eternal priesthood that is driven by the power of an endless life. The Order of Melchizedek exists beyond the perimeters of death in the realms of eternity.

There are also those who believe that *Melchizedek was Shem*, the son of Noah. They say that Shem was both a king and a priest, and that he received this priesthood from his father Noah. This belief stands on thinner ice than those who believe that Melchizedek was the first Adam returning in his glory. Here is why:

- The Bible clearly sets out the genealogy of Noah's family in the book of Genesis, which includes Shem. This in itself clearly disqualifies Shem from being the Melchizedek who met Abram in the valley of Shaveh. Once again the apostle Paul is quite clear that this Melchizedek who met Abram in the valley of the kings "had no earthly genealogy or beginning of days." There is no way God would use someone whose natural genealogy could be so easily proven to represent an eternal priesthood that is not of this world.

- Finally, if Melchizedek were Shem the son of Noah, it would mean that he would have had to have lived a very long time. If this were the case, it is highly probable that his appearance in the book of Genesis would have been duly noted, before and after Genesis 14. The fact that Melchizedek is not mentioned in the historical accounts of the book of Genesis except for this one meeting with Abram suggests that he was not Shem. Furthermore, the Bible does tell us when Shem died. Again, the apostle Paul is clear in letting us know that this Melchizedek had "no beginning of days or end of life."

Then there are those who believe that the Melchizedek who met Abram when he was returning from the slaughter of the kings was *the king-priest of the ancient City of Salem*. I admit that this school of thought is much more plausible than the previous two concerning the identity of this mysterious priest.

I personally believe that the king-priest over the ancient City of Salem was not the one who commissioned Abram in Genesis 14, even though he was certainly a priest of Jehovah. The Melchizedek priesthood which was stationed in the ancient City of Salem was merely a "shadow and forerunner" of the true heavenly Order of Melchizedek priesthood of our Lord Jesus Christ.

There are three more reasons why I believe that the Melchizedek who met Abram in the Valley of Shaveh was not the same Melchizedek who ruled the earthly City of Salem (Jerusalem).

- In the prophetic vision of King David in Psalm 110, David makes it very clear that the Order of Melchizedek is an eternal priestly ministry of Christ that has always existed in the realms of eternity before God created the world.

- After the fall of Adam, every human being born of a woman has been born a slave to sin, in terrible need of a Savior. I just do not see how God can pattern the eternal priestly ministry of Christ after a sin-compromised earthly priesthood. The supernatural never bows to the natural. The natural can be patterned after the supernatural but never the other way around. The Melchizedek priesthood in ancient Salem was patterned after the heavenly.

- The Bible teaches that all have sinned and come short of the glory of God. (See Romans 3:23.) If the Melchizedek who met Abram in the Valley of Shaveh was a mere mortal, I fail to see how he could possibly assume such a lofty title as the king of righteousness and prince of peace.

- While I agree that there was a king-priest over the ancient City of Salem who represented the eternal priesthood of Christ, I do not believe that he is the one who brought Abram into a living covenant with God. This is because the writer of Hebrews makes it quite clear that the Melchizedek who met Abram

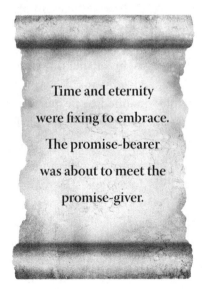

Time and eternity were fixing to embrace. The promise-bearer was about to meet the promise-giver.

in Genesis 14 was greater than Abram. If the Melchizedek who met Abram was a mere mortal, then it would mean that there was a man on earth who was greater and of a superior spiritual pedigree than Abram. If this were the case, then Abram is not qualified to be the father of many nations and the spiritual father of the New Creation. The "greater" is always more honorable and more blessed than the "lesser." Melchizedek, the king-priest of the ancient City of Salem, was therefore more suited to be the father of many nations and the spiritual father of the New Creation than was Abraham. If we insist that the Melchizedek who met Abram was a mere mortal who was stationed here on earth, then we also have to conclude that Abram was not the best candidate to be "the father of many nations."

Which leads us to what I believe is the most probable identity of the Melchizedek who intercepted Abram in the kings' valley. My extensive study on this subject has convinced me that the Melchizedek who met Abram in the Valley of Shaveh was different in both glory and stature from the earthly Melchizedek. I believe that this heavenly man was actually Christ manifesting Himself in bodily form to Abram before the virgin birth.

Perhaps this is what Jesus meant when He told the astounded Jews of His era that, "Abraham saw my day!" (See John 8:56.) What the Bible tells us in Genesis 14 is that this man was the "King of Salem," which corresponds to the heavenly City of Jerusalem. The Bible also tells us that this man was also the "King of righteousness," a term that is only befitting of Christ. The very name Melchizedek means "King over the whole domain of righteousness." Who else is fully qualified to properly assume the lofty title of "King of righteousness" other than the Lord Jesus Christ?

The Bible also tells us in Genesis chapter 14 that this man whom Abram met when he was returning from the slaughter of the kings was also the "Priest of God Most High." The man carried "bread and wine" which he offered to the stunned Abram. Abram was so impressed with this awesome man that he gave Him a tenth of all the spoils. This priestly man seemed to know everything about Abram. He even told Abram why he triumphed over such a mighty foreign army with only 318 men who were trained in his own house. Melchizedek informed Abram that the God of heaven and earth had sent his warring angels ahead of him into the battlefield. By the time Abram got to the camp of his enemies, their fate had already been delivered into his hands.

HEAVENLY BREAD AND WINE

Before Melchizedek left the scene, He blessed Abram, who was the custodian of the Covenant of Promise. The fact that this man blessed Abram proves that He was more powerful and loftier than Abram. Melchizedek also gave Abram the supernatural bread and wine that he had brought with Him from His eternal priestly Order. Bread and wine are the eternal emblems of the priestly Order of Melchizedek. We will discuss the spiritual implications of these spiritual emblems later, but I want to draw your attention to a very interesting declaration that Jesus made in the New Testament about Himself:

> Jesus replied, "I am the **bread** of life. Whoever comes to me will never be hungry again. Whoever believes in me will never be thirsty" (John 6:35).

> And he took a cup of wine and gave thanks to God for it. He gave it to them and said, "Each of you drink from it, for this is my blood, which confirms the covenant between God and his people. It is poured out as a sacrifice to forgive the sins of many" (Matthew 26:27-28).

SAYING NO TO THE KING OF SODOM

After Abram returned from his victory over Kedorlaomer and all his allies, the king of Sodom went out to meet him in the valley of Shaveh (that is, the King's Valley) (Genesis 14:17).

While Abram was returning from the slaughter of the kings from the East, news of his glorious victory reached the ears of the king of Sodom. The king of Sodom drove in his royal chariot to intercept Abram on his victorious return. The "king of Sodom" represents a demonic system that wants to corrupt every Kingdom business man and woman in the marketplace. Abram did not know that the king of Sodom was riding ferociously toward him, but the Lord did. The setting of the time and timing God chose to introduce Abram to the priestly Order of Melchizedek is very significant indeed. The perfect spiritual timing of Melchizedek's appearance in Abraham's life will shed light on the awesome power of this eternal priestly order. It was no coincidence that God in His infinite wisdom chose to intercept Abram's life just before the king of Sodom reached him. God was determined to touch Abram before the devil's greatest agent had a chance to do so.

> *The king of Sodom said to Abram, "Give back my people who were captured. But you may keep for yourself all the goods you have recovered." Abram replied to the king of Sodom, "I solemnly swear to the LORD, God Most High, Creator of heaven and earth, that I will not take so much as a single thread or sandal thong from what belongs to you. Otherwise you might say, 'I am the one who made Abram rich'"* (Genesis 14:21-23).

Remember that Sodom was more wicked than any of the countries of the East. Sodom made Egypt look like it was a paradise of righteousness. Please bear in mind that the Egyptians were no saints, they were hardcore idol worshippers. They worshipped Pharaoh, frogs, lice, the river Nile, just to name a few, and yet the people of Sodom made the Egyptians look like saints. The people of Sodom were ultra social liberals who did not believe in any kind of divine or moral restraint.

This was the same king whose royal chariots were charging ferociously toward Abram who was headed toward the Valley of Shaveh, also known as the King's Valley. This valley became the showdown stage for the confrontation between two kings from two different kingdoms. The divine confrontation was between the king of Sodom, who was the personification of the devil, and Melchizedek, King of Jerusalem and Priest of God Most High who represented the Kingdom of God.

When the king of Sodom finally reached Abram, he was a moment too late. The King of Jerusalem and High Priest of God Most High had already intercepted Abram, and Abram had been fully introduced to the priestly Order of Melchizedek. Abram had already partaken of the bread and wine of this heavenly Order and had been changed from the inside out. There was a divine power working inside his spirit and mind like he had never known before. When the king of Sodom tried to bribe him, Abram refused his luring offer. Abram told the king of Sodom that he had nothing that Abram desired, even to the shoelaces of the people of Sodom whom he had rescued in battle. Abraham's obedience coupled with his encounter with the priestly Order of Melchizedek gave him the power to rise above the seductive power and influence of the king of Sodom. In so doing, Abram side-stepped the demonic agencies that were driving the king of Sodom.

Abram's encounter with Melchizedek's priesthood gave him the supernatural power to resist every demonic entity that was coming against him through the king of Sodom. This divine encounter also gave Abraham the power to say "NO" to a very lucrative business proposal that the king of Sodom presented him, which was worth multiplied millions of dollars. I have seen too many good ministers and businessmen who have been destroyed like flies because they failed to say "NO" to the seductive influence of the king of Sodom (symbolic of Satan and this world system).

TITHES OF HONOR

Melchizedek blessed Abram with this blessing: "Blessed be Abram by God Most High, Creator of heaven and earth. And blessed be God Most High, who has defeated your enemies for you." Then Abram gave Melchizedek a tenth of all the goods he had recovered (Genesis 14:19-20).

One of the defining moments in the encounter that Abram had with Melchizedek, the High Priest of God Most High, had to do with the covenant exchange that took place between Melchizedek and Abram. The Bible tells us that Melchizedek, who was representing the Godhead in this supernatural transaction, gave Abram sacred bread and wine. Abram, on the other hand, who was representing humanity in this heavenly transaction, responded by sowing tithes of honor into this divine priesthood.

We will not discuss the deep and profound spiritual implications of this divine exchange between the Order of Melchizedek and Abram in this chapter. At this point I will simply say that tithing under the Order of Melchizedek is very different and much more honorable than the way tithing is taught today by many of the proponents of Malachi 3:8-12. Regrettably, both the revelation and attitude behind Abram's tithing are unmistakably missing in many of the popular methods of tithing. Understanding the Order of Melchizedek will both restore and upgrade the technology of tithing in the global Church.

A CHANGED NAME

Rachel was about to die, but with her last breath she named the baby Ben-oni (which means "son of my sorrow"). The baby's father, however, called him Benjamin (which means "son of my right hand") (Genesis 35:18).

Names were very important to people of the ancient world, but they were even more important to the Jewish people. The Jews believed that a person's name was a "sign post" of the person's:

- Inherent nature, character.
- Prophetic calling.
- Spiritual capacity.
- Destiny.

Jacob, for instance, was no stranger to the spiritual struggles that were induced into his life by the name that his father Isaac had given him. Jacob means "one who supplants." The online thesaurus dictionary defines the word *supplant* as "to take the place of (another), as through force, scheming, strategy, or the like."

When we observe Jacob's earlier life before God changed his name to Israel, he lived like a true supplanter. He deceived his brother Esau and coerced him to sell his firstborn birthright. In another matrix of deception in collaboration with his mother, Jacob became part of a plot to deceive his father. Isaac wanted to bestow the blessing of the firstborn upon his favorite son, Esau. When Rebecca, his wife, heard of it, she connived with scheming Jacob to impersonate Esau and steal the blessing. This is exactly what Jacob did.

When the deception behind his scheme was discovered by his ailing father and elder brother, there was great turmoil in the household. Esau was so angry that he plotted to kill his younger brother. When Jacob learned of this plot, he ran into exile to Syria. When we observe the earlier part of Jacob's life, we can clearly see that in many scenarios he was either supplanting someone else or he was the one being supplanted. It was a vicious cycle of pain and betrayal.

Keeping what we have observed in mind, we can appreciate why Jacob responded so quickly in renaming his last born son, when his dying wife gave him a cursed name. As Rachel's life was passing into eternity, she whispered the newborn son's name, "Ben-oni" meaning "the son who causes sorrow." Jacob knew from his own experience that such a name would marginalize the boy in life and hinder him from fulfilling his God-given destiny. Jacob quickly replaced it with the name Benjamin, which means "son of my right hand." The phrase "son of my right hand" in the ancient world conveyed the picture of a high-ranking official in any kingdom, second only to the reigning king. Bible history shows us that the tribe of Benjamin became one of the most powerful and elite tribes of Israel.

> When we observe the earlier part of Jacob's life, we can clearly see that in many scenarios he was either supplanting someone else or he was the one being supplanted. It was a vicious cycle of pain and betrayal.

When Melchizedek, the priest of God Most High, intercepted Abram in the Valley of Shaveh, he was known as Abram. Abram means "exalted father." Even though this was a fairly decent name, it was nevertheless a far cry from the great name that God had promised him when he migrated from Ur of the Chaldeans. God had a greater and more powerful name for Abram.

> Now the LORD had said to Abram: "Get out of your country, from your family and from your father's house, to a land that I will show you. I will make you a great nation; I will bless you and make your name great; and you shall be a blessing (Genesis 12:1-2 NKVJ).

When God promised Abram that he would make his name great, he was already known as Abram (exalted father) by many who were close to him. It follows then that the name Abram was not the "great" name God had promised to bestow upon him. But something very supernatural happened to the spiritual matrix of his name when he met Melchizedek in the Valley of Shaveh.

> *Then Melchizedek king of Salem brought out bread and wine; he was the priest of God Most High. And he blessed him and said: "Blessed be Abram of God Most High, Possessor of heaven and earth; and blessed be God Most High, Who has delivered your enemies into your hand"* (Genesis 14:18-20 NKJV).

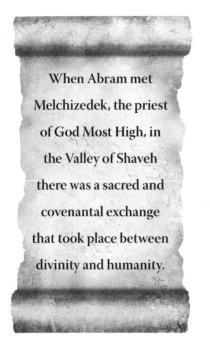

Melchizedek was the priest of God Most High. I want you to take note of this important phrase, "of God Most High." This powerful phrase refers to the spiritual order, rank, and title of Melchizedek, this king-priest was "of God Most High." There was no earthly order, rank, and title that rivaled the extreme loftiness of this king-priest.

When Abram met Melchizedek, the priest of God Most High, in the Valley of Shaveh there was a sacred and covenantal exchange that took place between divinity and humanity. Melchizedek (a foreshadow of Christ) served Abram with sacred bread and wine. After Abram partook of this covenantal meal, Melchizedek proceeded to bless Abram. The question that quickly comes to mind: "What was the blessing that Melchizedek gave to Abram in this covenantal exchange?" The answer is hidden in Genesis 12 verse 2, the blessing of a great name that God had promised. *The blessing of a changed name marked Abram's entrance into a higher level of spiritual stature.*

> When Abram met Melchizedek, the priest of God Most High, in the Valley of Shaveh there was a sacred and covenantal exchange that took place between divinity and humanity.

When Melchizedek the prophetic king-priest blessed Abram, he supernaturally added the "of God Most High" part of His lofty title to Abram's name. He was no longer simply Abram, he was now "Abram of God Most High." In other words, Abram's spiritual order, rank, and title had changed permanently to that "of God Most High." After this glorious meeting with Melchizedek "Abram of God Most High" was for all practical purposes the loftiest and most powerful man on earth. God gave him a name which was more valuable than any corporate brand name that you could ever think of.

> *What's more, I am changing your name. It will no longer be*
> *Abram. Instead, you will be called Abraham, for you will be the*
> *father of many nations* (Genesis 17:5).

Interestingly enough, the name Abraham, which carries the meaning "father of many nations," is the singular equivalent of the phrase, "Abram of God Most High." The "ha" sound in Abram's new name was the Hebrew equivalent of the name "Yahweh." The name "Yahweh" simply means "God Most High." This change in name from "Abram" to "Abraham" greatly changed the course of Abraham's life, and assured Abraham of a place of eternal greatness in God's Kingdom. The name that means "father of many nations" established the fact that what God had started with Abraham would not die or end with him.

The "of God Most High" part of his new great name also exponentially increased Abraham's spiritual capacity in God. When he was called Abram, his destiny and spiritual capacity were largely about his personal stake. As Abram, he was the "exalted father." This name assured him of achieving personal greatness but it did not guarantee him an ongoing posterity. It does not matter how exalted a father is, if he has no family of his own to preserve his posterity, he is limited to a certain extent. But when Melchizedek the king-priest added the expression "of God Most High" to his name, he removed every conceivable limit on Abraham's spiritual capacity to be fruitful in God's Kingdom. Melchizedek's priesthood gave Abram the power to become the "father of a multitude of nations" by simply changing his name. Christ's Order of Melchizedek priesthood will remove any boundary of limitation on the businesses of Kingdom business men and women who are submitted to this Order.

As in Abraham's case, God also wants to give us a great name. He wants to give us unforgettable divine encounters with His presence that will drastically change the internal spiritual configurations of our lives. *God want us to have very real divine encounters with Jesus Christ who is our present-day Melchizedek.* If we are truly the seed of Abraham and Jesus Christ is the High Priest after the Order of Melchizedek, then we have to admit that God set a prophetic pattern for us to follow in Abraham. As in Abraham's case, we cannot enter our promise of greatness without having intimate communion with our High Priest, even the Lord Jesus Christ. As in Abraham's case, God wants us to live by the sacred bread and wine of the Order of Melchizedek.

> *As they were eating, Jesus took some bread and blessed it. Then he broke it in pieces and gave it to the disciples, saying, "Take this and eat it, for this is my body." And he took a cup of wine and gave thanks to God for it. He gave it to them and said, "Each of you drink from it, for this is my blood, which confirms the covenant between God and his people. It is poured out as a sacrifice to forgive the sins of many* (Matthew 26:26-28).

LIFE APPLICATION SECTION

MEMORY VERSES

As they were eating, Jesus took some bread and blessed it. Then he broke it in pieces and gave it to the disciples, saying, "Take this and eat it, for this is my body." And he took a cup of wine and gave thanks to God for it. He gave it to them and said, "Each of you drink from it, for this is my blood, which confirms the covenant between God and his people. It is poured out as a sacrifice to forgive the sins of many" (Matthew 26:26-28).

REFLECTIONS

Why were names so important to the Jewish people?

Explain the significance of the covenantal exchange that took place between Abram and Melchizedek.

How does this covenant exchange affect Kingdom business men and women in the marketplace?

ABRAM MEETS MELCHIZEDEK

JOURNAL YOUR PERSONAL NOTES ON THIS CHAPTER

77

CHAPTER FOUR

The King of Sodom

After Abram returned from his victory over Kedorlaomer and all his allies, the king of Sodom went out to meet him in the valley of Shaveh (that is, the King's Valley) (Genesis 14:17).

And with many other words he testified and exhorted them, saying, "Be saved from this perverse generation" (Acts 2:40 NKJV).

W E WILL NOW EXAMINE how the Order of Melchizedek is designed to deliver us from being corrupted by the demonic sodomic system, *which is the principle of perversity that is inherent in all man-made institutions.* I will show you how the Order of Melchizedek is designed to preserve Kingdom citizens who have vocations in a marketplace environment which is controlled by secularism. If you are a Kingdom business man or woman I admonish you to prayerfully read this chapter. Please remember that Sodom was the most morally bankrupt nation among the countries of the East during Abraham's era. The people of Sodom and Gomorrah made the Egyptians look like saints.

The people of Sodom were ultra social liberals who did not believe in heeding to any kind of divine restraint. Some of today's churches have been overtaken by the doctrine of demons, which come in the form of a message of "greasy grace" that refuses to condemn sin in the church for fear of losing people who have not yet made up their minds to become disciples of Christ.

This chapter takes an introspective look at the king and people of Sodom to uncover what they represent, prophetically speaking. I will also show you how the Order of Melchizedek gives us the power to rise above the seductive influence of the demonic sodomic system. This is especially critical for those with vocations in the marketplace.

The following is a glossary of what the king of Sodom represents prophetically—a snap shot of the underlying essence of this demonic sodomic system.

- The king of Sodom was the king of an ultra liberal society in which every boundary of morality in the structure of the nation had been removed. This reminds me of the Sprite commercial which says "Obey your thirst!" In Sodom, everybody obeyed their thirst, whatever it was. This is the direction that the United States of America is sliding towards rapidly and the frontline of this culture war is the marketplace.

- The king of Sodom was the king of a nation that celebrated every form of sexual perversion, including homosexuality and bestiality. Sexual perversity is quite prevalent in the marketplace today. They are many Kingdom business men and women, even pastors, who are struggling with an addiction to pornography that they contracted in the marketplace. Unholy sexual affairs between CEOs and their secretaries are rampant in the marketplace, even among the so called "Christian businessmen." Most advertising campaigns for the selling of goods and services in the marketplace have strong sexual overtones.

- The king of Sodom also represents the diabolical mismanagement of seed, through inappropriate sexual intercourse. This diabolical mismanagement of seed causes the seed of future apostles, prophets, pastors, presidents, and so forth to die in an instrument that God never designed for procreation. This is not what God intended in the beginning when He created male and female as procreators of the second generation. This is the same spirit which deceives many Kingdom business men and women, causing them to mismanage the financial resources (seeds) that are supposed to be used to advance the Kingdom. They end up purchasing multimillion dollar luxury mansions in foreign lands that they only visit once a year. This diabolical mismanagement of Kingdom financial resources will come to an end, when Melchizedek's priesthood intercepts the power of the king of Sodom over His Kingdom citizens in the marketplace.

- The king of Sodom completely destroyed the "mountain of family" within the structure of his nation. This would explain why Lot's daughters did not see anything wrong with having sex with their own father. (The mountain of family is what many call the institution of family.) Across the nations of the world there is a relentless attack on the institution of family in the marketplace. The primary victim of this relentless demonic attack on the family is the traditional definition of marriage.

- The king of Sodom also represents ill-gained financial resources, which were obtained by using demonic technology (corruption). The demonic sodomic system is behind the systemic corruption that is prevalent in many corporate boardrooms and corridors of government. Only those who are of the Order of Melchizedek can live above the reach of this demonic system. Kingdom business men and women must never allow themselves to participate in corrupt practices in order to secure a business contract. We must remember that we serve a God who can supply superabundantly in the worst economic conditions. If Kingdom business people engage in corruption they are opening the door for the devil to plunder their entire corporation.

- The king of Sodom was a prophetic picture of the spirit of the anti-Christ. The spirit of the anti-Christ is the spirit that stands opposed to the advancement of the Kingdom of God and to anything that is Christ-like. Kingdom business men and women must never be ashamed of identifying themselves with the Kingdom of God in the marketplace. They must hold steadfast to both the values and the principles of the Kingdom and God will make sure that "all of these things" (profits) will be added to them.

- The king of Sodom was so devoted to operating in spiritual darkness that the spirit of Satan manifested itself very powerfully in his life. The demonic sodomic system is behind much of the "Satanism" and infatuation with witchcraft that pervades most western nations. The king of Sodom (the devil) is behind the explosion of psychic phenomenon in the marketplace today. CEOs and some police departments are now consulting with psychics, when they should be consulting with God's prophets. Where are the "Josephs" and the "Daniels" who can bring the spirit of prophecy to the marketplace?

- The king of Sodom is a prophetic representation of the spirit of Babylon, which is the principal spirit behind the systems of this world. The spirit of Babylon is an adulterous, covenant breaking spirit. This is the same spirit which is behind much of the backstabbing and double dealing that is prevalent in corporate boardrooms and in the corridors of government. It is also the same spirit that causes many corporate women to sleep with their male counterparts in order to climb the corporate ladder. The Order of Melchizedek can save Kingdom citizens from being trapped in this perversity. The Order of Melchizedek will teach Kingdom business men and women how to honor all of their verbal and contractual agreements with their vendors, creditors and business partners. You would be surprised just how untrustworthy many so called "Christian business men" really are!

THE COUNTRY OF SODOM

So the LORD told Abraham, "I have heard a great outcry from Sodom and Gomorrah, because their sin is so flagrant. I am going down to see if their actions are as wicked as I have heard. If not, I want to know" (Genesis 18:20-21).

Sodom was so obnoxiously wicked that God decided to come down from Heaven to check it out for Himself. The flagrant nature of the sin and sexual perversity in this wicked country had reached the ears of a holy God. The people of Sodom, under the guidance of the king of Sodom, had transformed

Sodom into a "hell house." Sodom had become a little satanic empire here on earth. It had become the base of operations for fallen angels and every foul spirit imaginable. Every sexual sin you can think of, including homosexuality and bestiality, were practiced freely in this wicked nation.

According to Roget's Thesaurus, *bestiality* means "sexual relations between a person and an animal or sodomy." The very name Sodom tells us just how depraved and sexually perverse this ancient country was. Some of the people of Sodom were having sex with animals and the king of Sodom did not see anything wrong with this. It's not surprising that God came down to visit this wicked country just like He had come down to see the building of the tower of Babel.

> *But before they retired for the night, all the men of Sodom, young and old, came from all over the city and surrounded the house. They shouted to Lot, "Where are the men who came to spend the night with you? Bring them out to us so we can have sex with them!" So Lot stepped outside to talk to them, shutting the door behind him. "Please, my brothers," he begged, "don't do such a wicked thing. Look, I have two virgin daughters. Let me bring them out to you, and you can do with them as you wish. But please, leave these men alone, for they are my guests and are under my protection"* (Genesis 19:4-8).

Interestingly enough, what we call the "gay lifestyle" originated in this ancient city, which God judged by burning it to the ground with fire and brimstone. The sin of homosexuality was one of the sins for which this ancient city was judged. I love gays very deeply with the love of God. I am very opposed to demeaning or demonizing those who are gay, but the constitution of the Kingdom (the Bible) prohibits such a lifestyle. What amazes me is how some so-called Christian churches that claim that the Bible is their final authority in matters of doctrine waver on this important subject. Following is a quote from the editorial page of *Charisma* magazine's February 2007 issue that underscores how the seductive and corrupting influence of the king of Sodom is creeping into the life stream of the global Church.

> *A while later Jay let the world know what he really believes. He told Radar magazine: "This sounds so churchy, but I felt like*

God spoke to my heart and said (homosexuality) is not a sin."
So I am blowing the whistle. This is an official apostasy alert. In
case you haven't noticed, Jay is not the only voice in the blogo-
sphere claiming that God has changed His mind about homo-
sexuality. The Episcopal Church voted to ordain a gay bishop in
2003. Many gay affirming churches are sprouting up in Middle
America – including some that claim to be Pentecostal. In fact,
the founder of the largest gay denomination in the country, Troy
Perry, was raised in the Church of God of Prophecy.

What Troy Perry, Jay Bakker and the Episcopalians are offer-
ing America is a new religion that guarantees no hell and
requires no holiness. It's a limp spineless Christianity that can-
not confront sin for fear of being "judgmental." It is an impo-
tent gospel which tells people who wrestle with homosexuality
that they might as well indulge. It welcomes everyone with a
polite "come as you are" mantra, but in the end is incapable
of breaking the power of addic-
tion or sexual dysfunction. It uses
feel-good words such as "tolerance,"
"acceptance," and "grace," terms
that sound hip and sexy in today's
permissive culture. It is a golden
calf, shiny and seductive, forged by
those whose goal is to invent a new
morality. This "gay-affirming gos-
pel" is a toxic heresy that must be
addressed boldly from our pulpits
in 2007. I pray that there is enough
moral backbone left in the church
to face this challenge.[1].

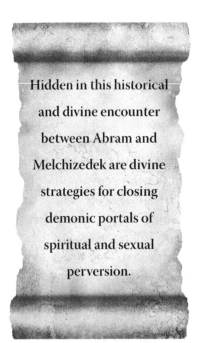

Hidden in this historical
and divine encounter
between Abram and
Melchizedek are divine
strategies for closing
demonic portals of
spiritual and sexual
perversion.

I normally don't include such long quotes in my books, but this one is far too important to quote out of context. The author emphasizes how the seductive influence of the king of Sodom (the devil) is trying to redefine the fundamental tenets of the gospel of our Lord Jesus Christ. This underscores why we need to rediscover and tap into the power of the priestly Order of Melchizedek.

The Order of Melchizedek is the only spiritual order that God has made available to New Testament believers that has the power to intercept the seductive power and corrupting influence of the king of Sodom. The Order of Melchizedek is the only spiritual priesthood which has the power to deliver every person who is struggling with the sin of same-sex attraction. The divine interception of Abram by Melchizedek, the priest of God Most High, right before the king of Sodom intercepted him, has far-reaching spiritual implications for the present day ministry of the Church. Hidden in this historical and divine encounter between Abram and Melchizedek are divine strategies for closing demonic portals of spiritual and sexual perversion in our generation.

Sexual perversity in our generation has reached a frightening peak. Everything on television is driven by overtures of sex and sexuality. Our generation's obsession with sex has now taken over the advertising industry. Almost every other marketing ad on television is either driven by an almost nude model or has strong sexual overtones. Even car sales advertisements display almost nude women sitting on the car or truck. The woman is told to look into the camera seductively and challenge the viewing audience to run to the dealership to buy the automobile being advertised.

The subliminal message behind many of these commercials is simple but hellishly dangerous: "Buying this car (furniture, candy bar, beer, grill, whatever) is like having sex with this beautiful, almost-naked woman." Living in such a sexually driven and perverse generation such as ours requires that we have a personal encounter with God Most High. We need a supernatural encounter with God that will effectively purge sexual lust out of our system.

In recent years we have seen the sad and unfortunate destruction of some of the greatest men and women of God of our generation because of sexual scandals. Multimillion dollar ministries and businesses that were touching the lives of multiplied millions with the gospel of the Kingdom were cut short when it was discovered that the man (in most cases) or the woman at the top of the organization had been caught in an unholy sexual affair.

In light of the devil's plan to flood the earth's spiritual atmosphere with the wickedness of sexual perversity, we cannot overemphasize the importance of the Order of Melchizedek in our lives. There is a supernatural grace available to us under this royal-priestly order to rise above sexual perversity and walk in purity. I am convinced that if Melchizedek's priesthood had not intercepted Abram, the king of Sodom would have succeeded in seducing him. After all, Abram had miserably lost a spiritual battle to the king of Egypt when he sold his wife to save his life. (See Genesis 12:10-12.)

DON'T GO DOWN TO EGYPT

One of the critical dangers we are most likely to face on our spiritual journey is the danger of aborting our prophetic destiny during periods of transition. When the devil saw that Abram and Sarai were moving forward in their God-given destinies, he created an artificial drought around Abram's habitat. We must remember that the first heaven which is responsible for controlling natural times and seasons here on earth is in a fallen state, which means that this part of the heavens can be easily manipulated by demonic powers.

When we make decisions that impact our destiny based on external stimuli, we may be walking into demonic entrapment. This is exactly what happened to Abram and Sarai. When Abram saw that the wells of water that he needed to sustain his livestock had dried up, he panicked. In his panic he made a hasty decision and migrated to Egypt. *This demonically engineered decision placed him on the pathway of death and destruction.* Kingdom business men and women must be careful not to allow dollars and cents to override the counsel of the Lord just to make a buck. In many cases the devil is in the details. "Sign here and all your problems are over" could translate into years of heart wrenching pain and regret.

A MARRIAGE IN CRISIS

As mentioned previously, when Abram got to the borders of Egypt, he broke the covenant of marriage with his wife and brought her into a covenant of lies to protect himself. In Egypt his dear wife was almost raped by the king of Egypt who wanted to sleep with her. In exchange for exploiting Sarai sexually,

Abram and his nephew Lot were given an abundance of male and female servants. The king of Egypt also gave him plenty of livestock, gold, and silver from the treasuries of Egypt. It must have looked great on his business portfolio!

Had Abram known that this tainted business deal with the king of Egypt had set him on a collision course with the king of Sodom, he probably would have made a better decision. Had God not intervened, Sarai would have been raped by the king of Egypt and Abram would have been killed by Pharaoh once he discovered that Abram had actually deceived him. This is why being of the Order of Melchizedek is so important. This kingly-priesthood of our Lord Jesus Christ will preserve our lives and families if we truly submit ourselves to it. Instead of being killed, Abram and Sarai were given an eviction notice to leave Egypt. Abram and Lot left with a lot of money and material possessions from the treasuries of Egypt. Unfortunately their ill-gained wealth had come at a terrible price.

> Sexual perversity in our generation has reached a frightening peak. Everything on television is driven by overtures of sex and sexuality.

LOT MOVES TO SODOM

Abram's decision to move to Egypt during the time of famine (economic recession) had mudded his relationship with his nephew, Lot. Whenever we disobey God in our decision-making process, the spiritual consequences of our spiritual inaccuracy almost always manifest in the arena of our closest personal or business relationships. This was certainly the case between Abram and Lot. As soon as they returned from Egypt with the bounty taken from the treasuries of Egypt, there was serious strife and division between their two corporations. The presence of spirits of strife and division in our closest relationships is always a sign that demonic agencies are swimming in the "spiritual wells" we are drinking from.

The strife between Abram's and Lot's herdsmen quickly became hostile. Abram called for a truce. Abram told Lot that there was no need for them to fight over land (business contracts) because they were family. *Kingdom business men and women must never fight each other "filthy lucre," because there are no shortages of resources in the economy of the Kingdom.* Even though Abram had seniority, he gave Lot the power of first choice concerning the land. (Coincidentally, when we come into a place of spiritual maturity, we can do more with the "leftovers" than most people can do with a whole pie.) The intervention of God that Abram had just experienced in the land of Egypt was still fresh on his mind. He remembered how God had delivered his wife from Pharaoh's bedchamber and spared his own life. This powerful intervention of God had left an indelible mark on Abram's spirit. He was beginning to appreciate the power of the God who had called him out of Babylonia. This is why he refused to fight with Lot over the issue of land.

On the other hand, Lot did not know how to make spiritual decisions from his spirit-man. *Kingdom business men and women who master the art of listening to the Lord before making major business decisions, will never lose money in any business deal.* Lot, on other hand, simply looked at the evidence that was presented to him by his natural senses and decided to pitch his tent (business) near the wicked country of Sodom. The plains surrounding Sodom and Gomorrah at that time were very fertile and richly supplied with water. Lot thought that he had hit the jackpot. From the outside it appeared as if Lot had made a great spiritual and business decision, but it was actually disastrous. Lot did not know that his path toward Sodom was on a collision course with the wrath of God.

> The presence of spirits of strife and division in our closest relationships is always a sign that demonic agencies are swimming in the "spiritual wells" we are drinking from.

If Lot had known that his decision to live near Sodom would one day cause him to lose everything that he had worked for all his life, he would have been terrified. Had he known that his decision to settle in the plains of Sodom would one day transform his dear wife into a pillar of salt and force his two daughters to commit incest, he would have been horrified. His decision to move to Sodom brought him under the power and influence of the king of Sodom. Unfortunately, Lot did not have the spiritual stamina and stature to effectively resist the powerful demonic influence of the king of Sodom.

Lot's carnal decision to live near Sodom unknowingly also placed Abram on a collision course with the seductive and corruptive power of the king of Sodom. Lot was the small fish that the devil used as spiritual bait to draw in Abram, the big fish. The devil knew that the promise of God to bless all the nations of the world was entrusted to Abram. It was Abram the devil wanted; Lot was simply collateral damage. The devil knew that Abram loved his nephew and would not hesitate to come to his rescue.

FIGHTING ON THE LOSING SIDE

The king of Sodom represents in a prophetic sense the spirit of the anti-Christ. This is why persecution from the world will rise against Kingdom citizens who are not afraid of identifying with Christ in the marketplace. When Lot and his family established residence in Sodom, they did not know that the judgment of this wicked nation had already been set in stone in the corridors of eternity. Lot had placed himself on the pathway of death and destruction.

When we identify ourselves with the king of Sodom and not with the King of Jerusalem (Jesus Christ), we are setting ourselves up for defeat and destruction in the future. So-called Christian business men and women who do not know how to conduct business in the economy of the Kingdom are going to be easy prey for the demonic sodomic system. It grieves me deeply to see how many pastors are watering down the gospel message in order to attract larger crowds. These carnal decisions are aligning pastors and their church members with the spirit of this world. Driven by an unholy desire to prosper at all costs, some pastors and business leaders have placed themselves in very compromising positions. Some of these spiritual leaders do not know that they are fighting on the same side as the king of Sodom (Satan), because of their lust for power and money. The only sure protection we have from being overtaken by the power of the king of Sodom is to yield ourselves to the authority and will of the High Priest of the Order of Melchizedek, our Lord Jesus Christ.

When we align ourselves with the spirit of this world and begin to eat from the same plate that this diabolical spirit is feeding from, we will suffer in the judgment of this wicked system. The king of Sodom was already quarantined for death and destruction by divine decree. *The rampant greed and corruption within this world's economic system has already placed the sentence of death on the world's systems of commerce.* Lot's close association with the king and people of Sodom made him become a partaker of this wicked nation's impending judgment. Lot went into Sodom a wealthy, righteous business man, but he came out a financially bankrupt and backslidden preacher of righteousness. Please do not fight on the same side as the king of Sodom in your desire to have a mega ministry or business. I am not opposed to anybody having a mega ministry or business, but we must make sure that the spiritual technology we are using to grow our ministry or business is not borrowed from Sodom!

DIVINE INTERCEPTION

After Abram returned from his victory over Kedorlaomer and all his allies, the king of Sodom went out to meet him in the valley of Shaveh (that is, the King's Valley). And Melchizedek, the king of Salem and a priest of God Most High, brought Abram some bread and wine. Melchizedek blessed Abram with this blessing: "Blessed be Abram by God Most High, Creator of heaven and earth. And blessed be God Most High, who has defeated your enemies for you." Then Abram gave Melchizedek a tenth of all the goods he had recovered (Genesis 14:17-20).

We are living in very dangerous times. The sovereignty of nations is constantly being threatened by international terrorism. For many of us who live in the United States, we will never forget the horrors of September 11, 2001, that brought the portals of terror right to our doorsteps. Rogue nation dictators, such as in North Korea and Iran, are determined to build nuclear weapons, and are telling the world that they want to wipe Israel off the face of the earth.

The growing threat of terrorism posed by the rapid rise of radical Islamists and the rise of rogue dictators has forced world powers like the United States of America, Great Britain, Russia, and China to invest heavily in nuclear missile interception technology. This technology specializes in enhancing the ability of nations to intercept nuclear missiles that might be launched against them by some fanatical terrorists. This technology has given nations such as the United

States the military capability to defuse a nuclear missile in midair rendering it useless in regard to its original objective.

Thousands of years before the powers of the West thought of developing this powerful technology, God had already secured this spiritual technology for Kingdom citizens. To help you appreciate the intercepting capability of the priestly Order of Melchizedek, I will define *intercept* from Roget's Dictionary.

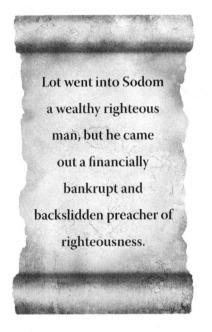

Lot went into Sodom a wealthy righteous man, but he came out a financially bankrupt and backslidden preacher of righteousness.

Intercept means:

1. To take, seize, or halt (someone or something on the way from one place to another); cut off from an intended destination: to intercept a messenger.

2. To see or overhear (a message, transmission, etc., meant for another).

3. To stop or check (passage, travel, etc.): to intercept the traitor's escape.

4. To take possession of (a ball or puck) during an attempted pass by an opposing team.

5. To stop or interrupt the course, progress, or transmission of.

6. To destroy or disperse (enemy aircraft or a missile or missiles) in the air on the way to a target.

7. To stop the natural course of (light, water, etc.).

8. To intersect.

9. Obsolete. To prevent or cut off the operation or effect of.

10. Obsolete. To cut off from access, sight, etc.

I hope that you are as excited as I am at the far-reaching spiritual implications of what it means for you and I to be *intercepted* by God before we are overrun by a demonic nuclear missile. *Divine interception means that God apprehends us before we get taken by the enemy!* After Abram soundly defeated the kings from the East that had plundered Sodom, news of his resounding victory reached the ears of the king of Sodom. The king of Sodom quickly informed the keeper of the royal chariots to mount his horses because they were going to intercept Abram on his return. The king of Sodom put on his royal garments and fumed himself in the oils and fragrances which were offered in worship to his demon gods. With the smell of hell oozing from his body, the king of Sodom drove his chariots like a mad race-car driver to the finish line. He was in a demonic hurry to intercept Abram, but he was too late.

Moments before the king of Sodom and his diplomatic entourage from the land of Sodom arrived, Melchizedek, High Priest of God Most High, intercepted Abram. Many scholars believe that this king-priest was a pre-incarnation manifestation of Christ. This priestly man, who was also the prophetic representation of the eternal priesthood of our Lord Jesus Christ, intercepted Abram just before the king of Sodom got to him. The divine encounter between Abram and Melchizedek was so powerful and life changing that Abram did something that he had never done before. *Abram gave this Priest of God Most High, his first tithe.* As mentioned previously, there is more discussion about tithes of honor that Abram gave to this king-priest in Chapter Ten. I have also discussed these tithes of honor in great detail in my book, *The Return of the Lost Key: Tithing under the Order of Melchizedek.* What is very important to understand is that Abram would have fallen to the seductive power of the king of Sodom, had he not been intercepted by the priesthood of Melchizedek.

Do Not Make a Deal with the King of Sodom

Moments after Melchizedek's departure, the chariots of the king of Sodom screeched to a halt, shooting speckles of dust into the air. The king of Sodom dismounted and in royal pomp, walked toward Abram. The king of Sodom had heard of Abram but he had never met him until now. The king of Sodom gave Abram a hideous smile and offered him a deal that he felt Abram could not refuse. Had the king of Sodom succeeded in manipulating Abram into signing the demonic contract, God would have had to look for another man to do what He had called Abram to do. This is how serious the confrontation between Abram and the king of Sodom was to Abram's future destiny and God's purpose for humankind.

The king of Sodom told Abram to give his people back. But he told Abram that he could keep the money that the foreign invaders had stolen from the treasuries of Sodom. If Abram had been like some of today's ecclesiastical and marketplace ministers he would have taken the bounty from the treasuries of Sodom. He would have televised it as testimony of a great financial miracle. Fortunately Abram had just been introduced to the Order of Melchizedek. This one encounter with the Order of Melchizedek had opened his spiritual eyes and helped his spirit to properly discern the king of Sodom's hidden demonic agenda. In a prophetic sense, Abram saw all the poisonous snakes that were hidden in the money bags that the king of Sodom was offering him. Had Abram taken the money from the treasuries of Sodom, he would have opened a spiritual portal for devils to enter his life.

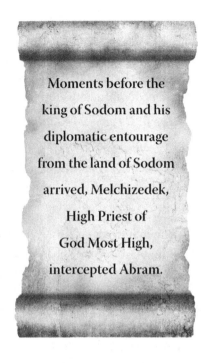

Moments before the king of Sodom and his diplomatic entourage from the land of Sodom arrived, Melchizedek, High Priest of God Most High, intercepted Abram.

How many great spiritual leaders and kingdom businessmen do you know of who have caved in to the king of Sodom? Some of these spiritual leaders and businessmen are selling their souls to a demonic system for an extra buck! The scandalous fall of great televangelists in the 1980s and 1990s rocked the entire church world. The men who were heading these ministries failed to say "NO" to the seductive offers of the king of Sodom. In light of such scandals that have tarnished the image of the Church and hurt the cause of Christ, you cannot convince me that spiritual leaders in the Body of Christ do not need to submit themselves to the Order of Melchizedek.

Instead of taking the money the king of Sodom had offered him, Abram emphatically and publicly told the king of Sodom that his answer was a resounding and heartfelt, "NO!" Abram told the king of Sodom that there was nothing that he owned in all of Sodom that Abram desired for himself or his business. *This means that there is a more excellent way of acquiring real Kingdom wealth without compromising Kingdom values and principles.* Abraham then proceeded to tell the King of Sodom the two main reasons why he had turned down his demonically engineered offer.

The first reason revealed the source of Abram's power.

> *Abram replied to the king of Sodom, "I solemnly swear to the LORD, God Most High, Creator of heaven and earth, that I will not take so much as a single thread or sandal thong from what belongs to you* (Genesis 14:22-23).

The main reason why Abram refused the offer of money from the hands of the king of Sodom was based upon the fact that he had just established a covenant of tithe with God through Melchizedek who was the Priest of God Most High. This one divine encounter with Melchizedek's priesthood had shown him that God was his source for everything he needed to fulfill the prophetic assignment upon his life. *This awesome encounter with the heavenly king-priest had completely shut down the wells of greed inside the chambers of his sanctified soul.* The glitter of the gold and silver from the treasuries of Sodom had suddenly lost their lustrous appeal. Abram was a changed man.

The second reason unmasked the hidden demonic agenda behind the offer of the king of Sodom.

> *...Otherwise you might say, 'I am the one who made Abram rich'* (Genesis 14:23).

The second reason that underscores why Abram refused to take money from the hands of the king of Sodom was based upon another very important consideration. Abram knew through personal experience that when you take money from the devil there will always be hell to pay in the near future! Abram had made a similar mistake once when he had stretched out his hands to take the gold and silver that the king of Egypt had offered him at the time.

Years later after Abram took the "hush money" from the treasuries of the king of Egypt, He was stalked constantly by rumors that said that the king of Egypt was boasting and telling people that he was the one who had made Abram rich. These stories caused Abraham tremendous pain and embarrassment.

Fortunately when the king of Sodom showed up and offered him the same deal, he was able to discern that this particular financial offer by the king of Sodom was more sinister and spiritually poisonous than that of the king of Egypt. The covenant communion of the sacred bread and wine that he had received at the hands of Melchizedek had infused him with a keen sense of spiritual awareness and discernment! This is why New Testament believers need to be aware of what is available to them under the eternal priestly Order that our Lord Jesus Christ presides over.

SNAKES IN MONEY BAGS

Abram's ability to reject the generous offer of the king of Sodom also has far-reaching spiritual ramifications for the seed of Abraham. According to the principle of apostolic succession, we were all (born-again believers) in the spiritual loins of Abraham when he said "NO" to the king of Sodom and rose above the seductive power of the gold and silver of this world. This means that if we tap into the same grace that Abram discovered when he met Melchizedek, the seductive power of mammon will be broken over our lives and business practices! Nevertheless, this will not happen unless we become accurately connected to the Order of Melchizedek.

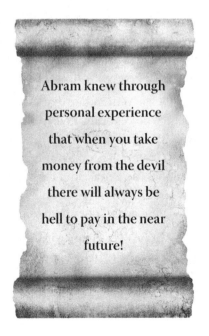

Abram knew through personal experience that when you take money from the devil there will always be hell to pay in the near future!

Nothing has destroyed more good ministries and business men than the seductive and corrupting influence of money and sex. The corridors of human history are plastered with tragic stories of great men and women of God who had great world-shaking ministries. But some of these servants of God and their ministries were destroyed when they failed to say, "NO" to the king of Sodom. During the apex of their success story and national notoriety, the chariots of the king of Sodom (the devil) stopped at their doorsteps. *The king of Sodom made them an offer they*

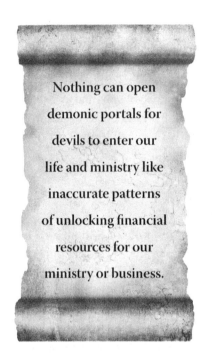

Nothing can open demonic portals for devils to enter our life and ministry like inaccurate patterns of unlocking financial resources for our ministry or business.

failed to refuse. The scandalous fall of their ministries now plagues us all.

Some great ministries that are commanding a large following presently have also fallen to the power of the king of Sodom. They have become contaminated by the demonic sodomic system. Even though their mega ministry may look very appealing from the outside to the undiscerning eye, the process of spiritual decline in the lives of these modern-day gospel greats has already begun. *Only God and the devil know that they are carrying snakes in their money bags.* The machinery of death is already at work in the internal matrix of their glamorous ministries or businesses.

Nothing can open demonic portals for devils to enter our life like inaccurate patterns of unlocking financial resources for our ministry or business. We must remember that just because something works does not mean it is right. We can manipulate the saints or our business partners for money and make them give us whatever we want. This demonic behavior in us will only set us up for death and destruction in our future destiny.

Please remember that Abram and Lot became very wealthy almost overnight when Abram lied to Pharaoh. Abram told the king of Egypt that Sarai was his sister instead of his wife. The king of Egypt with a mouth dripping with sexual lust for Sarai, gave Abram and Lot an abundance of gold, silver, livestock, and male and female servants. *For a short season, Abram's lie worked miracles for him.* He got blessed by cheating a king and manipulating his wife into lying against her own conscience.

Abram left Egypt with the bounty he had made by lying to Pharaoh and placing his wife in a very compromising situation. Abram thought he got away with it. Nothing could have been further from the truth. Resources gained from using demonic technology always come filled with snakes. These demonically engineered snakes are preprogrammed by the enemy to strike and inject us with their poison at a strategic time in our future destiny when we are the most vulnerable. This attack of the enemy usually happens at a time when the devil knows that he can cause the most damage to the cause of Christ.

One of the snakes that was in the money bags the king of Egypt gave to Abram was a young Egyptian maid named Hagar. *The devil had set her up as his trump card. She was a ticking time bomb in Abraham's future destiny.* When she finally exploded in Abraham and Sarah's lives, she produced an Ishmael in Abraham's bloodline. The consequences of this costly mistake in Abraham's life are still being felt and played out on the global scene thousands of years later, as evidenced each day in the news media. Reports of continuing violent clashes between Palestinian Arabs (the natural descendants of Abram's Ishmael) and neighboring Jews in Israel are common place. May God help us to take our place in the Order of Melchizedek.

LIFE APPLICATION SECTION

Memory Verses

When the palace officials saw her, they sang her praises to Pharaoh, their king, and Sarai was taken into his palace. Then Pharaoh gave Abram many gifts because of her—sheep, goats, cattle, male and female donkeys, male and female servants, and camels. But the Lord sent terrible plagues upon Pharaoh and his household because of Sarai, Abram's wife. So Pharaoh summoned Abram and accused him sharply. "What have you done to me?" he demanded. "Why didn't you tell me she was your wife? Why did you say, 'She is my sister,' and allow me to take her as my wife? Now then, here is your wife. Take her and get out of here!" (Genesis 12:15-19).

Reflections

Why did Lot move to Sodom and how did his life end up?

Write what the "demonic sodomic system" means to you.

_____

_____

_____

_____

_____

_____

_____

_____

Who does the king of Sodom represent prophetically and how does this impact you in the Marketplace?

_____

_____

_____

_____

_____

_____

_____

_____

JOURNAL YOUR PERSONAL NOTES ON THIS CHAPTER

CHAPTER FIVE

Heavenly Bread
and Wine

WHAT IS EVEN MORE SIGNIFICANT and exhilarating than what we've covered so far, is that the Lord Jesus Christ whom we now know is the High Priest of the priestly Order of Melchizedek, restored the priestly Order of Melchizedek to the Jewish nation when He instituted the sacrament of Holy Communion. In so doing, Jesus made the royal priesthood of Melchizedek the only legitimate priesthood for New Testament believers and placed the last death nail on the Levitical priesthood. The royal priesthood of Melchizedek was to become the priesthood that would service the "New Creation." During the Last Supper, Jesus gave His apprentice apostles the same spiritual elements of bread and wine that Melchizedek had offered to Abram in Genesis 14:18-20.

The *"bread and wine"* which Melchizedek offered to Abram was no simple meal of natural sustenance. This food had the very nature of *eternity* within its substance. It not only provided something powerful for Abram, but also to his posterity in the generations that were yet to come. These benefits also apply to present day believers who are now grafted into the fold of God by the blood of Jesus Christ.

The word "Bread" comes from the Hebrew term *Lechem,* meaning: *Food; especially bread or the grain used for making it.* (Strong's) The term *Lechem* comes from the Hebrew word *Lacham,* meaning: *To battle to destruction; to eat or devour.* It means to make war, prevail and overcome. This is why God promised to deliver Abram's enemies into his hand!

Therefore, the *bread* represents supernatural strength to prevail in battle! This is what was given to Abram and all those who live under the Order of Melchizedek!

The word *wine* comes from the Hebrew term *Yayin,* meaning: To effervesce (to bubble like fermenting wine) (Strong's). The bubbling "gas" which is released from fermenting wine is steadily generating and increasing in volume. This "wine" represents the supernatural increase of God upon the life of Abram and his descendents. "Increase" is the heritage of Abram and his people!

THE LAST SUPPER

> *As they were eating, Jesus took some bread and blessed it. Then he broke it in pieces and gave it to the disciples, saying, "Take this and eat it, for this is my body." And he took a cup of wine and gave thanks to God for it. He gave it to them and said, "Each of you drink from it, for this is my blood, which confirms the covenant between God and his people. It is poured out as a sacrifice to forgive the sins of many* (Matthew 26:26-28).

Jesus was in essence prophesying to His apprentice apostles and to every demonic principality in the heavenly realms that He was instituting a new order of priesthood. By His enactment of the sacrament of Holy Communion, Jesus was making an announcement that He was the High Priest after the Order of Melchizedek. What is most exciting is the spiritual timing of the reenactment of this priestly Order of Melchizedek by the Lord Jesus Christ. It happened just before He was betrayed and crucified. This means that when the Lord Jesus was betrayed, crucified, and resurrected, He was no longer operating under the Levitical priestly Order which answers to the Mountain of Law (Mount Sinai in Arabia). Jesus was operating under the priestly Order of Melchizedek, which is an infinitely higher priesthood that only answers to the heavenly Father.

This would explain why Jesus Christ's betrayal, sufferings, crucifixion, resurrection, and ultimate ascension all became infinitely more powerful and redemptive than they would have been had they occurred under the Levitical priesthood. This would also explain why Jesus Christ did not defend Himself or beg for mercy from Pontius Pilate when He stood in his judgment hall. Jesus did not beg for help because doing so would have meant submitting the infinitely higher Order of Melchizedek to the infinitely lower orders of human government.

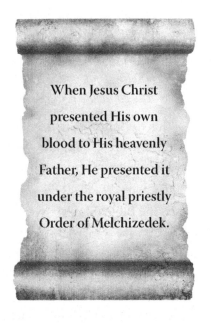

When Jesus Christ presented His own blood to His heavenly Father, He presented it under the royal priestly Order of Melchizedek.

This would also explain why Jesus never returned to the temple in natural Jerusalem when He rose from the dead. His blood of atonement could not be taken to the Mercy Seat of the temple inside natural Jerusalem. His atoning blood had to be taken to the temple of God Most High in spiritual Jerusalem—the mother of us all. This means that when Jesus Christ presented His own blood to His heavenly Father, He presented it under the royal priestly Order of Melchizedek. This would explain why the blood of Jesus has tremendous redeeming power for the people who are called to live under this eternal royal priestly Order.

As we continue our extensive study of the Order of Melchizedek, I will explain in great detail the spiritual ramifications and present-day applications of the sacred bread and wine that Melchizedek gave to Abram. We need to know what God has made available to us in the sacrament of Holy Communion. What is the eternal significance of the sacred bread and wine? How does the spiritual digestion of these two sacred elements affect us today? These are very important questions to consider.

THE SACRED BREAD

After Abram returned from his victory over Kedorlaomer and all his allies, the king of Sodom went out to meet him in the valley of Shaveh (that is, the King's Valley). And Melchizedek, the king of Salem and a priest of God Most High, brought Abram some bread and wine. Melchizedek blessed Abram with this blessing: "Blessed be Abram by God Most High, Creator of heaven and earth. And blessed be God Most High, who has defeated your enemies for you." Then Abram gave Melchizedek a tenth of all the goods he had recovered (Genesis 14:17-20).

This Scripture tells that there was a divine covenant exchange that took place between Abram and Melchizedek, the king-priest. Melchizedek gave Abram bread and wine and Abram gave Him tithes of honor. Let us examine the prophetic implications of the sacred bread and wine.

In the Bible there are seven prophetic representations of the sacred bread that Melchizedek gave to Abram. By examining the seven prophetic representations we quickly come to terms with the critical importance of this sacred bread of the Order of Melchizedek. Bread in the Bible symbolizes the following seven prophetic dimensions.

1. The Doctrine of the Kingdom of God

*Jesus also used this illustration: "The Kingdom of Heaven is like the yeast a woman used in making **bread**. Even though she put only a little yeast in three measures of flour, it permeated every part of the dough"* (Matthew 13:33).

Many churches today are out of touch with Jesus Christ's primary message. I believe that the global Church's obsession with the idea of going to heaven has robbed it of the primary passion and mission of Jesus Christ. What is adamantly clear when we examine the message and ministry of Jesus is that He was never obsessed with the idea of getting people to heaven. *His primary message was about restoring the reality and influence of the Kingdom of heaven here on earth.*

Contrary to what many so-called Christians believe, God created man to live here on earth. God never created humankind for the ultimate purpose of transferring his residence from the earth to heaven. The truth of the matter is that if Adam and Eve had never sinned, there would have been no need for anyone to go to heaven. Heaven only became God's temporary transition home for His people after Adam's sin introduced death to planet Earth.

*Seek the **Kingdom** of God above all else, and live righteously, and he will give you everything you need* (Matthew 6:33).

*Jesus replied, "I tell you the truth, unless you are born again, you cannot see the **Kingdom** of God." "What do you mean?" exclaimed Nicodemus. "How can an old man go back into his mother's womb and be born again?" Jesus replied, "I assure you, no one can enter the **Kingdom** of God without being born of water and the Spirit"* (John 3:3-5).

Many of us would be very surprised if we did extensive research to examine just how many times Jesus spoke about the Kingdom of God. Jesus spoke about the Kingdom of God with much greater frequency than most churches do today. Jesus knew that God created humankind for the ultimate purpose of establishing God's Kingdom rule here on earth. Jesus did not come to our planet to simply atone for the sins of humankind. His work of atonement was designed to remove the gulf of separation that sin had placed between God and humankind. Once this gulf of separation has been removed, we can then be used by God to establish the Kingdom of God here on earth.

*Now it came to pass, as He was praying in a certain place, when He ceased, that one of His disciples said to Him, "Lord, teach us to pray, as John also taught his disciples." So He said to them, "When you pray, say: Our Father in heaven, hallowed be Your name. Your **kingdom** come, Your will be done on earth as it is in heaven* (Luke 11:1-2 NKJV).

His primary message was about restoring the reality and influence of the Kingdom of heaven here on earth.

Perhaps no other passage in the synoptic gospels captures and crystallizes the essence of Jesus Christ's divine mission on earth like the Lord's Prayer. In the Lord's Prayer, Jesus makes it clear that New Testament praying must be driven by a deep desire to see God's Kingdom established on earth. This is why I believe that when we partake of the bread of the Order of Melchizedek, God will fill us with the doctrine of the Kingdom. Our passion to see the message of the Kingdom of God spread to the ends of the earth will expand exponentially. I am convinced that churches and businesses that are patterned after the Order of Melchizedek are very Kingdom minded and Kingdom driven.

2. **The Life or Body of Christ**

> *As they were eating, Jesus took some **bread** and blessed it. Then he broke it in pieces and gave it to the disciples, saying, "Take this and eat it, for this is my body"* (Matthew 26:26).

> *Jesus replied, "I am the **bread** of life. Whoever comes to me will never be hungry again. Whoever believes in me will never be thirsty"* (John 6:35).

When Melchizedek, the priest of God Most High, gave Abram the sacred bread, He was giving him much more than the doctrine of the Kingdom. The bread that He gave to Abram was "Christ." Christ is the "Life" of the sacred bread that Melchizedek gave to Abram. Abram's time of Holy Communion with Melchizedek in the Valley of Shaveh was a prophetic foreshadowing that no human being can effectively function in the Order of Melchizedek without partaking of the incorruptible life of Christ.

3. *Deliverance from Demonic Oppression*

> *And behold, a woman of Canaan came from that region and cried out to Him, saying, "Have mercy on me, O Lord, Son of David! My daughter is severely demon-possessed." But He answered her not a word. And His disciples came and urged Him, saying, "Send her away, for she cries out after us." But He answered and said, "I was not sent except to the lost sheep of the house of Israel." Then she came and worshiped Him, saying, "Lord, help me!" But He answered and said, "It is not good to take the **children's bread** and throw it to the little dogs." And she said, "Yes, Lord, yet even the little dogs eat the crumbs which fall from their masters' table"* (Matthew 15:22-27 NKJV).

Ever since Adam and Eve's messy encounter with the devil in the Garden of Eden, the warfare between humankind and demons has only escalated. What is clear from observing this demons-against-humankind warfare is that the devil hates humankind with an unimaginable passion because we were created in the image of God and the devil hates God.

The widespread demonic oppression of the masses by demonic powers is evidence of this ongoing warfare between the Kingdom of Light and the kingdom of darkness. Cases of mental, emotional, and physical oppression have reached an all-time high. Both Christians and Kingdom citizens are not completely immune to these subversive attacks of the enemy if they do not know how to release the power of God.

When the king of Sodom arrived, he came on the scene accompanied by an avalanche of evil spirits from the underworld.

When the Canaanite woman came crying to Jesus because her daughter was grievously oppressed by demons, Jesus rebuffed her. He told her that it was not wise to take the "children's bread" (believers) and give it to the dogs (non-believers). Remember, this woman wanted Jesus to cast out the evil spirit that was oppressing her daughter. She was looking for deliverance. This passage proves that deliverance from demonic oppression is the children's bread (born-again believers).

This passage in the book of Matthew proves that deliverance from demonic oppression is a covenant right of God's children. The bread that Melchizedek gave to Abram was also the *bread of deliverance from demonic oppression.* It did not take long for Abram to discover how the bread of the Order of Melchizedek can deliver a person from demonic powers. When the king of Sodom arrived, he came on the scene accompanied by an avalanche of evil spirits from the underworld. But these demonic spirits could not touch or infect Abram with their poison because he had already partaken of the bread of deliverance. This is why I advise Kingdom business men and women to have Holy Communion with their staff every week. They will get more business done this way and increase their company's profitability.

I really believe that New Testament churches that are either afraid of teaching on deliverance or do not believe in it are not patterning themselves after the Order of Melchizedek. The deliverance ministry is an integral part of the New Creation order of the Melchizedek priesthood. Jesus Christ who is the High Priest of the Order of Melchizedek cast more devils out of people than any other man in history. How can we fully represent Jesus Christ if we do not believe in His deliverance ministry?

4. **God's Manifested Presence**

Place the **Bread** *of the Presence on the table to remain before me at all times* (Exodus 25:30).

There is simply nothing more glorious or precious than the manifest presence of God. Biblical history teaches us that the greatest men and women of the Bible had one key thing in common. They all shared a deep and abiding passion for the presence of God. Abram knew the power of the manifested presence of God. Moses begged God to show him His glory. The high priest Eli died instantly when he heard that the Ark of God's presence had been captured by the Philistines.

King David danced himself out of his clothes when the Ark of God's presence returned to Israel. The apostle Peter walked in such a high level of the manifest presence of God that sick people who stepped into his shadow were healed instantly. The sacred bread that Melchizedek, the king-priest, gave to Abram was the "Bread of His presence." After Abram partook of it, the manifest presence of God in his life increased greatly. I truly believe that churches and businesses that are patterned after the Order of Melchizedek are very passionate about celebrating the manifest presence of God. These churches or people are not satisfied with church as usual. They have a driving desire to see God manifest Himself in His temple.

5. **The Word of God**

During that time the devil came and said to him, "If you are the Son of God, tell these stones to become loaves of bread." But Jesus told him, "No! The Scriptures say, 'People do not live by bread alone, but by every **word** *that comes from the mouth of God'"* (Matthew 4:3-4).

Words are very important. They communicate desires and clarify purpose. Words are as important to both spiritual and natural life as oxygen is to the human body. Just like a critical lack of oxygen is lethal to the human body, a critical lack of words can kill spiritual or natural relationships. *Words are important because God created the heavens and the earth by using words.* What's more, the Bible tells us that Christ is the "eternal Word" that was in the beginning with God.

The sacred bread that Melchizedek gave to Abram in the Valley of Shaveh was also symbolic of the bread of the Word of God. When Abram partook of this sacred bread, he was actually ingesting Christ—the life giving Word of God—into his spiritual DNA. The psalmist tells us in Psalm 119:11 KJV that "Thy word have I hid in my heart, that I might not sin against thee." This passage makes the summation that when our hearts are richly filled with the Word of God, living in sin will not be an option.

This was certainly the case in Abram's case. When the king of Sodom tried to tempt him with a luring offer, the Word of God that he had ingested when he consumed the sacred bread rose up inside him to curb the power of sin. Abram gave the king of Sodom a clear "NO" answer. I truly believe that no church or New Testament believer can operate effectively in the royal priesthood of Melchizedek without having a passion for the Word of God. In order to function in this priestly Order of Melchizedek, we must rightly divide the Word of Truth and allow the Word of God to dwell in us richly. Especially those of us who spend a majority of our time in a marketplace environment that is full of devils.

6. **Spiritual Nourishment or Spiritual Prosperity**

*So He said to them, "When you pray, say: Our Father in heaven, hallowed be Your name. Your kingdom come, Your will be done on earth as it is in heaven. Give us day by day our **daily bread***" (Luke 11:2-3 NKJV).

*But Jesus told him, "No! The Scriptures say, 'People do not live by bread alone, but by **every word** that comes from the mouth of God*" (Matthew 4:4).

In these two Scripture passages, the Lord Jesus Christ makes it quite clear that He wants His people to live by the "daily bread" that comes from the mouth of God. This daily bread is the Spirit of revelation. It is the rhema Word of God. This daily bread may come in the form of a Bible passage that the Holy Spirit quickens for us for that particular day or it may be a personal prophetic message that God may speak to our heart. The daily bread is an unplanned spontaneous word that grabs hold of our spirit.

> *When Jesus came to the region of Caesarea Philippi, he asked his disciples, "Who do people say that the Son of Man is?" "Well," they replied, "some say John the Baptist, some say Elijah, and others say Jeremiah or one of the other prophets." Then he asked them, "But who do you say I am?" Simon Peter answered, "You are the Messiah, the Son of the living God." Jesus replied, "You are blessed, Simon son of John, because my Father in heaven has revealed this to you. You did not learn this from any human being"* (Matthew 16:13-17).

This passage from Matthew further underscores the difference between *Logos* and *Rhema*. Jesus turned to His apprentice apostles and asked them two important questions. "Who do the people say that I am?" The disciples began to tell Him what the people were saying about Him. Then Jesus asked them a second question. "Who do *you* say that I am?" Simon Bar-Jona turned to Jesus and told Him that He was the Christ, the Son of the Living God. Jesus quickly responded by informing Peter that flesh and blood had not revealed this to him, but the Father who is heaven.

After identifying who Jesus Christ really was by the spirit of revelation, Jesus changed Simon's surname from Bar-Jona to Peter. The name Bar-Jona means "one who is unstable as a reed." On the other hand, the name Peter means "a small, stable stone." *The moral of this story is that it is impossible for our old nature to change apart from the spirit of revelation.* When Melchizedek gave Abram the sacred bread, He was also *imparting the spirit of revelation* inside Abram's spirit. When this supernatural download was complete, Abram was a changed man.

I truly believe that churches or believers who are patterned after the Order of Melchizedek appreciate the importance of "accessing" the Spirit of revelation. I also believe that the Order of Melchizedek is saturated with the Spirit of revelation. When a church begins to function properly in this Order of Melchizedek, the church will be flooded with the Spirit of revelation. Such a church will be full of people who have been changed from the inside out.

7. **Natural Nourishment or Material Prosperity**

> *In the sweat of your face you shall eat **bread** till you return to the ground, for out of it you were taken; for dust you are, and to dust you shall return"* (Genesis 3:19 NKJV).

> *...and the seven years of famine began to come, as Joseph had said. The famine was in all lands, but in all the land of Egypt there was **bread*** (Genesis 41:54 NKJV).

God created man as a triune being, consisting of spirit, soul, and body. Since man is also a physical being, he has inherent physical needs that cannot be ignored. Humankind has a deep need for water, food, clothing, and shelter. If these fundamental physical needs are ignored, they can lead to all kinds of social ills. Said simply, humankind functions better in a community of shared prosperity, where everybody's physical needs have been met. I have yet to meet a people group on earth who enjoys poverty.

> *Beloved, I wish above all things that thou mayest prosper and be in health, even as thy soul prospereth* (3 John 2 KJV).

The sacred bread that Melchizedek the king-priest gave to Abram was also symbolic of God's supernatural provision to meet all of Abram's physical needs. *The sacred bread released a spirit of financial and material prosperity in Abram's life.* Since Jesus Christ is our king-priest after the Order of Melchizedek, we must expect financial and material prosperity to flow into our lives. Jesus became "poor" that we might become "rich" through the riches of His grace toward us. I truly believe that churches and businesses that are patterned after the Order of Melchizedek do not suffer from a poverty mentality. They know that they need a substantial amount of money to advance God's Kingdom agenda here on earth.

The Sacred Wine

*And Melchizedek, the king of Salem and a priest of God Most High, brought Abram some bread and **wine** (Genesis 14:18).*

The second vital spiritual element that Melchizedek gave to Abram when he intercepted him in the King's Valley was the sacred wine. Understanding the prophetic symbolism of this sacred wine ushers in a whole new dimension of life-giving revelation. Based upon the prophetic writings of the holy writ, wine symbolizes the following:

1. **The Spirit of the Kingdom of God**

   And do not get drunk with wine, for that is debauchery; but ever be filled and stimulated with the [Holy] Spirit. Speak out to one another in psalms and hymns and spiritual songs, offering praise with voices [and instruments] and making melody with all your heart to the Lord, At all times and for everything giving thanks in the name of our Lord Jesus Christ to God the Father (Ephesians 5:18-20 AMP)

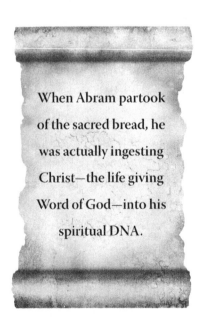

When Abram partook of the sacred bread, he was actually ingesting Christ—the life giving Word of God—into his spiritual DNA.

But if I am casting out demons by the Spirit of God, then the Kingdom of God has arrived among you (Matthew 12:28).

We have already established that the "Kingdom of God" is the primary ingredient of the true message of the Gospel and the only message that Jesus preached. But God's method for establishing His Kingdom here on earth is through the Person and work of the Holy Spirit. *The Holy Spirit is the spiritual Governor and Administrator of the Kingdom of God on earth.*

In the Garden of Eden, Adam and Eve did not lose a religion; they lost a Kingdom.

So the most important ministerial assignment of the Holy Spirit is to restore the Kingdom of God to our troubled planet. The sacred wine that Melchizedek the King-priest gave to Abram represents the indwelling presence of the Holy Spirit. The Holy Spirit is the Spirit of the Kingdom of God. He is the One who drives the machinery of the Kingdom of God on earth. By giving Abram the sacred wine, Melchizedek wanted Abram to be saturated with the Spirit of the Kingdom (the Holy Spirit).

It is impossible to effectively advance the Kingdom of God on earth if we are not filled with the Spirit of Christ. We must be filled with the Holy Spirit to overflowing if we are serious about becoming "power brokers" in the Kingdom of God. I truly believe that churches and businessmen who are patterned after the Order of Melchizedek cannot help but be Kingdom driven and Kingdom minded. Unfortunately many pastors and Christians (born-again believers who are still trapped in the Christian religion) are too focused on building their personal empires than advancing the Kingdom of God.

2. Spiritual Intoxication

He ties his foal to a grapevine, the colt of his donkey to a choice vine. He washes his clothes in wine, his robes in the blood of grapes. His eyes are darker than wine, and his teeth are whiter than milk (Genesis 49:11-12).

So they were all amazed and perplexed, saying to one another, "Whatever could this mean?" Others mocking said, "They are full of new wine." But Peter, standing up with the eleven, raised his voice and said to them, "Men of Judea and all who dwell in Jerusalem, let this be known to you, and heed my words. For these are not drunk, as you suppose, since it is only the third hour of the day (Acts 2:12-15 NKJV).

When I was still living in Zambia (located in Central Africa), I lived for a couple of years with an alcoholic uncle who was a good person, although he was quite stingy when he was sober. But when he got drunk, he metamorphosed into a ridiculously generous person. When he was drunk you could have asked him to sign over the title deeds to his house and he would have done it!

When he got drunk, my uncle became loud, joyous, generous, and overly courageous. He was quite fun to be around. The Bible compares the effects that strong wine has over humankind's five senses to the effects that being filled with the Holy Spirit has upon our spiritual senses. When we are filled with the wine of the Holy Spirit, Saint Paul tells us that our hearts will be filled with singing and melody.

Just like being drunk with wine overpowers the normal reactions of our physical senses, being filled with the wine of the Holy Spirit has the same effect over our spiritual and physical senses. How many miracles and spiritual victories have been lost because God's people allowed the dictates of their five senses to abort what God was doing in their lives? It is no wonder we need to be intoxicated by the wine of the Spirit.

I noticed that whenever my uncle was drunk, he was not at all fearful. To the contrary, he was overly courageous. While highly intoxicated he acted like he had no cares in the world. I don't know about you, but personally I need to be constantly intoxicated with the wine of the Holy Ghost. *I find that whenever I am intoxicated with the Spirit, walking by faith is much easier.* I find that I forgive easily and that I am not at all fearful of what the future holds. The sacred wine that Melchizedek gave to Abram also symbolized the process of being intoxicated with the Holy Spirit.

3. **The Blood of Jesus**

> *And he took a cup of wine and gave thanks to God for it. He gave it to them and said, "Each of you drink from it, for this is my blood, which confirms the covenant between God and his people. It is poured out as a sacrifice to forgive the sins of many"* (Matthew 26:27-28).

The shedding of the blood of Jesus Christ on Calvary's cross was the greatest offering of love that God ever gave to humankind. The redeeming power of the blood of Jesus is limitless. The blood of Jesus is "covenant-blood;" without it we can never access the covenant of mercy that God established with Abraham. Whenever and wherever God sees the blood of Jesus flowing, there He postpones or cancels His impending judgment.

And they have defeated him by the blood of the Lamb and by their testimony. And they did not love their lives so much that they were afraid to die (Revelation 12:11).

The writer of the Apocalypse tells us that the covenant blood of Jesus has tremendous power over the devil and his hierarchy of evil spirits. The precious blood of Jesus Christ has power to silence the ravaging power of sin in human life. *The sacred wine that Melchizedek the King-priest gave to Abram also symbolized Abram partaking in the awesome benefits of the blood of the Covenant.* Jesus called His blood, the true drink offering.

I believe that churches and Kingdom businessmen who are patterned after the Order of Melchizedek hold the blood of Jesus in very high esteem. Many of their worship services are centered on celebrating the offering of the blood of Jesus. When Abram drank the sacred wine, he was in essence symbolically drinking the blood of Jesus, which saves and sanctifies. Glory to God in the highest!

> God's method for establishing His Kingdom here on earth is through the Person and work of the Holy Spirit. The Holy Spirit is the spiritual Governor and Administrator of the Kingdom of God on earth.

4. **The Anointing of the Holy Spirit**

*Then the Lord awoke as from sleep, like a mighty man who shouts because of **wine*** (Psalm 78:65 NKJV).

*These people are not drunk, as some of you are assuming. Nine o'clock in the morning is much too early for that. No, what you see was predicted long ago by the prophet Joel: 'In the last days,' God says, 'I will **pour out my Spirit** upon all people. Your sons and daughters will prophesy. Your young men will see visions, and your old men will dream dreams"* (Acts 2:15-17).

Jesus began His earthly ministry by announcing His anointing. He clearly described the type of anointing that was upon His life through the enablement of the Holy Spirit. Here is what Jesus said about His anointing.

> *"The Spirit of the LORD is upon me, for he has anointed me to bring Good News to the poor. He has sent me to proclaim that captives will be released, that the blind will see, that the oppressed will be set free, and that the time of the LORD's favor has come* (Luke 4:18-19).

Jesus said that the anointing upon His life was to help Him accomplish the following:

- Preach the Gospel to the poor.
- Proclaim liberty to the captives.
- Open the eyes of the blind.
- Heal those who are bruised emotionally and mentally.
- Proclaim the year of the Lord's favor.

The moral of this story: if Jesus Christ our Savior and High Priest needed the anointing of the Holy Spirit to fulfill His Kingdom assignment, we need it too. Personally, I have heard enough dry sermons and have attended enough dry services that I cannot stand anointing-less services any more. When Melchizedek, the priest of God Most High, gave Abram the sacred wine, He was anointing Abram's service in the Kingdom of God.

I believe that churches and believers who are patterned after the Order of Melchizedek have a high regard for the anointing of the Holy Spirit. There is an ongoing effort to increase the anointing in churches that are patterned after this royal priesthood of Melchizedek. I also believe that we can never function effectively in the Order of Melchizedek if we do not hold the anointing of the Holy Spirit in high esteem.

5. **The Joy of the Lord**

> *And **wine** that maketh glad the heart of man, and oil to make his face to shine, and bread which strengtheneth man's heart* (Psalm 104:15 KJV).

*Go thy way, eat thy bread with joy, and drink thy **wine** with a merry heart; for God now accepteth thy works* (Ecclesiastes 9:7 KJV).

God wants all of His people, especially His spiritual leaders, to serve Him with joy. I am tired of talking to ministers of the gospel who give the impression that serving the Lord is an odious task. Nothing should be further from the truth. *Jesus told us that His yoke of ministry is easy and its burden is light.* (Matthew 11:28-29.) This expression by Jesus means that working and living for God is supposed to be a joyful endeavor.

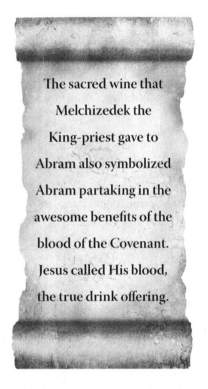

The sacred wine that Melchizedek the King-priest gave to Abram also symbolized Abram partaking in the awesome benefits of the blood of the Covenant. Jesus called His blood, the true drink offering.

> *And Nehemiah continued, "Go and celebrate with a feast of rich foods and sweet drinks, and share gifts of food with people who have nothing prepared. This is a sacred day before our Lord. Don't be dejected and sad, for the joy of the LORD is your strength!"* (Nehemiah 8:10)

The prophet Nehemiah tells us that the "joy of the Lord is your strength." This means that the spiritual strength that we need to serve the Lord is found in living and serving in the joy of the Lord. Many pastor's children (nicknamed PKs) have no desire to serve God in the so-called full-time ministry because they see how their parents struggle to exhibit the joy of serving God. The sacred wine that Melchizedek gave to Abram also represents an offering of the joy of the Lord. Under this royal priesthood of Melchizedek, God will saturate our spirits with His sacred wine until we are able to serve Him with joy. Churches and believers who are patterned after the Order of Melchizedek will know the pleasure and strength that comes with the joy of the Lord.

6. **The Generational Blessing**

Isaac said to Esau, "I have made Jacob your master and have declared that all his brothers will be his servants. I have guaranteed him an abundance of grain and wine—what is left for me to give you, my son?" (Genesis 27:37).

Now there was a man named Naboth, from Jezreel, who owned a vineyard in Jezreel beside the palace of King Ahab of Samaria. One day Ahab said to Naboth, "Since your vineyard is so convenient to my palace, I would like to buy it to use as a vegetable garden. I will give you a better vineyard in exchange, or if you prefer, I will pay you for it." But Naboth replied, "The LORD forbid that I should give you the inheritance that was passed down by my ancestors" (1 Kings 21:1-3).

If you have been saved long enough, you have probably been bombarded with many teachings on breaking generational curses. It seems to me that many teachers of the Word have placed an undue emphasis on studying generational curses, and have done too little research on *generational blessings*. God is a generational God. When He starts something, He seldom finishes it in that same generation; He carries it forward to the ensuing generations.

In the ancient world in which Abram lived, you could not pass on the blessing of generational wine without owning a vineyard. In this context the blessing of wine became a symbol of a generational blessing. King Ahab, the wicked husband of Jezebel, saw the beautiful vineyard of Naboth and wanted it for himself. He begged Naboth to sell it to him, but Naboth refused because it was an inheritance from his ancestors.

When Melchizedek the King-priest offered Abram the sacred wine, He was in actuality imparting the "generational blessing" of the Kingdom of God. God wanted this generational blessing to pass on from Abram to all of His spiritual and natural descendants. *When we pattern our ministries after the Order of Melchizedek, we will become very generational in our thinking.* This generational mentality will radically affect how we approach the subject of Kingdom advancement and wealth creation. God is looking for churches that are patterned after the Order of Melchizedek.

LIFE APPLICATION SECTION

MEMORY VERSES

The Spirit of the LORD is upon me, for he has anointed me to bring Good News to the poor. He has sent me to proclaim that captives will be released, that the blind will see, that the oppressed will be set free, and that the time of the LORD's favor has come (Luke 4:18-19).

REFLECTIONS

What does the wine and bread that Melchizedek gave to Abram represent?

Can you explain the effects that being drunk with the Holy Spirit are supposed to have on our spiritual and physical senses?

How can the phenomenon of being drunk with the Holy Spirit affect your disposition in the Marketplace?

JOURNAL YOUR PERSONAL NOTES ON THIS CHAPTER

CHAPTER SIX

The Order
of Aaron

A WHILE BACK MY WIFE AND I were guests in the beautiful home of one of our dear friends who pastors a thriving church in Tulsa, Oklahoma. She is a well-known national and international prophetess. We were sitting in her gorgeous kitchen, talking about things pertaining to the Kingdom of God.

Suddenly the presence of the Lord came upon her and she gave me that "prophetic bull's-eye look," which seemed to be saying, *Francis, God wants to talk to you, now!* She started to prophesy into my life and here is part of the prophecy from the Spirit of God... *God has called you to teach the Body of Christ roots and origins. Many people in the Body of Christ do not like roots and origins, but you do, says the Lord. God is going to use you to show the Body of Christ that if the roots and origins of something they are doing are satanic, they cannot make them godly no matter what they do to them!*

ROOTS AND ORIGINS

When I left her house, what she had prophesied to me was ringing in my spirit like a fire alarm which had been set off by the presence of a consuming fire. All I kept hearing in my spirit were the words, *You have been called to teach the Body of Christ roots and origins.* Suddenly, God was all over me like a mother chicken hovers over her eggs. He started conversing with me. God began to show me some of my past experiences—both good and bad. God showed me how everything that I have gone through was skillfully designed to bring me to a place were I could experientially and conceptually understand the type of call that God had placed upon my life. The prophecy I had just received brought focus to what has always been in my life, but was somehow hidden from me.

God spoke to my spirit and said, "Son I have surely called you to teach the Body of Christ about the roots and origins of divine and demonic technologies and how they work!" As the light of God's glory exploded in my spirit, I started to see some of my past experiences in a new light. I was amazed to see the handwriting of God even on some very painful experiences that I had gone through. I will share with you one of those experiences, and hope it will shed light on the subject of roots and origins and how they affect us in the realm of the Spirit.

In October 2002, my wife and I flew to Malaysia to attend a school of ministry hosted by Dr. Jonathan David. At this school, Dr. David called my wife and me out of about a hundred pastors who had gathered from all over the world. He started to prophesy over us. The heart of the prophetic word was, *God is calling you to plant a church.*

When we flew back to the United States, we began planning our church plant. We were living in Oklahoma City at the time. Around this same time, a woman from Chicago who had attended one of my revival services there, called me. She asked me when I was going to start a church in Chicago. Judging from how well-attended my Chicago conferences had been in the past, I knew I had an adequate following in the city of Chicago. So I took the call from this woman as a sign from God to start a church in Chicago. *But as soon as I announced to my wife that we were moving to Chicago, a strange uneasiness crept into my spirit.* Unfortunately I ignored the uneasiness that was building inside my spirit and explained it away as simply the fear of moving across state lines. How I wish this was the case.

When we arrived in Chicago, things started to go wrong almost immediately. First and foremost, the house we moved into was shrouded in a bitter legal controversy. The self-professing Christian real estate agent who had found us the house conveniently forgot to tell us that the house we were moving into was already in foreclosure proceedings.

Second, our new church plant was not growing as fast as we had anticipated. What's more, the Chicago businesswoman who had called to ask us to start a church in Chicago, only attended one of our church services, then disappeared. The church offerings were terribly low, so I was forced to attack our savings to support us and a church that I had started in the power of the flesh. Within a couple of months we had exhausted our savings and things were getting desperate. The increased spiritual tension coupled with the ensuing financial crisis caused my wife and I to start arguing a lot. Our home was not a home of peace during that short but painful excursion to Chicago.

In the midst of all of this housing and marital turmoil, the same uneasiness I had felt before we left Oklahoma City grew stronger. The mounting spiritual uneasiness robed me of the little bit of joy I got out of the dismal successes we were experiencing in the growth of the new church plant. In my spirit I kept hearing God say things like, *You are not supposed to be here. This is not the place I have called you to. No matter what you do here My blessing on your life will be limited at best!*

In desperation, I called Dr. Jonathan David in Malaysia, whom I highly respect as a true prophet of God and father in the faith. I asked him, in reverse, to pray and see if I was supposed to be in Chicago. He agreed and told me to call him back within two weeks.

During those two weeks I prayed and repented a gazillion times for having missed God. I was desperate. *I was begging God to reconsider and bless what I was doing in Chicago.* I negotiated with God desperately and asked Him to remember just how sincere my heart was in my service to Him. My efforts to move on God to

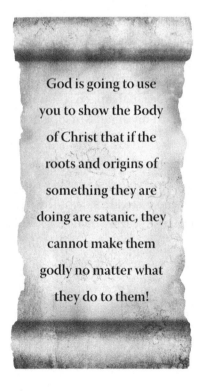

God is going to use you to show the Body of Christ that if the roots and origins of something they are doing are satanic, they cannot make them godly no matter what they do to them!

change His mind fell on deaf ears because my predicament had nothing to do with how pure and sincere my heart was before God. Instead it had everything to do with the *spiritual roots and origin* of the church I was asking Him to bless.

When the two weeks were up, I called Dr. David and asked him to tell me what God had told him. He said that God had told him that "if I stayed in Chicago I would be able to build the church, but I would always struggle." He went on to tell me that while he was praying for me, he "saw a vision of a throne of glory rising out of the state of Texas" and the Lord told him that "the church which He had called me to build was in Texas and not Chicago!"

God also told him that if I moved to Texas, He would give me a great church and a spiritual base from which my ministry would have a lasting impact on the whole United States. When I got off the phone with Dr. David, I knew I had a huge decision to make. The church I was leading in Chicago had now grown to about 34 members. It did not take much time to make my decision. God allowed the devil to overplay his hand to show me the dangerous position I was in, in the realm of the Spirit.

On a rainy and icy day, I decided to drive to Calumet City to visit some pastor friends of mine. I stopped at a traffic light. When it turned green, I quickly made my turn and I was horrified to see that heading right for me in my lane at a very high speed was a huge emergency ambulance truck, coming directly toward my small Mitsubishi Gallant!

If I have ever smelled death, I truly smelled it that day. Out of sheer panic and chemical reflex, I swerved to the right to get out of harm's way and collided head-on with a stationary car that was waiting for the traffic light to turn green on the opposite side of the street. The big emergency ambulance truck missed my small car by inches. My small car was a wreck, but I was alive, without any scratches. I was terrified. The Spirit of God spoke to my heart and said, *If you do not leave Chicago, you will surely die here!*

I called my wife and told her that we were leaving Chicago. I told her that I was going to close the church we had started. She was very relieved. When Sunday came I humbly stood before our church members and asked for their forgiveness for misleading them and thinking that I could be their spiritual shepherd outside the perfect will of God. I told them that I had founded the church on a spirit of rebellion to the inner witness of the Holy Spirit, who had tried to warn me not to leave Oklahoma City.

I told them that no matter how sincere I was or they were in our service to God, God was not going to place His full blessing on our church. This is because the true spiritual roots and origins of our church-plant were based upon a spirit of rebellion to God's authority! I begged them to forgive me and to release me from the responsibility of being their pastor—they did, with tears of regret. The people wept bitterly because they truly loved my wife and me. Seeing their tears of regret made me even more determined to get back into God's perfect will for my life, so they could also discover theirs.

This painful experience taught me the seriousness of *spiritual roots and origins* in the Kingdom of God. My experience in Chicago also helped me to appreciate the importance of having the global Church transition from the Levitical model (Order of Aaron) of doing ministry to the Order of Melchizedek model. The priestly ministry of many churches today has roots in a Levitical priestly system.

LORD, CAN ISHMAEL BECOME ISAAC?

Then Abraham bowed down to the ground, but he laughed to himself in disbelief. "How could I become a father at the age of 100?" he thought. "And how can Sarah have a baby when she is ninety years old?" So Abraham said to God, "May Ishmael live under your special blessing!" But God replied, "No—Sarah, your wife, will give birth to a son for you. You will name him Isaac, and I will confirm my covenant with him and his descendants as an everlasting covenant" (Genesis 17:17-19).

We see this same powerful prophetic principle concerning spiritual roots and origins played out in a most revealing way in the life of Abraham. God had made a covenant promise to Abraham that he would give him a son who would be born through Sarah. When God first gave this prophetic promise to Abraham and Sarah it was much easier for them to believe it. They were both relatively young. Then months turned into many years of waiting. *Along the way, Sarah herself gave up the hope of becoming a mother in her old age, so she devised a plan that was in actuality the kiss of death.* Sarah decided to help God fulfill His word of promise by telling Abraham to sleep with her Egyptian maid Hagar so that the child that she would bear would be Sarah's.

I imagine that Sarah did not have a difficult time selling her new idea to her aging husband. How often does an old married man get the blessing of his wife to sleep with a beautiful 18-year-old maid? Abraham was probably in Hagar's tent long before Sarah could have second thoughts. From the outside, Sarah's plan looked brilliant. But she and Abraham had walked into a demonic trap. They made a monumental error that would haunt them for the rest of their lives.

> *So Abram had sexual relations with Hagar, and she became pregnant. But when Hagar knew she was pregnant, she began to treat her mistress, Sarai, with contempt. Then Sarai said to Abram, "This is all your fault! I put my servant into your arms, but now that she's pregnant she treats me with contempt. The LORD will show who's wrong—you or me!"* (Genesis 16:4-5)

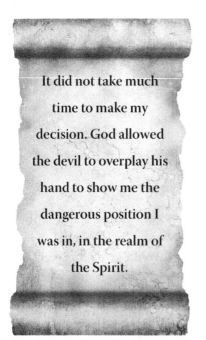

It did not take much time to make my decision. God allowed the devil to overplay his hand to show me the dangerous position I was in, in the realm of the Spirit.

Like a rattlesnake forced into a corner, Sarah's brilliant plan quickly backfired and struck at the core of her marriage to Abraham. The son born through her Egyptian maid whom she had thought would bring her great joy only brought sorrow and death into her life. The ensuing spiritual tension caused Abraham and Sarah to begin to have marital problems and infighting. The true roots and origins of what they had created were paving a way for devils to attack them.

Sarah wondered why her sincere and well-thought-out plan to help God turned so terribly wrong. The answer is found in understating spiritual roots and origins. If something has its roots and origins in a satanic power play, there is little we can do to change the true nature of what the thing really is. *Hagar's son, Ishmael, was born out of a spirit of self-will and rebellion to God's authority.* There was no way this child could bring the fullness of joy and laughter which God had promised would come with the birth of Isaac. The spiritual roots and origins of Abraham's Ishmael went all the way back to the ten gods of Egypt, not to mention the devil himself who was the principal spirit behind Egyptian idolatry.

When the appointed time came for God's Isaac to be born, Abraham had a difficult time releasing his faith because he was so enamored with the child that he had produced by his own power. Abraham actually interceded for Ishmael. He asked God to have Ishmael replace Isaac. God would not hear of it. God refused to hear of it because Abraham did not know the spiritual ramifications of what he was asking. *He did not know that when something is built on demonic technology, its root system is rooted in hellish operations.* No matter what God did to Ishmael, Ishmael would have remained at best, half divine and half devilish. Ishmael was a mixed blessing.

This is precisely why I have serious issues with the popular Malachi 3:8-12 tithing model, because I know that it originates out of the Mountain of Law and its roots are steeped in legalism. Malachi's tithing model describes a Levitical tithe which was paid in accordance with the law. This means that no matter how we try to spiritualize and decorate the Malachi tithe to make it applicable to New Testament believers, its true spiritual roots and origins will always lead us back to the Mountain of Law.

Once we head back to the Mountain of Law the fruit the mountain produces, which is *legalism,* will inevitably creep into our internal motivation for serving God. This Levitical mindset on the part of many church leaders has bred legalism into the inner workings of the Church's priestly ministry. Unfortunately, the works of the Law will quickly crush and snuff out the precious embers of the flames of grace inside our hearts. Just look at how well-meaning men and women of God curse God's people from the pulpit whenever they start talking about the giving of tithes and offerings. The Order of Melchizedek is a loftier priesthood than the Order of Aaron and it is not based upon the dictates of the Mosaic Law. The Order of Melchizedek is based upon *the Word of oath* or *faith-pledge* that God made to Christ in Psalm 110:4. This means that the priestly ministry of the Order of Melchizedek functions better in an atmosphere of faith and not law.

> *The LORD has taken an oath and will not break his vow: "You are a priest forever in the order of Melchizedek"* (Psalm 110:4).

THE PRIESTLY ORDER OF AARON

> *Call for your brother, Aaron, and his sons, Nadab, Abihu, Eleazar, and Ithamar. Set them apart from the rest of the people of Israel so they may minister to me and be my priests* (Exodus 28:1).

There are only two priestly Orders which God ever gave to His people—the priestly Order of Aaron (commonly known as the Levitical priesthood) and the priestly Order of Melchizedek. For this reason both of these priesthoods are very important to God's revealed will for His people. The priestly Order of Aaron came out of the Mountain of Law which is Mount Sinai where God gave Moses the Covenant of Law. The following is a summarized overview of the spiritual characteristics of the Order of Aaron.

1. *The priestly Order of Aaron was based on the Mountain of Law.*

   > *So if the priesthood of Levi, on which the law was based, could have achieved the perfection God intended, why did God need to establish a different priesthood, with a priest in the order of Melchizedek instead of the order of Levi and Aaron?* (Hebrews 7:11)

2. *The priestly Order of Aaron derived all its high priests from the sons of Aaron.*

   > *"Now take Aaron your brother, and his sons with him, from among the children of Israel, that he may minister to Me as priest, Aaron and Aaron's sons: Nadab, Abihu, Elemazar, and Ithamar"* (Exodus 28:1 NKJV).

3. *The priestly Order of Aaron was commanded to receive a tithe of their brethren according to the Law.*

   Now the law of Moses required that the priests, who are descendants of Levi, must collect a tithe from the rest of the people of Israel, who are also descendants of Abraham (Hebrews 7:5).

4. *The tithe under the priestly Order of Aaron was simply payment for priestly services rendered to the people.*

   As for the tribe of Levi, your relatives, I will compensate them for their service in the Tabernacle. Instead of an allotment of land, I will give them the tithes from the entire land of Israel (Numbers 18:21).

Tithing under the Levitical priesthood was intricately connected to service. It was a payment to the priesthood for services rendered. On the other hand, tithing under the Order of Melchizedek is based upon the *principle of honor.* We will discuss this principle of honor in more detail in Chapter Ten.

Whenever I hear spiritual leaders tell their people to *"pay their tithes,"* I know instantly that they are trapped in a Levitical priestly mindset because under the Levitical priesthood *"tithes were paid out"* in the same way one would pay an electric bill that is due. Under the Order of Melchizedek, tithes are never paid out, they are always "given" in honor.

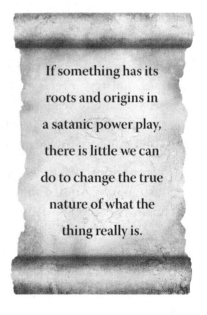

If something has its roots and origins in a satanic power play, there is little we can do to change the true nature of what the thing really is.

5. *Under the priestly Order of Aaron, the priesthood was only chosen from the tribe of Levi.*

   So if the priesthood of Levi, on which the law was based, could have achieved the perfection God

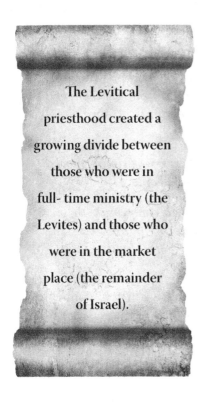

The Levitical priesthood created a growing divide between those who were in full- time ministry (the Levites) and those who were in the market place (the remainder of Israel).

intended, why did God need to establish a different priesthood, with a priest in the order of Melchizedek instead of the order of Levi and Aaron? (Hebrews 7:11)

Under the Levitical priesthood, members of the other eleven tribes of Israel could never be admitted to the priesthood. The priesthood was passed on as a right of birth to the sons of Levi. Women who were also born into the tribe of Levi were not included in the staffing of the priesthood. The Levitical priesthood created a growing divide between those who were in full- time ministry (the Levites) and those who were in the marketplace (the remainder of Israel).

A quick look at how many Christian denominations there are quickly exposes the fact that many of today's church leaders are not operating after the Order of Melchizedek. They function more like Old Testament Levites. How many of these church leaders use the phrase full-time ministry to refer to their vocation, while simultaneously separating themselves from those in the church who are serving God in the marketplace? What's more, how many Christian denominations have problems fully admitting God's daughters (women) into the priesthood?

There are spiritual leaders in the Body of Christ who go to great lengths to demonstrate why women should not be given full covenant rights to the New Testament priesthood. Many of these leaders are experts at misinterpreting the teachings of the apostle Paul because they fail to understand Paul's teachings on the Order of Melchizedek. If anybody knew that the New Testament priesthood of Melchizedek gives both men and women full covenant rights to the priesthood, it was the apostle Paul.

6. *Under the priestly Order of Aaron the priests were responsible for teaching the Jewish nation how to abide by the Mosaic Law.*

   "The words of a priest's lips should preserve knowledge of God, and people should go to him for instruction, for the priest is the messenger of the LORD of Heaven's Armies. But you priests have left God's paths. Your instructions have caused many to stumble into sin. You have corrupted the covenant I made with the Levites," says the LORD of Heaven's Armies (Malachi 2:7-8).

7. *Under the priestly Order of Aaron, the priests had no owner- ship of land.*

   And the LORD said to Aaron, "You priests will receive no allot- ment of land or share of property among the people of Israel. I am your share and your allotment" (Numbers 18:20).

Under the Old Testament, Jewish nation land ownership was synonymous with business ownership. The Jewish people were mainly farmers and shep- herds. *To receive an allotment of land under the Old Testament was tanta- mount to being given a chance to do business.* This means that anybody who was given an allotment of land was immediately ushered into the marketplace. All the tribes of Israel, except the tribe of Levi, were given a specific allot- ment of land. Their provision and sustenance was predicated upon their ability to exploit the natural resources of the land. Said simply, every tribe in Israel except the Levites, were engaged in business. Said in another way, 90 percent of the citizenry in Israel were found in the marketplace, whereas the remaining 10 percent (Levites) did priestly ministry!

The tribe of Levi (the priesthood) was not given any allotment of land by divine decree, which completely took the Levites (the priesthood) out of the marketplace. Beyond this, the divine decree that God imposed upon the Old Testament Levitical priesthood also paralyzed the business gene in the entire bloodline of the priesthood.

What is sad and regrettable is that there are New Testament pastors who belong to the Order of Melchizedek, yet are trapped in a Levitical mindset and spiritual structure that has completely annihilated the business gene in many of these leaders. This would explain why only a few spiritual leaders can truly preach messages that can really help their people succeed in business. For the most part, messages preached every Sunday morning in the global Church are more primed towards getting people to heaven than helping them to do business (occupying) on earth until Christ returns.

It is also quite regrettable that many Kingdom business people find more "Word" at secular motivational seminars to inspire them to achieve greatness than at their local church. To add insult to injury, many people in the church who are serving God in the marketplace are told constantly that they are not in full-time ministry. How is that for inspiration? This is why books such as the one you are reading are needed to help reform the Church and "loose the priesthood" into the purposes of God.

8. *Under the priestly Order of Aaron, the high priest could only come into the Holy of Holies once a year.*

> *But only the high priest ever entered the Most Holy Place, and only once a year. And he always offered blood for his own sins and for the sins the people had committed in ignorance* (Hebrews 9:7).

Under the Levitical priestly Order, access to the *Shekinah* or manifest presence of God was quite restrictive. Apart from the high priest, very few if any of the people of Israel ever had the opportunity to bask in the manifest presence of God. Even for the presiding high priest, entering the Holy of Holies, which was the residency of the manifest presence of God, was also quite scary. Tinkling bells were attached to the priestly garments of the high priest when he entered the Holy of Holies. These bells were designed to alert the priests serving in the holy place whether the high priest was dead or alive. How would you like to enter God's presence not knowing whether you will come out alive?

> *So then, since we have a great High Priest who has entered heaven, Jesus the Son of God, let us hold firmly to what we believe. This High Priest of ours understands our weaknesses, for he faced all of the same testings we do, yet he did not sin. So let us come boldly to the throne of our gracious God. There we will receive his mercy, and we will find grace to help us when we need it most* (Hebrews 4:14-16).

The spiritual technology for accessing the presence of God under the Levitical priestly system was quite frightening and highly restrictive. This is in direct contrast to the spiritual technology for accessing the manifest presence of God under the Order of Melchizedek, which is the royal priesthood of Jesus Christ. Under the New Testament Order of Melchizedek priesthood, *every blood-washed believer can freely access the presence of God without fearing for their lives.* Accessing the *Shekinah* or manifest presence of God is no longer the birthright of a privileged few.

9. *Under the priestly Order of Aaron, a curse as prescribed by the Mosaic Law was placed upon those who withheld their tithes and offerings from the house of God.*

> *"Should people cheat God? Yet you have cheated me! But you ask, 'What do you mean? When did we ever cheat you?' You have cheated me of the tithes and offerings due to me. You are under a curse, for your whole nation has been cheating me"* (Malachi 3:8-9).

Under the Levitical priesthood, the spiritual consequences for withholding tithes and offerings from the house of God were quite grave and binding. God promised that those who were found guilty of robbing God of His tithes and offerings would be punished with a "curse." This curse was based upon and pre-scribed by the Mosaic Law. It is important to note that this curse did not come directly from the mouth of God; it was based on the dictates of the covenant of Law. Imagine being told that if you did not pay your tithes, you would be cursed by the Law. How would such a decree inspire tithes and offerings given from an inspired heart?

> *But Christ has rescued us from the curse pronounced by the law. When he was hung on the cross, he took upon himself the curse for our wrongdoing. For it is written in the Scriptures, "Cursed is everyone who is hung on a tree." Through Christ Jesus, God has blessed the Gentiles with the same blessing he promised to Abraham, so that we who are believers might receive the prom-ised Holy Spirit through faith* (Galatians 3:13-14).

Preachers and teachers who apply the dictates of Malachi 3:8-12 to New Testament believers whenever they are exacting the tithe are in gross error.

I am not suggesting that spiritual leaders cannot exact the tithe in the New Testament. I am simply suggesting that the technology of exacting the tithe from New Testament believers is very different from the technology of exacting the tithe that was used by the Levitical priestly Order. I explain in great detail how church leaders can exact the tithe from post-Calvary New Testament believers in my book titled *The Return of the Lost Key: Tithing under the Order of Melchizedek*.

What is adamantly clear is that Christ redeemed all post-Calvary New Testament believers from the curse of the Law. No self- and Bible-respecting teacher would argue that Christ did not fully redeem post-Calvary New Testament believers from the curse of the Law. If this is the case, why is it that many New Testament preachers and teachers completely ignore Galatians 3:13 whenever they are collecting tithes and offerings? As a senior pastor, I know the importance of tithes and offerings to the financial stability of the local church. But the truth of the matter is that the church's usage of Malachi 3:8-12 has hurt the case for tithing far more than it has helped it. I rest my case.

10. ***The priestly Order of Aaron was ordained by God to minister to the Jewish nation who lived under the Mosaic Covenant of Law.***

Fasten the two stones on the shoulder-pieces of the ephod as a reminder that Aaron represents the people of Israel. Aaron will carry these names on his shoulders as a constant reminder whenever he goes before the LORD (Exodus 28:12).

The Levitical priestly Order was only designed to service the spiritual needs of the Jewish nation. This priesthood became the custodians of the Mosaic Law. On the other hand, the New Testament priestly Order of Melchizedek has the power to service both Jews and Gentiles who profess their faith in Christ. It is a loftier priesthood and has spiritual custody over the New Covenant.

11. ***The priestly Order of Aaron did not extend beyond the natural borders of Israel. This is why Jews who were in captivity had to pray facing the direction of Jerusalem in order to get their prayers answered.***

But when Daniel learned that the law had been signed, he went home and knelt down as usual in his upstairs room, with its windows open toward Jerusalem. He prayed three times a day, just as he had always done, giving thanks to his God (Daniel 6:10).

12. *The priestly Order of Aaron was responsible for offering gifts and sacrifices to God for the remissions of the sins of the Jewish nation.*

When these things were all in place, the priests regularly entered the first room as they performed their religious duties. But only the high priest ever entered the Most Holy Place, and only once a year. And he always offered blood for his own sins and for the sins the people had committed in ignorance (Hebrews 9:6-7).

13. *Under the priestly Order of Aaron, the high priest had to offer gifts and sacrifices for his own sins and that of the people.*

He is the kind of high priest we need because he is holy and blameless, unstained by sin. He has been set apart from sinners and has been given the highest place of honor in heaven. Unlike those other high priests, he does not need to offer sacrifices every day. They did this for their own sins first and then for the sins of the people. But Jesus did this once for all when he offered himself as the sacrifice for the people's sins (Hebrews 7:26-27).

14. *The priestly Order of Aaron was designed to be a transitional priestly Order, until the arrival of the priestly Order of Melchizedek through our Lord Jesus Christ.*

But now Jesus, our High Priest, has been given a ministry that is far superior to the old priesthood, for he is the one who mediates for us a

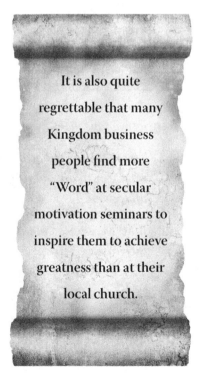

It is also quite regrettable that many Kingdom business people find more "Word" at secular motivation seminars to inspire them to achieve greatness than at their local church.

*far better covenant with God, based on better promises. If the
first covenant had been faultless, there would have been no need
for a second covenant to replace it* (Hebrews 8:6-7).

It is quite clear from biblical history that the priestly Order of Melchizedek
preceded the birth of Levi and the Levitical priestly Order. What is also quite
clear from the Word of Truth is the fact that the Levitical priesthood was a
"transitional priesthood," which was meant to pass away with the death and
resurrection of the Lord Jesus Christ.

The fact that God introduced Abram to the royal priesthood of Melchizedek
400 years before the birth of the Levitical priesthood, is quite telling. It underscores the fact that God had always intended for the Order of Melchizedek to
be the eternal priesthood of Abraham's spiritual descendants. The Church's
obsession with Malachi chapter 3 has made it quite difficult for many believers
to transition from a Levitical mindset to the Kingdom mindset of the Order
of Melchizedek.

15. *The priestly Order of Aaron was constantly harassed by the
spirit of death.*

> *There were many priests under the old system, for death pre-
> vented them from remaining in office. But because Jesus lives
> forever, his priesthood lasts forever* (Hebrews 7:23-24).

16. *The priestly Order of Aaron is an earthly priesthood, which
ministers from outside the eternal structures of the Kingdom
of heaven.*

> *If he were here on earth, he would not even be a priest, since
> there already are priests who offer the gifts required by the law.
> They serve in a system of worship that is only a copy, a shadow
> of the real one in heaven...* (Hebrews 8:4-5).

17. *The priestly Order of Aaron was constantly harassed and
held hostage by the personal and inherent weaknesses of its
high priests.*

The law appointed high priests who were limited by human weakness. But after the law was given, God appointed his Son with an oath, and his Son has been made the perfect High Priest forever (Hebrews 7:28).

18. **The priestly Order of Aaron was harassed constantly by generational spirits and curses, because it was based upon an earthly ancestry.**

Every high priest is a man chosen to represent other people in their dealings with God. He presents their gifts to God and offers sacrifices for their sins. And he is able to deal gently with ignorant and wayward people because he himself is subject to the same weaknesses. That is why he must offer sacrifices for his own sins as well as theirs (Hebrews 5:1-3).

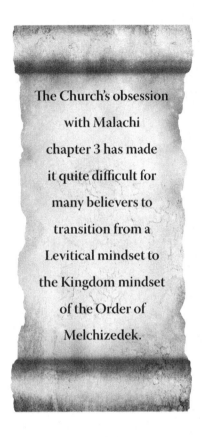

The Church's obsession with Malachi chapter 3 has made it quite difficult for many believers to transition from a Levitical mindset to the Kingdom mindset of the Order of Melchizedek.

19. **Under the priestly Order of Aaron, only priests from the tribe of Levi could come near the presence of God.**

"From now on, no Israelites except priests or Levites may approach the Tabernacle. If they come too near, they will be judged guilty and will die" (Numbers 18:22).

As previously mentioned, the spiritual technology for accessing the manifest presence of God under the Levitical Order of priesthood was quite frightening and highly restrictive. This is certainly in direct contrast to the New Testament Order of Melchizedek priesthood, where every born-again believer in Christ can access the glory of God.

LIFE APPLICATION SECTION

Memory Verses

This Melchizedek was king of the city of Salem and also a priest of God Most High. When Abraham was returning home after winning a great battle against the kings, Melchizedek met him and blessed him. Then Abraham took a tenth of all he had captured in battle and gave it to Melchizedek. The name Melchizedek means "king of justice," and king of Salem means "king of peace" (Hebrews 7:1-2).

Reflections

Why did God raise the Levitical priesthood and for how long?

Write three differences between the Levitical priesthood and the Order of Melchizedek.

JOURNAL YOUR PERSONAL NOTES ON THIS CHAPTER

CHAPTER SEVEN

The Order
of Melchizedek

The LORD has taken an oath and will not break his vow: "You are a priest forever in the order of Melchizedek" (Psalm 110:4).

IT IS AN ETERNAL ORDER

MY CO-HOST FOR OUR TV TALK SHOW "The Kingdom in the Marketplace" on one of our broadcasts asked me a very important question that really needs to be answered. "Dr Myles why is the Order of Melchizedek an Order?" Here was my response. The Order of Melchizedek is an Order, because God always sets a governing order around anything that He has ever created. This principle sets the premise for the "Law of Divine Order." By definition, "Order" is *a condition in which each thing is properly disposed with reference to other things and to its purpose; methodical or harmonious arrangement.* This definition is very sobering and revealing, as it unmasks why the Order of Melchizedek is an eternal "Order" before it is anything else. It is an eternal order which governs everything that God ever created in nature, including fallen angels. This is why the devil and his gang of demons are so terrified of the global Church rediscovering the Order of Melchizedek. The Order of Melchizedek is the highest order in all of creation because it is the eternal royal priestly order of Christ before He came to the planet through the virgin birth. Since the Order of Melchizedek is the highest spiritual order, it controls the following orders: "angelic orders, the order of mankind, the order of divine law, all man-made social, political and religious orders, scientific orders, and demonic orders just to name a few.

The priestly Order of Melchizedek is the highest priestly Order that God has ever established for His people. When Jesus Christ rose from the dead, He took the blood of the cross and presented it to His heavenly Father as a peace offering. By the offering of His blood, Jesus secured a permanent pathway into the Holy of Holies for all eternity, for all of God's people. Jesus then sat down at the right hand of God and put on His eternal mantle as the High Priest after the Order of Melchizedek.

Unfortunately many of God's children do not know much about the Order of Melchizedek and what's available to them through this awesome royal priesthood, chiefly because of inaccurate patterns of tithing which have been established in the global Church.

THE TESTIMONY OF AN APOLOGETIC APOSTLE

...Indeed, if others have reason for confidence in their own efforts, I have even more! I was circumcised when I was eight days old. I am a pure-blooded citizen of Israel and a member of the tribe of Benjamin—a real Hebrew if there ever was one! I was a member of the Pharisees, who demand the strictest obedience to the Jewish law. I was so zealous that I harshly persecuted the church. And as for righteousness, I obeyed the law without fault (Philippians 3:4-6).

The salvation of the apostle Paul and his subsequent transition from Judaism to the Kingdom is one of the most important historic events in the prophetic history of the New Testament church. No single person has contributed more to the cause of Christ and His Kingdom than Paul of Tarsus. His supernatural conversion to Christ is clearly recorded in the book of Acts and canonized in the Holy Scriptures. The apostle Paul, through the vehicle of apostolic and prophetic technology, is responsible for many of the doctrines of the Church today. No well-meaning New Testament believer or theologian can ignore the testimony of Paul and his teachings.

Of the post-Pentecost apostles of the Lord Jesus Christ, none is as qualified as the apostle Paul to teach on the priestly Order of Melchizedek and outline its supremacy over the Levitical priesthood. Paul was a prolific writer and expert on Jewish laws and customs. His zeal for Judaism was unrivaled even among his peers. God could never have chosen a more qualified person to write an apologetic discourse in defense of the New Testament merits of the priestly Order of Melchizedek. Much of what we know about the nature, power, and scope of the Order of Melchizedek was revealed to this apostolic general. As such, we will begin deciphering what the Order of Melchizedek is all about using the written testimony of Paul, a great pillar of the faith.

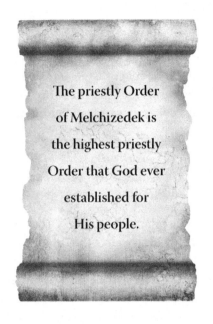

The priestly Order of Melchizedek is the highest priestly Order that God ever established for His people.

IT IS A MARKETPLACE AND PRIESTLY MINISTRY

The most unique aspect of the Order of Melchizedek is that, unlike the Levitical or Aaronic priestly Order, this eternal priestly Order is both a marketplace and priestly ministry. The High Priest of this eternal priestly Order is first and foremost a King who does priestly work. *As a King, His influence extends well beyond the boundaries of the temple, right into the marketplace.* All kings own everything that is within their kingdom. As a King-Priest, Jesus Christ has ongoing dual influence over both the services of His priests in the temple and the activities of His people in the marketplace.

In contrast, the high priest under the Levitical priesthood and his staff of priests were not permitted to engage in any form of secular business activity outside the normal activities of servicing the spiritual needs of the people of Israel. The only time that the Levites sought secular employment was when they were neglected by the other eleven tribes. *Moses made it very clear that God did not want the Levites to be involved in any form of secular business activity.* He wanted them to focus their energy on servicing the spiritual needs of the people of Israel and those of the temple of God. To ensure that this was the case, God gave the tithes of the remaining eleven tribes of Israel to the tribe of Levi as an everlasting inheritance.

> *As for the tribe of Levi, your relatives, I will compensate them for their service in the Tabernacle. Instead of an allotment of land, I will give them the tithes from the entire land of Israel* (Numbers 18:21).

Understanding the Order of Melchizedek will not only revolutionize how the Church exacts the tithe, *but it will also introduce the global Church to many creative ways of wealth creation outside the normal giving of tithes and offerings.* Unlike the Levitical priestly Order, the priesthood (members of the clergy) under the priestly Order of Melchizedek do not have to depend entirely on the tithes and offerings of the people to sustain the work of the ministry. Under the Order of Melchizedek, the tithes and offerings of the people are just two of the many streams of income that God has made available to the New Testament Church.

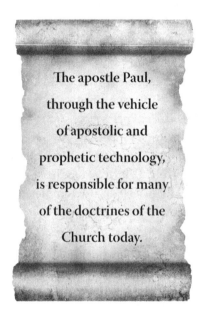

The apostle Paul, through the vehicle of apostolic and prophetic technology, is responsible for many of the doctrines of the Church today.

Under the priestly Order of Mel-chize-dek, senior pastors or founding apostles of churches can be just as involved in business as they are in ministering to the spiritual needs of the people in their church. *Under this eternal priestly Order, spiritual leaders can lead a church while managing a profitable business in the marketplace.* This dual involvement in ecclesiastical and marketplace ministry increases the scope and spiritual reach of the ministries of senior leaders who operate under the Order of Melchizedek.

Under the Order of Melchizedek, senior pastors or founding apostles of churches do not have to be limited to reaching only the people who step inside the four walls of the church building. The majority of lost souls are found in the marketplace. The apostle Paul is a classic example of this powerful synergy of marketplace and priestly ministry. Paul was able to reach far more people with the gospel because his ministry included the marketplace.

> *Then Paul left Athens and went to Corinth. There he became acquainted with a Jew named Aquila, born in Pontus, who had recently arrived from Italy with his wife, Priscilla. They had left Italy when Claudius Caesar deported all Jews from Rome. Paul lived and worked with them, for they were tentmakers just as he was. Each Sabbath found Paul at the synagogue, trying to convince the Jews and Greeks alike* (Acts 18:1-4).

Unfortunately many pastors in the Body of Christ are not aware that New Testament ministry is supposed to function after the Order of Melchizedek, so they are leading their churches under an Old Testament Levitical priestly mindset. The reason I know this is because many pastors are obsessed with tithes and offerings as the only method for raising money for the vision of their local church. These pastors stress themselves into a panic whenever they see that the tithes and offerings of the church are running low. This Levitical mindset has robbed many of these able pastors of many entrepreneurial endeavors that could effectively finance their vision in the Kingdom. The following quote underscores just how widespread and deeply rooted this Levitical mindset really is in many leaders in the Body of Christ.

> I was excited to attend my first pastoral roundtable, but that excitement turned quickly to frustration. After the laughs subsided, one pastor said, "You do not make money young man; you raise money. You have to get before your church and challenge them to give more. Teach your church to give."

> "Amen," the others responded.

> They went on to share with me fifty ways to handle an offering. I learned how to take an offering, receive an offering, and pull an offering. I have heard these methods echoed throughout the last twenty years.

Thus, everything I've learned from the church and in formal training about wealth-building can be summed up in two familiar words: Tithes and Offerings. That was the extent of the wealth knowledge I learned for many years.[1]

Since the New Testament Order of Melchizedek priesthood is both a marketplace and priestly ministry, telling believers who are serving God in the marketplace that they are not in full-time ministry is incorrect. This very common expression in the Body of Christ divides those in the so-called full-time ministry from believers who are serving God in the marketplace. This wrong theology is supported by the fact that many spiritual leaders in the Body of Christ are steeped in a Levitical mindset. *Under the Order of Melchizedek every believer is actively involved in full-time ministry in whatever vocation God has blessed them with.*

Understanding the Order of Melchizedek will not only revolutionize how the Church exacts the tithe, but it will also introduce the global Church to many creative ways of wealth creation outside the normal giving of tithes and offerings.

As we approach the prophetic establishment of Christ's millennial Kingdom, we are going to see the divine Kingdom invasion of the marketplace. This supernatural activity of God in the marketplace will come in the form of a "new prophetic company" of New Testament believers who have become awakened to the spiritual ramifications of belonging to the Order of Melchizedek. Like Joseph and Daniel, this prophetic company of Kingdom business men and women will turn the world upside down by taking over the seven mountains of Babylon (finance, business, law, media, sports/celebration, family, and church). Liberal Hollywood film makers are already nervous because God is raising men and women in the Kingdom to produce tomorrow's blockbuster films.

It Is an Eternal Priesthood

...without father, without mother, without genealogy, having neither beginning of days nor end of life, but made like the Son of God, remains a priest continually (Hebrews 7:3 NKJV).

The LORD has sworn and will not relent, "You are a priest forever according to the order of Melchizedek" (Psalm 110:4 NKJV).

The first thing that the apostle Paul and King David tell us about the priestly Order of Melchizedek is that unlike the priestly Order of Aaron, this priesthood *is an eternal or everlasting priesthood.* This powerful priestly Order exists in an infinite eternal state which cannot be improved upon because everything in this realm is completely perfect—there is nothing missing or broken in this spiritual Order. The fact that the priestly Order of Melchizedek is eternal has far-reaching spiritual implications. It means that there is simply no end to the level and quality of representation we can expect from this glorious Order when we yield ourselves to it.

It Is Built on the King's Righteousness

For this Melchizedek, king of Salem, priest of the Most High God, who met Abraham returning from the slaughter of the kings and blessed him, to whom also Abraham gave a tenth part of all, first being translated "king of righteousness," and then also king of Salem, meaning "king of peace," (Hebrews 7:1-2 NKJV).

The second thing that the apostle Paul tells us about the priestly Order of Melchizedek is that this priesthood is built around and upon the righteousness of its High Priest. The Bible tells us that this Melchizedek was King of righteousness. It isn't simply that this great priest Melchizedek was righteous, but rather that He reigns over the whole sphere of righteousness! Imagine this: anything righteous that you can think or dream of, He reigns over it.

This is in direct contrast to the priestly Order of Aaron in which the high priests themselves were constantly wrestling with personal sin and weaknesses. Under the Order of Melchizedek the High Priest has complete control over sin, and He lives in complete righteousness and reigns over it. Righteousness in Scripture has three prongs—it is being in right standing with God, man, and the devil. If we are in right standing with God but are not in right standing with our wives or neighbors, we are not walking in the fullness of our righteousness. If we are in right standing with God and man but are in wrong standing with the devil, we are still not walking in the fullness of our righteousness. The priestly Order of Melchizedek has the power to make all of its subjects completely righteous.

It Exists in an Eternal State of Peace

For this Melchizedek, king of Salem, priest of the Most High God, who met Abraham returning from the slaughter of the kings and blessed him, to whom also Abraham gave a tenth part of all, first being translated "king of righteousness," and then also king of Salem, meaning "king of peace," (Hebrews 7:1-2 NKJV).

The third thing that the apostle Paul shows us about this powerful priestly Order is that it exists in *a permanent state of peace and tranquility*. This priesthood presides over the kind of supernatural peace that surpasses human comprehension. It's difficult for us to truly imagine a life without the spirit of unrest and anxiety. This is because we live in a world where there is turmoil everywhere we turn. But when we bring ourselves under the priestly Order of Melchizedek, God will bring us into a place of supernatural rest and tranquility such as we have never experienced before. The word *peace* comes from the Hebrew word *Shalom* which means "nothing broken and nothing missing."

When we enter into this dimension of supernatural rest and tranquility, we will become the greatest demonstration of the power of God in the midst of a troubled world where all, including the rich, are in a constant state of unrest. People will gravitate to us wanting to know how they can drink from the same spiritual well we are drinking from, which has brought us so much peace and rest. Since the priestly Order of Melchizedek exists in a permanent state of peace, it has the power to restore whatever is broken or missing in our lives.

Jesus Christ is the High Priest

So also Christ did not glorify Himself to become High Priest, but it was He who said to Him: "You are My Son, today I have begotten You." As He also says in another place: "You are a priest forever according to the order of Melchizedek" (Hebrews 5:5-6 NKJV).

The fourth thing that the apostle Paul tells us about the priestly Order of Melchizedek is that in this eternal Order Jesus Christ is the presiding High Priest. In this Order, the High Priest never dies because He has an endless life and reigns over life and death. This High Priest is above the reach of death and moves in the realms of eternity. In this Order our High Priest is the sinless Son of God who lived and died for our sins and then rose from the dead. What a High Priest! He is worthy of all the glory and the honor.

The High Priest Is a King-Priest

Another very fascinating aspect of the priestly Order of Melchizedek is that in this Order the High Priest is both a Priest and a King. In the priestly Order of Aaron the high priest was simply that, a priest of God and no more. In the Order of Aaron, the High Priest had no kingly anointing and grace flowing through his life. He was operating on one spiritual cylinder, that of a priest. He could present the spiritual needs of the nation of Israel before God and make atonement for their sins, but he had no governmental authority over the nation of Israel.

Under the priestly Order of Melchizedek, the High Priest wears not only His priestly mantle but He also carries the spirit of government on His shoulders. This means that the scope of His spiritual

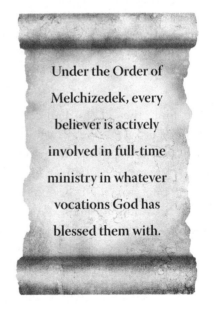

Under the Order of Melchizedek, every believer is actively involved in full-time ministry in whatever vocations God has blessed them with.

authority and the power that He exerts over the people that are under His priesthood are infinitely greater than the power the priesthood of Aaron exerted over the nation of Israel. This means that when we bring ourselves under the priestly Order of Melchizedek we will become shareholders in the spirit of governmental authority, which flows from the head of our Order. This is why Jesus said that under this priesthood, whatever we bind here on earth shall be bound in heaven and whatever we loose here on earth shall be given the same license in heaven. (See Matt. 16:19.) This is what I call packing power!

I have taught the people in my church to go around telling each other that they are *packing power*. When we truly bring ourselves under this priestly Order of Melchizedek we will become "walking powerhouses." Wherever we go, the power of God ought to explode into miraculous action. Under the Order of Melchizedek, we have no business walking in fear and defeat. Under this priestly Order, we truly become demon busters and world shakers!

Complete Dominion over the Power of Sin

He is the kind of high priest we need because he is holy and blameless, unstained by sin. He has been set apart from sinners and has been given the highest place of honor in heaven. Unlike those other high priests, he does not need to offer sacrifices every day. They did this for their own sins first and then for the sins of the people. But Jesus did this once for all when he offered himself as the sacrifice for the people's sins (Hebrews 7:26-27).

Since the fall of Adam and Eve, men and women have been ravaged by sin and its dreadful power. When sin entered the world it unleashed death agencies into the spiritual atmosphere of the fallen Adamic kingdom that we now call our world. These death agencies released by sin also corrupted the human gene pool, making every child born of a woman a prisoner of sin from their first breathing moment outside the womb. These death agencies released by sin also shortened our life expectancy here on earth and introduced unrest in the matrix of family relationships.

"Why are you so angry?" the LORD asked Cain. "Why do you look so dejected? You will be accepted if you do what is right. But

*if you refuse to do what is right, then watch out! Sin is crouching
at the door, eager to control you. But you must subdue it and be
its master." One day Cain suggested to his brother, "Let's go out
into the fields." And while they were in the field, Cain attacked
his brother, Abel, and killed him* (Genesis 4:6-8).

The showdown between God and Cain in Genesis chapter 4 began with
Cain's offering of disobedience, which was rejected by God for its inaccuracy.
This showdown culminated in the murder of Cain's young brother, Abel, show-
casing just how quickly sin had invaded man's sense of right and wrong. What's
worse, sin in Cain had raised its ugly head to the degree of challenging God's
supreme authority over the affairs of men.

Many generations later, men and women are still trying to control the raging power of sin in their lives, to no avail. Humankind continues to search desperately for a way to curb the evil residing within. Sin has taken a terrible toll
on the structure of family relationships, separating husbands from wives and
children from parents. There is nothing indecent or immoral that "Sin" will not
do. The more vile and horrifying an act is, the more "Sin" will do.

Many people do not know that the Bible teaches that "Sin" is an entity by
itself. As its own self-generating entity, Sin is more powerful than the devil
because the devil, who tempts the world with Sin, is also a slave to Sin. Actually
the devil was the first creation of God to become a slave to Sin. Since Lucifer
(the devil) became the first slave to Sin, he became the "express image" of the
invisible evil entity called Sin in the same way that Christ is the "express image
of the invisible" God. (See Hebrews 1:3.) Said in layman's terms, the devil is so
enslaved by Sin that he can never return to his original state of glory even if
he so desired it. His only option is to keep doing Sin's bidding until Sin lands
him into the lake of fire and brimstone and reduces the devil from a cherubim
angel (a four winged mighty angelic being) to a mere man. (See Isaiah 14:9-16
KJV.) The devil is like a heroine addict who knows that the drugs he is using are
destroying his person but is completely powerless to stop! He is truly a slave
to Sin.

Many Kingdom citizens (born-again believers) do not know what really
happened on the cross. They do not know the magnitude of what Jesus Christ
did through His death, burial, and resurrection. The reason for this is because
many teachers of the gospel have unmistakably placed the devil above the entity

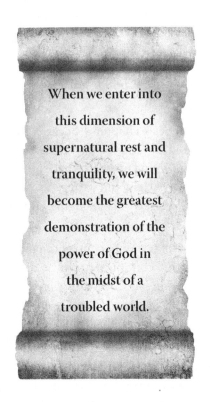

When we enter into this dimension of supernatural rest and tranquility, we will become the greatest demonstration of the power of God in the midst of a troubled world.

in nature called Sin. This is a gross error in the Church's theology. It is like mistaking the vice president of the United States for the president. In the kingdom of darkness, the devil is the vice president whereas the entity called Sin is the president. This is why the Bible calls "Satan" the Prince of darkness because *a prince is always the one next in line to the throne!* The devil is only a "king" over the demonic kingdom called Babylon the Great, which is currently, stationed in the second heaven. (See Isaiah 14:3-4, Revelation 12:7-9, 18:1-3.) Babylon the Great is a sub-demonic kingdom under the kingdom of darkness which drives the machinery of deception on earth, so that the souls of men can serve the entity called Sin.

When Jesus Christ went into the wilderness for forty days, He went to defeat the prince of darkness (see Matthew 4:1-9); but when He went to the cross (see 2 Corinthians 5:21), He went to destroy and conquer the strong man in the kingdom of darkness—the entity called Sin. When Christ conquered Sin and atoned for the Sin of humankind, the complete defeat of all principalities and powers was a foregone conclusion. (See Colossians 2:14-15.) The power of the devil, principalities and powers is rooted in Sin. Without it the devil is completely powerless. The following Scriptures clearly show that God treats Sin as its own self-generating evil entity in nature: Genesis 4:7, Ezekiel 28:15-16, 2 Corinthians 5:21, Romans 6:1-23, just to name a few). It is not within the scope of this book to give an effective treatise on this very important subject. Please read my book, *The Doctrine of Christ, Sin and the Devil!*

Sin has also taken its toll on the financial resources of many individuals and nations. Men and women motivated by the power of Sin have stolen the life savings of others and squandered them on the altar of personal greed. The recent exposure of the $50 billion fraud perpetrated by investment guru Bernie Madoff who robbed thousands of their life savings quickly comes to mind. Children have had their loving parents slaughtered by thieves who broke into their homes in search of money. *Sin has progressively reduced men and women in every way possible from being creatures of immense divine dignity into beasts of the field.* Hell is full of people serving their eternal sentence in unquenchable fires because they failed to use the power of God to break the power of Sin in their lives.

> The devil is like an heroine addict who knows that the drugs are destroying his person but is completely powerless to stop! He is truly a slave to Sin.

> *But there is another power within me that is at war with my mind. This power makes me a slave to the sin that is still within me. Oh, what a miserable person I am! Who will free me from this life that is dominated by sin and death? Thank God! The answer is in Jesus Christ our Lord...* (Romans 7:23-25).

The apostle Paul was no stranger to such personal struggles while he was trying to break the power of Sin over his life. He discovered that the more he tried to resist Sin in the power of his own flesh, the stronger the hold of Sin got on his life. A zealous follower of Judaism at the time, Paul discovered that the more he tried to obey the righteous demands of the Mosaic Law through his sheer force of will, the more rebellious and insidious the nature of Sin inside him became. *He found himself doing the very things that he had promised himself that he would never do.* Paul finally came to the sobering conclusion that the technology of sin and death had literally invaded every fiber of his being, making his body a body of Sin and death.

As a result of our personal struggles with Sin, many of us can appreciate the awesome power of being under a priestly Order where the High Priest has complete mastery over Sin and its insidious powers. Under the priestly Order of Melchizedek, the High Priest (Jesus) has never been defiled or adversely affected by Sin. As a result, He is able to invest in us the same supernatural grace to rise and live above the controlling power of Sin, when we yield to His priestly Order. Imagine coming into a season in your walk with the Lord where Sin is no longer an issue. This is the awesome power of living under the Order of Melchizedek. This type of prevailing grace over the *sin nature* is very much available to every New Testament believer under this priestly Order.

STEWARDING ABRAHAM'S SPIRITUAL INHERITANCE

But Christ has rescued us from the curse pronounced by the law. When he was hung on the cross, he took upon himself the curse for our wrongdoing. For it is written in the Scriptures, "Cursed is everyone who is hung on a tree." Through Christ Jesus, God has blessed the Gentiles with the same blessing he promised to Abraham, so that we who are believers might receive the promised Holy Spirit through faith (Galatians 3:13-14).

This powerful priestly Order of Melchizedek has been given the eternal privilege of stewarding the blessing of Abraham for the purpose of Kingdom advancement. Jesus Christ, who is also the High Priest after the Order of Melchizedek, has complete stewardship over Abraham's natural and spiritual inheritance and showers it on the people who live under His priestly Order.

POWER OVER THE SPIRIT OF DEATH

...by so much more Jesus has become a surety of a better covenant. Also there were many priests, because they were prevented by death from continuing. But He, because He continues forever, has an unchangeable priesthood (Hebrews 7:22-24 NKJV).

God told Adam and Eve that if they chose to disobey Him and ate from the Tree of the Knowledge of Good and Evil they would surely die. At the time God told them this, Adam and Eve could not comprehend the horrors of death because they had never seen anything die before. You can imagine the sense of horror and dismay that they must have experienced when they discovered the lifeless body of their son, Abel, who had been murdered by his own brother. Death agencies had struck close to home, and the emotional pain was almost unbearable. There is nothing more painful to a parent than the death of their child. Countless generations have wrestled with the angels of death while trying to make sense of the loss of loved ones.

> *Because God's children are human beings—made of flesh and blood—the Son also became flesh and blood. For only as a human being could he die, and only by dying could he break the power of the devil, who had the power of death. Only in this way could he set free all who have lived their lives as slaves to the fear of dying* (Hebrews 2:14-15).

Since the first funeral in the Garden of Eden, the fear of death has terrorized men and women for centuries. What is death? Death in its most basic form is the cessation of life or the absence of animation—the primary assignment of death agencies is to shut down the flow of life. If a marriage is filled with life and laughter, death agencies will look for ways to bring death into the marriage. The high rate of divorce in our modern societies is evidence that death agencies are working overtime to quarantine the flow of life. Death is more than a corpse lying in a casket; it's a demonic technology which stops the flow of life!

Jesus died to break the power that the devil had over the human race by manipulating us through our personal fear of death. Before the resurrection of Jesus Christ, death agencies terrorized the world using man's inherent fear of death. According to the apostle Paul, the priestly Order of Melchizedek has complete authority over the spirit of death. The Order of Melchizedek is the custodian for the divine technology—the Law of the Spirit of Life in Christ Jesus, which is infinitely superior to the demonic technology called the Law of Sin and Death. In the priestly Order of Aaron, the high priests kept changing because they could not serve forever by reason of death. Their ministerial assignments to the Jewish nation were always cut short by death.

When we bring ourselves under the priestly Order of Melchizedek, God will give us the power to conquer death and its auxiliary agencies. The priestly Order of Melchizedek will cancel and quarantine the sentence of death over our lives—spiritually, emotionally, and physically. Under this Order, death itself receives a sentence of death. Death is told to die!

There is no doubt that many people would pay astronomical amounts of money if a scientist invented a pill that contained the secret to the fountain of youth. A magic pill that, once swallowed, would arrest the machinery of death inside their bodies and reverse the aging process. I know that if such a pill was ever introduced, its originator would be a multibillionaire within hours of its release on the global market. There would be mass hysteria as the rich and famous fought their way to the front of the queue to buy the pill that would allow them to live longer. Such is the universal fear of death that exists in the inner sanctum of the human soul.

> *Then, when our dying bodies have been transformed into bodies that will never die, this Scripture will be fulfilled: "Death is swallowed up in victory. O death, where is your victory? O death, where is your sting?"* (1 Corinthians 15:54-55)

What multiplied millions of people on our planet do not know is that there is now a Priestly Order where the sentence and machinery of death at work in the human body can be restrained and even reversed. The miracle pill with the secret to the fountain of youth has already been invented under this Priestly Order of Melchizedek. It comes in the form of the divine bread and wine offered to the people who submit themselves to this powerful Priestly Order.

No Earthly Genealogy

> *...to whom also Abraham gave a tenth part of all, first being translated "king of righteousness," and then also king of Salem, meaning "king of peace," without father, without mother, without genealogy, having neither beginning of days nor end of life, but made like the Son of God, remains a priest continually* (Hebrews 7:2-3 NKJV).

You may have heard of the statement, "like father, like son" or "like mother, like daughter." You may have overheard someone say, "Dear God, this child is just as nasty as his father." The implied meaning is that the child and its father are cut from the same cloth; they have the same genetic tendencies or traits.

After the fall of Adam and Eve, who are the grandparents of the entire human race, Sin entered the world and corrupted the human gene pool. The technology of Sin unleashed the poison of demonic influence in the flow of the human bloodline.

The corruption caused by Sin when it entered the human gene pool caused the prophetic DNA, which God had given humankind, to mutate. Sin changed the inherent nature of the human genome making it more susceptible to demonic influences rather than the influence of the God kind of life. Like a nuclear torpedo, our DNA was reprogrammed to migrate toward death. Everything we do will, at some point, touch the peripherals of death. Our DNA as humans has mutated to the point that we will never be able to manifest the fullness of the God kind of life in our DNA without requiring a supernatural blood transfusion to flush out all the death agencies flowing in our bloodlines.

> *You must not bow down to them or worship them, for I, the LORD your God, am a jealous God who will not tolerate your affection for any other gods. I lay the sins of the parents upon their children; the entire family is affected—even children in the third and fourth generations of those who reject me* (Exodus 20:5).

Since our gene pool was corrupted by the entrance of sin in the human bloodline, our DNA became the best vehicle to transport demonic spirits and demonic tendencies from one generation to another. Demonic agencies had hit a home run. They had guaranteed themselves a sure transport between fathers and sons, mothers and daughters. The demonic spirits that were controlling parents had a sure license through the human gene pool to continue their tenancy in that particular family line even to the fourth generation.

Unless this demonic license through the human genome is revoked or restrained, the devil will have an upper hand in the destinies of our sons, daughters, and grandchildren. Unless this demonic license is canceled, the chance of our children fighting the same demons and demonic tendencies that we are fighting today is 100 percent. As a matter of fact, the longer demonic spirits operate within our bloodline the stronger the demonic technology becomes inside the chambers of our human genome.

The demonic hills we as parents fail to cross and conquer today will one day become great mountains of spiritual resistance in the days of our children.

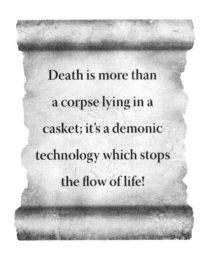

Death is more than a corpse lying in a casket; it's a demonic technology which stops the flow of life!

This is why my heart goes out to former President George W. Bush. The troubles he experienced trying to win the peace in the Iraq War had little to do with the genius of the commanders on the ground, and everything to do with the failure of his father, former President George H. W. Bush, who failed to take advantage of the opportunity he was given in the late 1980s to destroy Saddam Hussein and deliver the Iraqi people.

Years later when his son, George W. Bush, became president and went to war with Iraq, the playing fields had changed from the time when his father stood at the same frontiers. In the years it took for George W. Bush to get to Iraq, the demonic machinery and technology had changed the rules of engagement from the normal methods of combat to the unpredictable and suicidal tactics of zealous suicide bombers. I do not blame George W. Bush; I blame his father for failing to clear a hill in his day which later became a gigantic mountain in the days of his son.

The demonic pathway through the human genome has far-reaching spiritual implications. It means that if there have been struggles with child molestation or sexual perversion in a particular family, the genetic disposition of the descendants of this particular family will lean very heavily to the duplication of these insidious acts throughout the ensuing generations. This explains why the history of certain families is plastered with divorce and/or criminal issues. The same demonic agencies that had broken the marriages of their parents and grandparents are now destroying theirs. These cycles of sorrow, loss, and pain will continue until they are broken.

The answer to ending these cycles of death, destruction, and defeat is found in rediscovering our rightful inheritance under the Order of Melchizedek. The apostle Paul tells us that the priestly Order of Melchizedek has no earthly genealogy, ancestry or bloodline. Please remember that King David told us in Psalm 110:4, hundreds of years before the virgin birth of Jesus, that God had already told Christ that He was the High Priest after the Order of Melchizedek.

This prophetic decree from the book of Psalms implies that the priesthood of Melchizedek is based upon Christ's divinity even though it is tempered by His humanity.

> *Seeing then that we have a great High Priest who has passed through the heavens, Jesus the Son of God, let us hold fast our confession. For we do not have a High Priest who cannot sympathize with our weaknesses, but was in all points tempted as we are, yet without sin* (Hebrews 4:14-15 NKJV).

Even though the priestly Order of Melchizedek is based upon Christ's divinity, it is greatly influenced by His humanity. Without His humanity, Christ would have been a great High Priest who could not be touched by our infirmities (weaknesses). Christ's humanity is also the mitigating factor for His selection to the office of the High Priest, since every High Priest must be chosen from among men. But please understand that the underlying foundation and genesis of Christ's priestly Order is based upon His divinity and not His humanity. This is why Christ's Order of Melchizedek priesthood is infinitely higher than any earthly priesthood!

Christ's lofty position of honor and His lack of a traceable human genealogy have far-reaching spiritual implications for those who run for cover under His eternal priestly Order. Even though our Lord Jesus Christ shares in our humanity, the apostle Paul is quite clear that His priesthood is not of this world. Saint Paul makes it quite clear that the Levitical priestly Order was an earthly priesthood. This means then that Christ's priesthood is primarily based upon His divinity and not His humanity. This is why He has a heavenly priesthood.

> *If he [Jesus Christ] were here on earth, he [Jesus Christ] would not even be a priest, since there already are priests [Levites] who offer the gifts required by the law* (Hebrews 8:4).

Since His eternal priestly Order is based primarily upon His divinity and not His humanity, Christ has no earthly genealogy that can compromise His priestly Order. His priesthood can never be affected by demonic influences and tendencies that have established a strong pathway through the human genome. This means that when we come under this priestly Order of Melchizedek, *every generational curse that has been pursuing us through our bloodlines has to come to an abrupt end.* What a priestly Order! Most of the ministries who

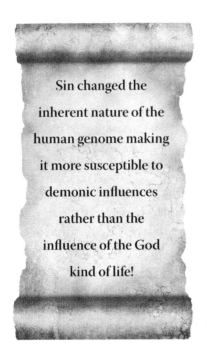

Sin changed the inherent nature of the human genome making it more susceptible to demonic influences rather than the influence of the God kind of life!

teach on breaking generational curses do not have a clear-cut revelation concerning the Order of Melchizedek. This is why they have a limited level of success in breaking generational curses over people's lives.

PRIESTLY ORDER SEALED WITH AN UNCHANGEABLE OATH

And inasmuch as He was not made priest without an oath (for they have become priests without an oath, but He with an oath by Him who said to Him: "The LORD has sworn and will not relent, 'You are a priest forever' according to the order of Melchizedek'") (Hebrews 7:20-21 NKJV).

We live in a world that is constantly changing and changing the people around us as the earth rotates on its axis. In the rapid changes that are taking place, we sometimes lose sight of vital principles that drive the engines of life. One of those vital principles, which sometimes gets lost in translation, is our ability to trust delegated authority. Many of us have seen leadership change hands so many times that we have become weary of trusting the engines of human leadership because we do not know who will be in power from one day to the next. This is especially true in democratic societies. In the United States, for instance, there is a change of leadership every four or eight years.

> *The law appointed high priests who were limited by human weakness. But after the law was given, God appointed his Son with an oath, and his Son has been made the perfect High Priest forever* (Hebrews 7:28).

People may like and trust the present structure of leadership but they are never sure whether the leaders that they trust in one day will be available to lead them in the next. This has caused many people to have very loose connections with authority figures, choosing rather to be laws unto themselves. In many cases the people's loose connections with their secular leaders usually translates into loose connections with their spiritual fathers and mothers in the Kingdom of God.

The frustrations of a constantly changing leadership structure and climate, was one of the horrifying things that plagued the people who lived under the priestly Order of Aaron. The high priests kept changing every few years as each previous high priest died away. Even more frightening was the fact that some very good and honorable high priests were sometimes replaced by a high priest who was corrupt and lacking in spiritual power. It's like being in a marriage where your wife or husband is constantly changing from one day to the next. How terrifying is that?

With great excitement, the apostle Paul tells us that under the priestly Order of Melchizedek, we never have to live in fear of a sudden change in the structure and climate of leadership. The structure of leadership and the eternal position of our presiding High Priest Jesus Christ has already been sealed by an unchangeable oath from the mouth of God.

Jesus Christ is the same yesterday, today, and forever (Hebrews 13:8).

Hebrews 13:8 means that under the priestly Order of Melchizedek we can fully surrender ourselves to our Leader, Jesus Christ, while He outworks His eternal purposes through our lives. The priestly Order of Melchizedek creates a spiritual climate in which people can establish very strong spiritual connections with their spiritual fathers and mothers in the Lord.

The Order of Melchizedek destroys the loose connections between the people and their shepherds. It unleashes strong spiritual connections between those who lead and those who follow. These supernatural dimensions of strong spirit connections and loyalty will help us establish strong father-son type of churches, which have the favor to possess, faith to prevail, and power to finish. Under the Order of Melchizedek we can truly build churches and businesses that can take the cities and impact the nations.

SUPERIOR TO THE LEVITICAL PRIESTHOOD

Consider then how great this Melchizedek was. Even Abraham, the great patriarch of Israel, recognized this by giving him a tenth of what he had taken in battle. Now the law of Moses required that the priests, who are descendants of Levi, must collect a tithe from the rest of the people of Israel, who are also descendants of Abraham. But Melchizedek, who was not a descendant of Levi, collected a tenth from Abraham. And Melchizedek placed a blessing upon Abraham, the one who had already received the promises of God. And without question, the person who has the power to give a blessing is greater than the one who is blessed. In addition, we might even say that these Levites—the ones who collect the tithe—paid a tithe to Melchizedek when their ancestor Abraham paid a tithe to him (Hebrews 7:4-7,9).

Consider that Paul's epistle to the Hebrews was written to the Jews who lived in Asia Minor and that it is the strongest and most intelligent apologetic epistle ever written by an apostle. This epistle was written to convince men and women of Jewish descent who were having a tough time walking away from the dictates of the Mosaic Law in their newfound faith. These Jewish believers kept mixing the Law with grace in their spiritual practices. We must remember that these Messianic Jews who were converting to a life of faith in Christ Jesus had spent over 4,000 years of their national history under the Levitical priesthood, and changing gears to a new priestly Order was no simple task.

This is why it was necessary for the apostle Paul to intelligently walk them through the writings of the Old and New Testaments and show them the utter superiority of the priestly Order of Melchizedek over the Levitical priesthood. Saint Paul had to show them that they were not abandoning their ancient Jewish faith in the God of Abraham, Isaac, and Jacob when they brought themselves under the priestly Order of Melchizedek.

The most important argument Paul presented to establish the surpassing superiority of the priestly Order of Melchizedek over the priestly Order of Aaron is that Abraham, the father of the Jewish nation, had himself tithed into this eternal priesthood of the Order of Melchizedek. This is significant because Abraham never ever tithed into the priestly Order of Aaron, a priesthood established on Mount Sinai over 400 years after Abraham's death.

The apostle Paul seals his argument when he states, That if Abraham who is the father of the Jewish nation tithed into Melchizedek, it also follows that Levi who was in the spiritual loins of Abraham when Abraham met Melchizedek also tithed into this powerful priestly Order. Paul's argument affected these Hebrew believers in a very profound way. They were beginning to realize that the tribe of Levi whose priesthood they had previously followed had also tithed into Melchizedek, when Levi was yet in the loins of their forefather Abraham. This is why I flinch when I hear preachers teach on tithing using Malachi 3:8-12 because I know that they are training New Testament believers to access the wrong priesthood concerning their tithes and offerings.

POWER TO ACHIEVE SPIRITUAL PERFECTION

Therefore, if perfection were through the Levitical priesthood (for under it the people received the law), what further need was there that another priest should rise according to the order of Melchizedek, and not be called according to the order of Aaron? Therefore He is also able to save to the uttermost those who come to God through Him, since He always lives to make intercession for them (Hebrews 7:11,25 NKJV)

The search for a perfect society is the motivating factor behind most world religions and political ideologies.

Ever since Adam and Eve opened the portals of time to the entrance of sin, death, and demons, men and women in every era have been in search of a utopian society where they would not have to deal with the idiosyncrasies of this broken down planet.

The search for a perfect society is the motivating factor behind most world religions and political ideologies.

The rise of Marxism—the philosophy of Karl Marx that gave birth to the ideology of communism—is the result of the global pursuit for a perfect or utopian society. Currently the United States is rocking from the shock waves of mass legal and illegal immigration because men and women worldwide want to live in a society where they can prosper and live in peace. They are invading the United States by the millions hoping to get their share of the great American dream.

> *For on the one hand there is an annulling of the former commandment because of its weakness and unprofitableness, for the law made nothing perfect; on the other hand, there is the bringing in of a better hope, through which we draw near to God* (Hebrews 7:18-19 NKJV).

This frantic search for a utopian society is not a foreign experience in the human pursuit for perfection. The formation of human civilizations and the ensuing industrial and technological revolutions are all by-products of this global search for a perfect society. Every little girl dreams of growing into a beautiful woman and marrying the most amazing man on earth and living happily ever after. I can imagine the feeling of emotional devastation and spiritual disillusionment some of these women go through once they are married and discover that their husband is the devil's first cousin.

How many times have politicians promised the masses a land of milk and honey while campaigning for office only to deliver stale bread and bitter drink after they are elected? Why is this so? The answer is simple. Once sin and death entered the world, the machinery of death has been working ceaselessly, and as such, whatever man touches or promises becomes a victim of this machinery of death.

The question that comes to mind is simply: *Is there a sure way of creating a perfect society?* The answer is a resounding *"YES"*! There is a spiritual technology for creating the perfect marriage and the perfect society and it is locked up in the priestly Order of Melchizedek. The apostle Paul concludes by telling the Hebrew believers that the Order of Aaron had no power to bring about the fulfillment of man's greatest search, the search for utopia. The Levitical priesthood had too many inherent flaws that made it impossible for the proper outworking of this spiritual technology. But under the priestly Order of Melchizedek, perfection in its purest form is a surety because this priestly Order already exists in a perfect state in the realms of eternity.

THIS PRIESTLY ORDER HAS ITS OWN LAW

For the priesthood being changed, of necessity there is also a change of the law. For He of whom these things are spoken belongs to another tribe, from which no man has officiated at the altar (Hebrews 7:12-13 NKJV).

God has laws that govern whatever He wants to do in the earth. When God established the Levitical priesthood, He gave Moses specific laws from the Mountain of Law (Mount Sinai), which regulated the priestly Order of Aaron. These specific laws were to govern the inflow and outflow of this priesthood and the way people tithed into it. These laws were then sealed and ratified by the blood of bulls and goats.

The apostle Paul shows us that the priestly Order of Melchizedek also has its own law that governs the outflow and inflow of this eternal priesthood. The law that the apostle Paul is referring to is the Law of the Spirit of Life in Christ Jesus. This is the primary law that governs the priestly Order of Melchizedek.

There is therefore now no condemnation to them which are in Christ Jesus, who walk not after the flesh, but after the Spirit. For the law of the Spirit of life in Christ Jesus hath made me free from the law of sin and death (Romans 8:1-2 KJV).

THE SPIRITUAL CURRENCY OF THIS PRIESTLY ORDER IS FAITH

But without faith it is impossible to please Him, for he who comes to God must believe that He is, and that He is a rewarder of those who diligently seek Him. (Hebrews 11:6 NKJV).

Whether you like the Roman Catholic Church or not, it is one of the most powerful religious institutions on planet Earth. This is because the Catholic church is the only church that I know of that has its own currency. I am a novice currency trader. I am very interested in how the exchange of goods and services creates currency movements across the global market. In the world we live in you cannot buy or sell if you do not have the right currency. The currency of the United States is the dollar; the pound sterling is the currency of Great Britain; the euro dollar is the currency of the European Union; and, South Africa has the rand, just to name a few. These different world currencies imply that if one is to do business, they have to convert their currency to the country that they wish to trade with.

The priestly Order of Melchizedek is the richest spiritual Order that God ever revealed to humankind. It has its own spiritual currency that enables all of those who are part of this priestly Order to buy and sell in God's Kingdom economy. With this currency those who operate in the priestly Order of Melchizedek can "buy" (appropriate) healing, peace, prosperity, and breakthrough, or "sell" (sow) their seed ideas and believe God for a harvest.

The spiritual currency of the priestly Order of Melchizedek is the *Spirit of Faith*. Faith is defined as "persuasion plus corresponding actions." Without the currency of faith, it is impossible to please God or be rewarded by Him for our efforts in His Kingdom economy. On the other hand, the spiritual currency for the Levitical priesthood was the letter of the Law. Faith is the spiritual currency that activates the blessing of Abraham for Kingdom citizens.

> *For if they which are of the law be heirs, faith is made void, and the promise made of none effect* (Romans 4:14 KJV).

FUNCTION TIED TO SPIRITUAL MATURITY

And God designated him to be a High Priest in the order of Melchizedek. There is much more we would like to say about this, but it is difficult to explain, especially since you are spiritually dull and don't seem to listen. You have been believers so long now that you ought to be teaching others. Instead, you need someone to teach you again the basic things about God's word. You are like babies who need milk and cannot eat solid food. For someone who lives on milk is still an infant and doesn't know

how to do what is right. Solid food is for those who are mature,
who through training have the skill to recognize the difference
between right and wrong (Hebrews 5:10-14).

The question that comes to mind, *Why is it that very few believers in the*
global Church have a clear-cut revelation about the Order of Melchizedek? The
answer is found in the fifth chapter of the book of Hebrews. According to the
apostle Paul who was given spiritual custody of this revelation concerning the
Order of Melchizedek, there are four main reasons why many believers in the
global Church do not quite understand the priestly Order of Melchizedek.

1. Spiritual Sensitivity

The apostle Paul lets us know that understanding the Order of Melchizedek
requires an acute sense of spiritual sensitivity. The priestly Order of Melchizedek
is not an earthly priesthood; it is a heavenly one. This royal priesthood cannot
be physically discerned, it must be revealed to the sensitive and seeking heart.
Living under this priestly Order of Melchizedek requires that we command a
place of intimacy with the Lord.

2. An Ear to Hear

In order to live under the priestly Order of Melchizedek, we must have
the ability to hear God's voice and accept a more excellent way of living. *If we*
are dull of hearing we will simply revert to doing business as usual. What God
has shown us about this powerful royal priesthood of Melchizedek will simply
disappear between the ears.

3. Requires a Change in Spiritual Diet

For us to become active participants in this powerful priestly Order, we
must be willing to change our spiritual diet. We must be willing to transition from drinking spiritual milk to eating the solid food of the Word of God,
because we become what we eat. Nothing saddens me more than to observe
the direction some ministers of the gospel are taking in order to attract larger
crowds. They are shifting from teaching the deep things of God to teaching the
milk of God's Word. *More and more pastors are abandoning their true spiritual*

mantles and aborting their prophetic destinies to this generation by becoming more like secular motivational speakers than preachers of righteousness.

What's even more depressing is that the masses of people who are following these self-made spiritual motivational gurus will remain spiritual babies with no power to cross into their spiritual inheritance because their spiritual fathers have refused to circumcise them with the Word so they can begin to chew on the meat of God's holy Word. For most of God's people, the Order of Melchizedek is readily available to them in the Holy Ghost, but only a few really know the transforming power of this royal priesthood of Jesus Christ in their everyday life.

4. Spiritual Training

Finally, the apostle Paul tells us that the other reason many of God's people live their lives without experiencing the power of the priestly Order of Melchizedek is due to the lack of spiritual training. Operating under the priestly Order of Melchizedek requires skill in the way we handle the Word of righteousness. This is why I wrote this book.

THE ETERNAL EMBLEMS OF BREAD AND WINE

And Melchizedek, the king of Salem and a priest of God Most High, brought Abram some bread and wine (Genesis 14:18).

As mentioned in Chapter Five, the priestly Order of Melchizedek has its own special emblems that act as prophetic logo for this divine priestly Order. It doesn't matter what part of the world you come from, you will most probably recognize the famous yellow golden arches of McDonald's fast food restaurants. Likewise, we should recognize the eternal emblems of the priestly Order of Melchizedek—they are bread and wine.

Wherever we see the enactments of these two emblems as part of spiritual communion, they are a prophetic sign that we can all access the priestly Order of Melchizedek. When Melchizedek appeared to Abram, intercepting him in the King's Valley, he brought with him bread and wine that he gave to Abram. Bread represents the doctrine of the Kingdom. Bread also represents the Body of Christ, while wine represents the Spirit of the Kingdom. The wine also represents the blood of Jesus. We have already discussed the spiritual benefits of the bread and wine that come from the Order of Melchizedek.

> *As they were eating, Jesus took some bread and blessed it. Then he broke it in pieces and gave it to the disciples, saying, "Take this and eat it, for this is my body." And he took a cup of wine and gave thanks to God for it. He gave it to them and said, "Each of you drink from it"* (Matthew 26:26-27).

THIS ORDER HAS ITS OWN HEAVENLY TEMPLE

> *Here is the main point: We have a High Priest who sat down in the place of honor beside the throne of the majestic God in heaven. There he ministers in the heavenly Tabernacle, the true place of worship that was built by the Lord and not by human hands* (Hebrews 8:1-2).

When Jesus rose from the dead, He took His own blood to the throne of God, which is located in spiritual Jerusalem, the holy city of God. The reason Jesus did not take His blood of atonement to the Mercy Seat in Solomon's temple in natural Jerusalem is quite obvious. The temple in earthly Jerusalem was designed to service the earthbound priesthood of Aaron. The temple in natural Jerusalem belonged to the Levitical priesthood.

As the High Priest of the priestly Order of Melchizedek, Jesus knew that the priestly Order of Melchizedek has its own spiritual temple located inside the city walls of the heavenly Jerusalem, which is the mother of us all. When Moses was instructed to build the Tabernacle in the wilderness, he was told emphatically to build it according to the pattern of the spiritual temple in heaven.

> *If he were here on earth, he would not even be a priest, since there already are priests who offer the gifts required by the law. They serve in a system of worship that is only a copy, a shadow of the real one in heaven. For when Moses was getting ready to build the Tabernacle, God gave him this warning: "Be sure that you make everything according to the pattern I have shown you here on the mountain"* (Hebrews 8:4-5).

SERVICES THE SPIRITUAL NEEDS OF ABRAHAM'S STAR-SEED

*But now Jesus, our High Priest, has been given a ministry that is
far superior to the old priesthood, for he is the one who mediates
for us a far better covenant with God, based on better promises*
(Hebrews 8:6).

The sand-seed of Abraham (the Jewish nation) were given the Levitical
priestly Order to service their spiritual needs in accordance with the Mosaic
Law. The first high priest of this priestly Order was Aaron, who was also Moses'
elder brother and chief spokesman. This Levitical priesthood had its own set of
laws and its own system of tithing. Malachi 3:8-12, for instance, was addressed
to the Jewish nation who lived under this priesthood.

On the other hand, Jesus Christ is the presiding High Priest of the eternal
royal priesthood of Melchizedek. This priesthood operates within the eternal
structures of the Kingdom of heaven. This Order of Melchizedek priesthood
is the one which services the spiritual needs of Abraham's star-seed. Every
New Testament believer lives and serves under this powerful priestly Order,
whether they know it or not.

SERVICED BY A STRONG ANGELIC AGENCY

*And when he brought his firstborn Son into the world, God said,
"Let all of God's angels worship him." Regarding the angels, he
says, "He sends his angels like the winds, his servants like flames
of fire"* (Hebrews 1:6-7).

One of the most stunning aspects of the priestly Order of Melchizedek is
that under this priesthood, angels are commanded to serve and worship the
High Priest. This is in striking contrast to the Levitical priestly Order. Under the
Levitical priesthood, the high priest had no jurisdiction over the angelic order.
Under the Levitical priesthood, angels worked in concert with the high priest as
he fulfilled the call of God upon his life. But the High Priest had no authority to
command the angels to do his bidding. Under the priestly Order of Melchizedek,
the entire angelic order belongs to our faithful High Priest. The angelic agency
bends to His every call and desire. What a powerful priestly Order! These holy

angels will stop at nothing to serve and protect the honor of the High Priest of the Order of Melchizedek. These angels have been known to kill kings of nations who failed to honor this High Priest who is also God Most High.

> *Now Herod was very angry with the people of Tyre and Sidon. So they sent a delegation to make peace with him because their cities were dependent upon Herod's country for food. The delegates won the support of Blastus, Herod's personal assistant, and an appointment with Herod was granted. When the day arrived, Herod put on his royal robes, sat on his throne, and made a speech to them. The people gave him a great ovation, shouting, "It's the voice of a god, not of a man!" Instantly, an angel of the Lord struck Herod with a sickness, because he accepted the people's worship instead of giving the glory to God. So he was consumed with worms and died* (Acts 12:20-23).

Acts 12:20-23 describes what happens to kings of nations who blatantly show disregard for the honor that is due the High Priest of this royal priestly Order. King Herod had chosen to resist and persecute the Church of the living God. He killed James the apostle, the brother of John, and then imprisoned the apostle Peter.

The spirit of the anti-Christ was manifesting itself through King Herod. On the day that he was officiating a peace treaty with the people of Tyre and Sidon, he acted like he was a god. With great pomp, King Herod bestowed upon himself the title and honor that is due only to God. Bewitched by his amazing charisma, the masses began to compare him to a god. In anger the angel of the Lord struck him with a sudden sickness. The angelic blow on King Herod was so powerful that he died instantly and began to decompose immediately. Worms began to ooze out of him in front of the now terrified crowd. The awesome power of the New Creation Order of Melchizedek priesthood of Christ was displayed before the masses.

The High Priest of the Order of Melchizedek has complete and absolute jurisdiction over the entire angelic order. We have seen from what's been revealed through the progressive revelation of Scripture that angels are holy and extremely powerful beings. Miraculous things happen whenever angels show up on the scene. Under the Order of Melchizedek there is no limit as to the number of angelic interventions that we can anticipate.

> *But while Peter was in prison, the church prayed very earnestly for him. The night before Peter was to be placed on trial, he was asleep, fastened with two chains between two soldiers. Others stood guard at the prison gate. Suddenly, there was a bright light in the cell, and an angel of the Lord stood before Peter. The angel struck him on the side to awaken him and said, "Quick! Get up!" And the chains fell off his wrists. Then the angel told him, "Get dressed and put on your sandals." And he did. "Now put on your coat and follow me," the angel ordered. So Peter left the cell, following the angel. But all the time he thought it was a vision. He didn't realize it was actually happening. They passed the first and second guard posts and came to the iron gate leading to the city, and this opened for them all by itself. So they passed through and started walking down the street, and then the angel suddenly left him. Peter finally came to his senses. "It's really true!" he said. "The Lord has sent his angel and saved me from Herod and from what the Jewish leaders had planned to do to me!" (Acts 12:5-11)*

When King Herod Agrippa killed the apostle James, John's brother, and saw that it increased his political clout with some influential leaders within the Jewish community, he proceeded to imprison Peter. Peter was an apostle who lived under the Order of Melchizedek. While Peter was bound up in the inner prison, a supernatural light shined in his cell. The supernatural light that pierced the darkness of night in his tiny cell was that of an angel who had been sent to deliver him.

The chains of imprisonment that were around Peter's hands and legs suddenly fell off, like one snaps a reed. The angel ordered Peter to follow him. As Peter followed the angel, all the prison gates opened of their own accord, and Peter found himself standing outside the prison in total freedom. Peter received a great deliverance from the priestly Order of Melchizedek, which services the spiritual needs of the star-seed of Abraham (born-again believers).

THE FUTURE OF ISRAEL AND THE ORDER OF MELCHIZEDEK

Then the angel of the LORD called again to Abraham from heaven. "This is what the LORD says: Because you have obeyed me and have not withheld even your son, your only son, I swear by my own name that I will certainly bless you. I will multiply your descendants beyond number, like the stars in the sky and the sand on the seashore..." (Genesis 22:15-17).

On Mount Moriah after his act of total obedience, Abraham was given two types of descendents—sand-seed and star-seed. The "sand-seed" descendents of Abraham are the people of the nation of Israel according to the flesh. The earthly genealogy of the Jewish nation can easily be traced back to Abraham.

The "star-seed" descendents of Abraham consist of men and women who have accepted Jesus Christ of Nazareth as their personal Lord and Savior. Abraham's star-seed descendants include both Jews and Gentiles who have responded positively to the preaching of the gospel. These star-seed descendants of Abraham are people from every nation who were not born again by the will of the flesh but by the will of God.

But to all who believed him and accepted him, he gave the right to become children of God. They are reborn—not with a physical birth resulting from human passion or plan, but a birth that comes from God (John 1:12-13).

The most important principle that is central to the dealings of God with humankind is that God always works on the basis of the *principle of continuance*. This means that God never makes covenant with sons, but with fathers. After God has established a covenant with the forefathers, He supernaturally transfers the blessings of the covenant He made with them unto the second generation. Based upon this same principle of continuance, or apostolic succession, the forefathers and the second generation always share the same calling and destiny.

The priests who collect tithes are men who die, so Melchizedek is greater than they are, because we are told that he lives on. In addition, we might even say that these Levites—the ones who collect the tithe—paid a tithe to Melchizedek when their ancestor Abraham paid a tithe to him. For although Levi wasn't born yet, the seed from which he came was in Abraham's body when Melchizedek collected the tithe from him (Hebrews 7:8-10).

In the Hebrews 7:8-10 passage, the apostle Paul is using this same *principle of continuance* to tell his fellow Jews that they would not be abandoning their ancient Jewish faith if they brought themselves under the New Testament priesthood of Melchizedek. To seal this important point, the apostle Paul told the Jewish believers that when Abraham their forefather met Melchizedek, the tribe of Levi (the tribe of the priesthood) was yet in the spiritual loins of Abraham. The apostle Paul said that Levi, who was given a commandment from God to collect a tithe according to the Law, also gave a tithe to Melchizedek because Levi was still in the loins of his father Abraham at the time of this God encounter.

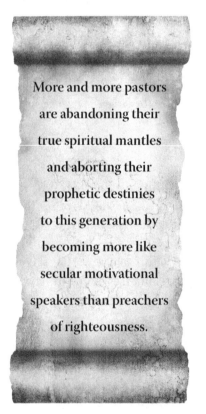

More and more pastors are abandoning their true spiritual mantles and aborting their prophetic destinies to this generation by becoming more like secular motivational speakers than preachers of righteousness.

This *principle of continuance* has far-reaching spiritual implications in explaining how the future of the Jewish nation is intricately tied to this priestly Order of Melchizedek. If Paul's arguments have any merit, it would follow then that the spiritual call and destiny of the Jewish nation will eventually lead them to a very personal encounter with Jesus Christ who is the Priest of God Most High after the Order of Melchizedek. This assumption is based upon the fact that when Abraham met Melchizedek and submitted his life to Him, all of his natural descendants (natural Israel) were still in his spiritual loins. *This means that Jewish DNA is prophetically predisposed to enter into the Order of Melchizedek.*

When this supernatural prophetic event happens, many Jewish people will instantly recognize and acknowledge Jesus Christ as the true Messiah. They will finally see Him as the Melchizedek of God who met their forefather Abraham in the Valley of Shaveh. When this powerful prophetic day in God arrives and the scales of spiritual blindness fall from the eyes of every living Jew, the apostle Paul says that *all Israel shall be saved!* The prophet Zechariah seems to be very much in agreement with Paul's conclusion.

> *Then I will pour out a spirit of grace and prayer on the family of David and on the people of Jerusalem. They will look on me whom they have pierced and mourn for him as for an only son. They will grieve bitterly for him as for a firstborn son who has died* (Zechariah 12:10).

When the Jewish nation has another defining God encounter with Melchizedek, Priest of God Most High, we are going to see the greatest world-wide revival ever. The most important facet of this great spiritual awakening is that the sand-seed of Abraham (the Jewish nation) will suddenly become the star-seed of Abraham.

The birth and resurrection of our Lord Jesus Christ set the spiritual path-way every Jewish person has to travel. Jesus Christ was born a sand-seed descendant of Abraham, but He was resurrected as Abraham's star-seed. Jesus was a Jew by natural birth, but he was declared the Son of God by the Spirit of resurrection.

The following Scripture from the book of Revelation strongly suggests that there is coming a day when the Jewish nation (who are the sand-seed descendants of Abraham) is going to be transformed by revelation into star-seed descendents of Abraham. When this supernatural event occurs, the influence of Israel over the nations of the world will no longer be just earthly but also heavenly. *The nation of Israel will become the woman clothed with the sun, whose head is surrounded by twelve stars.* Most scholars agree that the twelve stars of the woman in Revelation chapter 12 are the twelve tribes of Israel.

> *Then I witnessed in heaven an event of great significance. I saw a woman clothed with the sun, with the moon beneath her feet, and a crown of twelve stars on her head. She was pregnant, and she cried out because of her labor pains and the agony of giving birth* (Revelation 12:1-2).

LIFE APPLICATION SECTION

MEMORY VERSES

This Melchizedek was king of the city of Salem and also a priest of God Most High. When Abraham was returning home after winning a great battle against the kings, Melchizedek met him and blessed him. Then Abraham took a tenth of all he had captured in battle and gave it to Melchizedek. The name Melchizedek means "king of justice," and king of Salem means "king of peace" (Hebrews 7:1-2).

REFLECTIONS

What does the name Melchizedek mean?

What does the title King of Salem mean?

Write five characteristics of the Order of Melchizedek.

The Order of Melchizedek is both a priestly and marketplace ministry. What does this statement mean?

JOURNAL YOUR PERSONAL NOTES ON THIS CHAPTER

CHAPTER EIGHT

𝔄braham's Star-Seed

The LORD had said to Abram, "Leave your native country, your relatives, and your father's family, and go to the land that I will show you. I will make you into a great nation. I will bless you and make you famous, and you will be a blessing to others. I will bless those who bless you and curse those who treat you with contempt. All the families on earth will be blessed through you" (Genesis 12:1-3).

THE CALL OF ABRAM THE CHALDEAN (Babylonian) is one of the most important prophetic calls that God ever bestowed upon a man other than the Lord Jesus Christ. Adam was the beginning of the human race, but he also presided over the tragic fall of the entire human race. After many years of waiting and working behind the scenes, God found a man who was willing to allow God to form and fashion his life. Abram was that man.

As you know from previous chapters, Abram's name was later changed to "Abraham" when God transformed him into the father of many nations. *By divine election, Abraham became the father of a new race of people who live by faith and not by sight.* Abraham's personal journey of faith with God established the spiritual foundation for the coming of Jesus Christ, the last Adam. Abraham's obedience to God opened spiritual portals for God to invade the earth!

THE COVENANT OF ABRAHAM

"I will make a covenant with you, by which I will guarantee to give you countless descendants." At this, Abram fell face down on the ground. Then God said to him, "This is my covenant with you: I will make you the father of a multitude of nations! What's more, I am changing your name. It will no longer be Abram. Instead, you will be called Abraham, for you will be the father of many nations. I will make you extremely fruitful. Your descendants will become many nations, and kings will be among them! I will confirm my covenant with you and your descendants after you, from generation to generation. This is the everlasting covenant: I will always be your God and the God of your descendants after you" (Genesis 17:2-7).

After Abram had consistently maintained a testimony of faith and obedience, God made a covenant with him and changed his name to Abraham, which translates "Abram of God Most High" and carries the meaning "the father of many nations." Abraham was to be the father of the nation of Israel and also the father of the royal Kingdom nation whose maker and builder is God. This royal Kingdom nation consists of all followers of Christ who have accepted Him as Lord. God promised Abraham that even though he was well advanced in years, he would have a son with his wife, Sarah.

THE BIRTH OF ISAAC

The LORD kept his word and did for Sarah exactly what he had promised. She became pregnant, and she gave birth to a son for Abraham in his old age. This happened at just the time God had said it would. And Abraham named their son Isaac. Eight days after Isaac was born, Abraham circumcised him as God had commanded (Genesis 21:1-4).

The miraculous birth of Isaac marked the beginning of a new era in the dealings of God with Abraham. The birth of Isaac also initiated the release of a spirit of acceleration in God's plan to take back His inheritance in the nations of the world. Isaac was a very unique child because he was both a prophetic sign and a type of Christ. The birth of Isaac secured Abraham's inheritance in the nation of Israel. God also used the birth of Isaac to create a divine portal for the infusion of the Messianic Seed onto the human plane. The entrance of the Messianic Seed was the divine means through which Abraham would become the father of many nations. The Messianic Seed would turn men and women from the pathway of death onto the pathway of life.

THE OFFERING OF ISAAC

Some time later, God tested Abraham's faith. "Abraham!" God called. "Yes," he replied. "Here I am."

"Take your son, your only son—yes, Isaac, whom you love so much—and go to the land of Moriah. Go and sacrifice him as a burnt offering on one of the mountains, which I will show you." The next morning Abraham got up early. He saddled his donkey and took two of his servants with him, along with his son, Isaac. Then he chopped wood for a fire for a burnt offering and set out for the place God had told him about. So Abraham placed the wood for the burnt offering on Isaac's shoulders, while he himself carried the fire and the knife. As the two of them walked on together, Isaac turned to Abraham and said, "Father?"

"Yes, my son?" Abraham replied. "We have the fire and the wood," the boy said, "but where is the sheep for the burnt offering?"

"God will provide a sheep for the burnt offering, my son," Abraham answered. And they both walked on together (Genesis 22:1-3,6-8).

The offering of Isaac as a sacrificial lamb on Mount Moriah by his father Abraham, in total obedience to God, was one of the most significant prophetic events in Abraham's life. The offering of Isaac marked the fulfillment of Abraham's covenant of total obedience to God and established him as the father of many nations within the eternal structures of the Kingdom of heaven!

The most significant thing about the offering of Isaac to God lies in this powerful consideration: When Abraham offered Isaac as a sacrificial offering

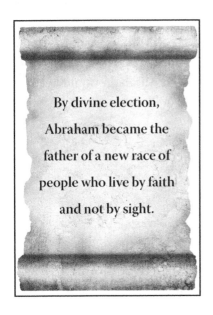

By divine election, Abraham became the father of a new race of people who live by faith and not by sight.

of obedience to God, the only priesthood that was revealed to Abraham at the time was the priestly Order of Melchizedek. We know for a fact that the Lord Jesus Christ is the High Priest after the Order of Melchizedek. It follows then, that when Abraham offered Isaac to God he offered his only son to God under the power of this eternal royal priesthood. This important consideration may explain why God was so moved by Abraham's faith and total obedience.

God was so moved by Abraham's faith and obedience that He thundered out of the heavens and swore that His covenant of blessing would never be removed from Abraham's life. Abraham's obedience in the offering of Isaac not only opened the door for the entrance of the Messianic Seed into the world, but it also established the priestly Order of Melchizedek as an everlasting priesthood for the "Seed of Abraham." When Abraham prophesied to Isaac and told him that *"God will provide himself a lamb"* (Genesis 22:8 KJV), Abraham's faith pulled Christ, the Messianic Seed, into the canals of time. Abraham's faith and obedience set Christ on course toward the redemption of the world.

WE ARE THE SEED OF ABRAHAM

In the same way, "Abraham believed God, and God counted him as righteous because of his faith." The real children of Abraham, then, are those who put their faith in God (Galatians 3:6-7).

Now to Abraham and his Seed were the promises made. He does not say, "And to seeds," as of many, but as of one, "And to your Seed," who is Christ (Galatians 3:16 NKJV).

The Bible says that we are the seed of Abraham. What does this mean? In order to answer this question we must first understand that Abraham was promised two types of seed. We must also understand why Christ is the ultimate Seed of Abraham. We also need to understand how the two types of seed Abraham was given on Mount Moriah unite in Christ—the true Seed of Abraham.

ABRAHAM'S TWO TYPES OF SEED

After Lot had gone, the LORD said to Abram, "Look as far as you can see in every direction—north and south, east and west. I am giving all this land, as far as you can see, to you and your descendants as a permanent possession. And I will give you so many descendants that, like the dust of the earth, they cannot be counted! (Genesis 13:14-16)

But you promised me, "I will surely treat you kindly, and I will multiply your descendants until they become as numerous as the sands along the seashore—too many to count" (Genesis 32:12).

1. The Sand-Seed of Abraham

The first strand of seed that God gave to Abraham in response to his faith and obedience was "sand-seed," a prophetic representation of Abraham's natural descendants. Sand is a natural product of the earth. These natural descendants of Abraham are the citizens of the nation of Israel. Since the nation of Israel has twelve tribes, these twelve tribes make up the sand-seed that Abraham was promised would occupy the land of present-day Palestine.

I will certainly bless you. I will multiply your descendants beyond number, like the stars in the sky and the sand on the seashore. Your descendants will conquer the cities of their enemies (Genesis 22:17).

"You have given me no descendants of my own, so one of my servants will be my heir." Then the LORD said to him, "No, your servant will not be your heir, for you will have a son of your

own who will be your heir." Then the LORD took Abram out-
side and said to him, "Look up into the sky and count the stars
if you can. That's how many descendants you will have!" And
Abram believed the LORD and the Lord counted him as righ-
teous because of his faith (Genesis 15:3-6).

2. The Star-Seed of Abraham

The second strand of seed that Abraham was given and promised by God
on Mount Moriah was "star-seed," a prophetic representation of Abraham's
spiritual descendants who are members of the Church of the firstborn (the
Body of Christ). This prophetic representation is based on the fact that stars
are found in the heavens and not on earth. Saint Paul, writer of the book of
Ephesians, tells us that the Body of Christ is seated in heavenly places in Christ
Jesus. (See Ephesians 2:6.)

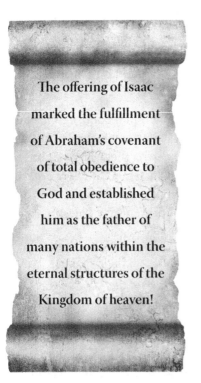

The offering of Isaac
marked the fulfillment
of Abraham's covenant
of total obedience to
God and established
him as the father of
many nations within the
eternal structures of the
Kingdom of heaven!

This group of star-seed descendants
consists of everyone who is a follower of
Christ regardless of race, ethnicity, nation-
ality, color of their skin, etc. Star-seed
descendants have accepted Jesus Christ
as their personal Lord and Savior and are
the true spiritual descendants of Abraham
who walked by faith and not by sight. They
are the ones the apostle Paul called the true
"Israel of God!" Star-seed descendants are
destined to inherit the Kingdom Of God.

Neither circumcision nor uncir-
cumcision means anything; what
counts is a new creation. Peace and
mercy to all who follow this rule,
even to the Israel of God (Galatians
6:15-16 NIV).

Since we now know that Jesus Christ
is the High Priest of the New Testament

Order of Melchizedek priesthood, I can confidently say that the priesthood that services the star-seed descendants of Abraham is the Order of Melchizedek. This means that every member of the Body of Christ whether they know it or not are members of the Order of Melchizedek. We who are saved and sanctified make up the royal priesthood of Melchizedek that the apostle Peter writes about.

> But you are a chosen generation, a royal priesthood, a holy nation, His own special people, that you may proclaim the praises of Him who called you out of darkness into His marvelous light (1 Peter 2:9 NKJV).

The sand-seed of Abraham was given Abraham's natural inheritance, which is Abraham's portion in the nations of the earth. God gave Abraham an inheritance in the nations because of his total obedience to God. God gave Abraham's descendants according to the flesh (the Jewish nation) the land of present-day Palestine for an everlasting inheritance. *Anyone who tries to give away the land of natural Israel is committing spiritual fraud and trespassing on God's territory!*

However, the power and influence of the nation of Israel was destined by God to extend well beyond the physical borders of Palestine. God told Abraham that his natural descendants (the Jewish nation) would be like sand by the seashore. Interestingly enough, sand is found on the shorelines of the seven continents of the world. The sand around the shorelines of the seven continents is a stunning prophetic proclamation to every demonic principality, that Abraham has an inheritance in all the nations of the world!

This is why no matter where you go in the world, it is impossible to escape the influence of Jewish technology and financial genius. In India, for instance, some of the high tech companies are front-corporations run and financed by Jewish businessmen. Even in the heat of Nazi tyranny, some Jewish people emerged from the holocaust with money that they had hidden in very ingenious ways. Even maniac Hitler's plan failed to snuff them off the face of the earth because Abraham's spiritual inheritance within the nations of the world was sealed by God as an everlasting covenant.

Interestingly enough, sand also acts as a "buffer" or beachhead between the waters of the seas and the landmasses of the seven continents. Without the sand, the continents would be flooded. I personally believe that the quickest way for nations to stop political, economic, spiritual, and natural tsunamis from destroying the structure of their nations is to adopt a favorable foreign policy toward the nation of Israel. God judges the nations of the earth based on how they treat the nation of Israel. Among all the nations of the world, Israel is the apple of God's eye. God destroyed the nation of Egypt based on how Pharaoh and his people treated the natural descendants of Abraham.

> *The LORD is a warrior; Yahweh is his name! Pharaoh's chariots and army he has hurled into the sea. The finest of Pharaoh's officers are drowned in the Red Sea. The deep waters gushed over them; they sank to the bottom like a stone* (Exodus 15:3-5).

The devastating tsunami in 2004 which killed over 200,000 people in Indonesia and other Arab regions that are mostly anti-Israel is quite telling. This particular tsunami was the most destructive in modern times, but the Bible records in Exodus another catastrophic tsunami, which destroyed Pharaoh and his entire army for terrorizing the sand-seed of Abraham. Nations that have a foreign policy favorable toward Israel are wise and well-advised. These nations will always attract the blessing of God. This is why the blessing of God continues to rest on the United States, despite her continuous moral decline.

The star-seed of Abraham who are the Church of the firstborn (Body of Christ) were given Abraham's spiritual inheritance. Abraham's spiritual inheritance is his God-given portion in the eternal structures of the Kingdom of heaven. This is why the Bible tells us that after Christ's ascension to the throne of His heavenly Father, He made us (the Body of Christ) to sit with Him in heavenly places.

> *For he raised us from the dead along with Christ and seated us with him in the heavenly realms because we are united with Christ Jesus* (Ephesians 2:6).

Abraham cried to God and told the Lord that He had given him no seed or offspring. Abraham told God that his servant Eliezer of Damascus was going to inherit all that God had given him because Abraham had no children of his own. God responded quickly. He took Abraham out of his tent and told him to look toward the heavens. When Abraham looked at the night sky, he saw more stars than he could count.

God told Abraham to look up because stars are found in the heavens. The more Abraham looked at the stars under the anointing of the Spirit, the more the stars began to look like spirit-children from every nation on earth. When Abraham saw in his spirit the billions of spiritual sons and daughters God was going to give him, Abraham believed God. This belief in God's ability to give him his star-seed descendants was counted for him as righteousness, and at that very moment Abraham became "the father of many nations!"

Stars are set as steady points of navigation in the heavens. When the pilgrims left the shores of Europe to come to what we now call the United States of America, their shipmasters depended on reading the positions of certain stars in order to chart their course toward the newfound land. Those who boarded ships led by captains who did not know how to navigate the sea by studying the patterns and positions of the stars got lost and died at sea.

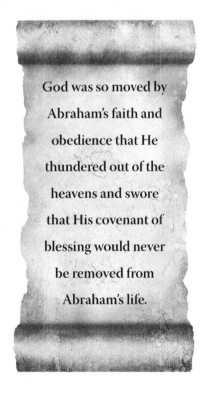

God was so moved by Abraham's faith and obedience that He thundered out of the heavens and swore that His covenant of blessing would never be removed from Abraham's life.

Jesus was born in Bethlehem in Judea, during the reign of King Herod. About that time some wise men from eastern lands arrived in Jerusalem, asking, "Where is the newborn king of the Jews? We saw his star as it rose, and we have come to worship him" (Matthew 2:1-2).

THE BIRTH OF A KING-STAR

When Christ was born in a manger in the city of Bethlehem, the magi from the

East saw His star in the sky and followed it for eight months, until it led them to Jesus. They brought Him Kingly gifts to worship Him. A bright eastern Star led the wise men to their Lord and Savior. Since we are Abraham's star-seed descendants, part of our spiritual inheritance lies in our ability to lead lost souls to the saving knowledge of our Lord and Savior by letting our light shine in their night season.

> *For I am not ashamed of this Good News about Christ. It is the power of God at work, saving everyone who believes—the Jew first and also the Gentile (Romans 1:16).*

The apostle Paul knew the eternal privilege of being one of Abraham's star-seed descendants through the finished work of Christ. Saint Paul knew that as a star-seed he was not ashamed to let the glorious light of the gospel shine through his life to reach the lost. Paul calls this shining of the gospel of the Kingdom into the spiritual darkness of lost souls, the power of God unto salvation. Paul was a Kingdom star who had no qualms about letting the light of Christ shine through him. The preaching of the gospel of Jesus Christ is the primary assignment of those who are of the Order of Melchizedek.

PROPHETIC SIGNS

> *Then God said, "Let lights appear in the sky to separate the day from the night. Let them mark off the seasons, days, and years. Let these lights in the sky shine down on the earth." And that is what happened. God made two great lights—the larger one to govern the day, and the smaller one to govern the night. He also made the **stars**. God set these lights in the sky to light the earth, to govern the day and night, and to separate the light from the darkness. And God saw that it was good (Genesis 1:14-18).*

God created stars to serve as signs in the heavens. Since we are Abraham's star-seed we must allow the precious Holy Spirit to use us as prophetic signs in other peoples' lives. People ought to know that when the spiritual descendants of Abraham (star-seeds) show up, something good is going to happen in their lives. We know that the power of a sign is not in itself but in the power of the entity it represents in the spirit world or natural world.

When Jesus stood under the sycamore tree that Zacchaeus was resting in, He instantly became a prophetic sign signaling that Zacchaeus's life would be changing for the better. By the time Jesus and His disciples left Zacchaeus's home, the man had been changed and the general public knew it. This is the type of priestly ministry that God has given to every New Testament believer under Christ's Order of Melchizedek priesthood. When Jesus hung on the cross before the whole world, He was a prophetic sign that the devil was defeated and that the sins of the world had been paid for.

TIMES AND SEASONS

God gave the stars the power to determine times and seasons. The stars of the heavens control the sequential flow of human calendar and of all natural seasons. Since we are the star-seed of Abraham, our entrance into people's lives must set an expiatory date on the works of the enemy. Our entrance into people's lives should open them up to a new season of breakthrough.

> *Nevertheless, that time of darkness and despair will not go on forever. The land of Zebulun and Naphtali will be humbled, but there will be a time in the future when Galilee of the Gentiles, which lies along the road that runs between the Jordan and the sea, will be filled with glory. The people who walk in darkness will see a great light. For those who live in a land of deep darkness, a light will shine* (Isaiah 9:1-2).

Because we are Abraham's star-seed, God has also appointed and anointed us to set nations on the calendar of God! God is not glorified when the spirituality and morality of nations continue to steadily decline while His church is trapped within the four walls of our glass paneled sanctuaries. God has already dared us to ask Him for the nations. (See Psalm 2) and promised to give us the heathens for our inheritance. Contrary to what many members of the Body of Christ believe, the times and seasons of a nation are not in the hands of politicians, they are in the hands of the global Church (God's ecclesia).

More than two decades ago, Nigeria was about 70 percent Muslim and about 30 percent Christian. Today this densely populated nation is about 65 percent Christian and about 35 percent Muslim. It is becoming increasingly difficult to become a president in Nigeria if you do not profess the Christian faith. The spiritual aggressiveness of the Church in Nigeria has placed that great country on the calendar of God. We must not forget that the Order of Melchizedek is a very governmental and militant priesthood because it is led by a conquering King—Jesus Christ.

DIVIDING THE DAY FROM THE NIGHT

Then God said, "Let lights appear in the sky to separate the day from the night. Let them mark off the seasons, days, and years" (Genesis 1:14).

God also gave stars the power to divide the day from the night. This passage of Scripture in Genesis is rich and implies that the day is always hidden in the night. So when our friends or nations are going through their night seasons and the devil is creating havoc in their lives, God will send us to them to separate the day of God that is trapped within their darkness. The light of Christ inside us will cause God to break out into their night season and show them a pathway of escape and recovery!

Anyone who tries to give away the land of natural Israel is committing spiritual fraud and trespassing on God's territory!

Let not your heart be troubled; you believe in God, believe also in Me. In My Father's house are many mansions; if it were not so, I would have told you. I go to prepare a place for you (John 14:1-2 NKJV).

Finally, since we are Abraham's star-seed, we must realize that we have been called to inherit Abraham's spiritual inheritance within the eternal structures of the

Kingdom of God. Since we are the heirs of Abraham's spiritual inheritance, our portion of the blessing of Abraham is far greater than the portion of the blessing of Abraham that was given to natural Israel. Abraham's spiritual inheritance consists of every spiritual blessing that is stored up in the *many mansions in My Father's house,* which Jesus spoke of in John 14:1-3.

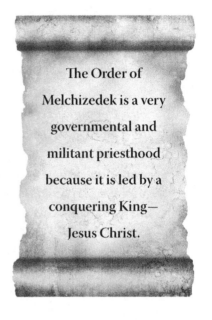

The Order of Melchizedek is a very governmental and militant priesthood because it is led by a conquering King—Jesus Christ.

Please remember that the highest and purest form of gold and silver is found in heaven. Gold is so abundant in the heavenly Kingdom that the streets of heaven are paved with gold! All of this heavenly gold is part of Abraham's spiritual inheritance, which God gave to his star-seed descendants. Knowing who we are as royal priests unto God after the Order of Melchizedek is vital. If Christ's ministry is patterned after the Order of Melchizedek, so should ours be.

LIFE APPLICATION SECTION

MEMORY VERSES

Then God said, "Let lights appear in the sky to separate the day from the night. Let them mark off the seasons, days, and years. Let these lights in the sky shine down on the earth." And that is what happened. God made two great lights—the larger one to govern the day, and the smaller one to govern the night. He also made the stars. God set these lights in the sky to light the earth, to govern the day and night, and to separate the light from the darkness. And God saw that it was good (Genesis 1:14-18).

REFLECTIONS

Who is Abraham's sand-seed and where is their current homeland?

_____

_____

_____

_____

Who is Abraham's star-seed?

_____

_____

_____

_____

_____

How does knowing that you are Abraham's star-seed affect your disposition in the Marketplace?

_____

_____

_____

_____

_____

_____

JOURNAL YOUR PERSONAL NOTES ON THIS CHAPTER

CHAPTER NINE

Jesus Christ: Our Royal High Priest

*T*HE GREATEST MINISTRY OF JESUS CHRIST *is not what He did during His short ministry excursion here on earth.* This statement might surprise and upset many people in the Church. I do not intend to diminish the ministry, suffering, crucifixion, and resurrection of Jesus Christ; but if the Church gets stuck basking in the work Jesus Christ did on earth without appreciating what Jesus Christ has become in His ascension, then the Church will forfeit Christ's ultimate divine mission.

> *[Christ Is Our **High Priest**] So then, since we have a great **High Priest** who has entered heaven, Jesus the Son of God, let us hold firmly to what we believe* (Hebrews 4:14).

The apostle Paul tells us that Christ's ultimate divine mission was to become the eternal High Priest of the New Creation order of priesthood. Everything Jesus Christ did (His suffering, crucifixion, and resurrection) while He was on earth was to restore the Kingdom of God and induct the "New Creation" into His eternal order of priesthood. *Being saved (born again) is not an end in itself, it is merely a step in the right direction.* Unfortunately many born-again believers act like being saved and attending church regularly is the sum total of Christ's mission. This mentality explains why many believers have not entered into the greater works of a people who belong to the Order of Melchizedek priesthood.

To help you appreciate why Christ's ongoing ministry as the High Priest of the New Creation Order of Melchizedek priesthood is so important, we will look at the history of earthly priesthoods.

THE HISTORY OF EARTHLY PRIESTHOODS

Earthly priesthoods go all the way back to the time that Adam and his sons were to bring offerings and sacrifices to the Lord God after their fall. One would think that the premise for priestly ministry today springs solely from that, but its origins really go back to eternity. That is why Jehovah already had His earthly priestly institution in place to bring Abraham into covenant with Himself, namely Melchizedek's Priesthood.

Based on the preceding, the title priest-king perfectly fit Melchizedek and his God-assigned purpose for being on the planet because all life back then revolved around deities. It was virtually impossible for a human to see himself or herself as godless; the concept of atheism was practically unthinkable and those that claimed it kept it to themselves. Ancient villagers and leaders considered being without a god a curse. This is what Jesus had in mind when He stated John 14:18. The word the King James Version renders "Comfortless" actually means parentless or fatherless. To be without a god was to signify that no deity wanted responsibility for a person's existence or security in life because he or she had so offended the deity (or the divine realm) to the point of being evicted from a divine family, as was the case with Cain.[1]

The concept of priesthoods was very common among the people of the ancient world. Godlessness was severely frowned upon because both kings and citizens alike believed that their national posterity relied heavily on their ability to communicate with their nation's deity through the deity's designated priesthood. In the kingdoms of the ancient world that Abraham was familiar with, everything revolved around pleasing the kingdom's deity.

The people of the ancient world believed that if they pleased their kingdom's deity they would guarantee prosperity in the kingdom economy and accelerate the expansion of their kingdom. They believed that if their deity was pleased with them, their deity would defend against invading armies and protect them from natural disasters. When Joseph was in Egypt, he married Asenath, the daughter of Potipherah priest of On. Obviously there was an earthly priesthood in Egypt.

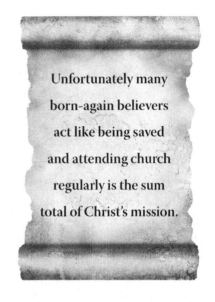

Unfortunately many born-again believers act like being saved and attending church regularly is the sum total of Christ's mission.

I particularly want to draw your attention to the fact that in the kingdoms of the ancient world, there was no separation of Church (priesthood) and State. The politics of the kingdom revolved around pleasing the desire of the nation's deity. The marketplace activities of the kingdom also revolved around pleasing the kingdom's deity. This means that all business practices and the nation's legal system were stamped with the philosophy of the kingdom's deity. All military campaigns and strategies had to seek the favor of the nation's deity.

> *Joshua and the elders of Israel tore their clothing in dismay, threw dust on their heads, and bowed face down to the ground before the Ark of the LORD until evening. Then Joshua cried out, "Oh, Sovereign LORD, why did you bring us across the Jordan River if you are going to let the Amorites kill us? If only we had been content to stay on the other side! Lord, what can I say now that Israel has fled from its enemies? For when the Canaanites and all the other people living in the land hear about it, they will surround us and wipe our name off the face of the earth. And then what will happen to the honor of your great name?"*

> *But the LORD said to Joshua, "Get up! Why are you lying on your face like this? Israel has sinned and broken my covenant! They have stolen some of the things that I commanded must be*

set apart for me. And they have not only stolen them but have lied about it and hidden the things among their own belongings. That is why the Israelites are running from their enemies in defeat. For now Israel itself has been set apart for destruction. I will not remain with you any longer unless you destroy the things among you that were set apart for destruction (Joshua 7:6-12).

Battles lost were signs that the kingdom citizens had fallen short of the kingdom deity's approval. To prevent future failures on the battlefield, both the king and his kingdom citizens went to their deity's designated earthly priesthood to discover the reasons for the deity's displeasure. Once the reason for the failure in battle was diagnosed, the king and his people would quickly make the appropriate atonement as prescribed by the deity to his earthly priesthood.

By now you are beginning to understand why I believe that Jesus Christ's greatest ministry is not the ministry He had while He was on earth—His greatest ministry is His present-day everlasting High Priesthood over the "New Creation." In His present-day ministry as the High Priest after the Order of Melchizedek, Christ's priesthood provides the "New Creation" (born-again Kingdom citizens) with a legitimate God-assigned priesthood. All the praying in the Church, all the preaching and all offerings of praise and worship would be both meaningless and powerless if the New Creation did not have access to a legitimate God-ordained priesthood. Christ's Order of Melchizedek priesthood is the only legitimate priesthood that God has sanctioned to service the spiritual needs of all Kingdom citizens.

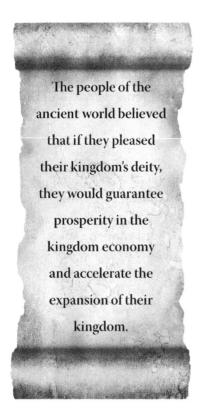

The people of the ancient world believed that if they pleased their kingdom's deity, they would guarantee prosperity in the kingdom economy and accelerate the expansion of their kingdom.

Now you understand why I made such a profound announcement concerning Christ's greatest ministry. Next we'll focus on what the Bible says about Christ's priesthood, examining its nature, powers, scope, and how it affects us today.

> *But you are a chosen generation, a royal priesthood, a holy nation, His own special people, that you may proclaim the praises of Him who called you out of darkness into His marvelous light* (1 Peter 2:9 NKJV).

The apostle Peter's description of the New Testament priesthood of Jesus Christ is probably one of the finest descriptions in the New Testament. Saint Peter says that Christ's eternal priesthood is a royal priesthood made up of God's own people who are both holy and chosen. The primary spiritual activity of this royal priesthood is to show forth the praises of Him (Christ) who called us out of darkness into His marvelous light.

The expression "royal priesthood" is quite telling. Nothing can be considered royal unless it is based upon royal lineage. In order to classify any priesthood as a royal priesthood, the presiding High Priest over the said priesthood has to be of royal blood. This means that the High Priest must either come from the family of kings or be a king himself. "Royal priesthood" also means that Peter was not referring to the Levitical priesthood. The tribe of Levi was definitely a priestly tribe, but there was nothing royal about it.

THE BIRTH OF A KING

> *Now after Jesus was born in Bethlehem of Judea in the days of Herod the king, behold, wise men from the East came to Jerusalem, saying, "Where is He who has been born King of the Jews? For we have seen His star in the East and have come to worship Him"* (Matthew 2:1-2 NKJV).

What is abundantly clear from reading the Scriptures is that Jesus Christ was first born a King before he became a Savior or Priest. Besides this, we know that Christ is the Eternal Word who was in the beginning with God. Christ therefore is the Eternal Word who is also God whom the apostle John describes in John 1:1. If Jesus Christ is God, it also means that He has always been a King in His divinity. The Scriptures are clear that God is the King over the whole of creation.

When Christ was born, He was also born into the royal lineage of King David because both Joseph and Mary were descendants of King David. This means that Jesus Christ is a King both in His divinity and in His humanity. This is why Christ's New Testament priesthood is so superior to the Old Testament Levitical priesthood and all other earthly priesthoods.

JESUS CHRIST: THE KING-PRIEST

[Jesus Is Greater Than Moses] And so, dear brothers and sisters who belong to God and are partners with those called to heaven, think carefully about this Jesus whom we declare to be God's messenger and **High Priest** *(Hebrews 3:1).*

The apostle Paul in his epistle to the Hebrews tells us that Jesus Christ has become the High Priest of everyone who is a partaker of the divine nature. Since it has been proven that Jesus Christ is a true King, it follows then that Christ's new order of priesthood has to be a royal priesthood. Since Jesus Christ is a King, His priestly ministry is greatly influenced by His kingship. It is impossible to separate His kingship from His priesthood.

Kings, by nature, own and control everything that is within the sphere of their kingdom. All the praying, preaching, and marketplace activities within a kingdom must reflect the personal will of the king. The priesthood of a king is designated to reflect and carry out the will of the king to all the citizens of the kingdom and to all aspects of the kingdom.

This means that Christ's priesthood has jurisdiction over the affairs of Kingdom citizens in the arenas of finance, business, law, media, sports/celebration, family, and church. This means that what Kingdom citizens do in the House of God (local church) and what they do in the marketplace are both holy and spiritual when they are done in accordance with the King's will.

Under Christ's New Testament Order of Melchizedek priesthood, we can be most assured that our Kingdom assignment is important and spiritual, whether it is carried out in the temple or in the marketplace. Under this Order of Melchizedek priesthood, we are all in full-time ministry even though for some (pastors) that ministry is primarily carried out in the House of God. On the other hand, full-time ministry for many others (marketplace ministers) may involve spending a majority of their time representing the Kingdom of God in the marketplace. It is quite regrettable when preachers of the gospel act like Kingdom citizens who spend a majority of their time in the marketplace are not "as spiritual as they are." This counter productive mindset stems from not understanding the nature and scope of Christ's New Creation priesthood.

All the praying, preaching, and marketplace activities within a kingdom must reflect the personal will of the king.

A MERCIFUL AND FAITHFUL HIGH PRIEST

*Therefore, it was necessary for him to be made in every respect like us, his brothers and sisters, so that he could be our merciful and faithful **High Priest** before God. Then he could offer a sacrifice that would take away the sins of the people* (Hebrews 2:17).

The apostle Paul tells us that even though Christ's priesthood is based upon His divinity, His humanity gave Him the proper perspective on the fragilities of the human condition. Before Christ became the "Word made flesh," He had no concept of what it feels like to wrestle with sin and temptation in the human body. But the apostle Paul tells us that Christ became a human being and wrapped human flesh around His divinity.

Once Christ became a man, that is to say both human and divine, He could be tempted by the devil. Christ's human condition made Him susceptible to the fragilities of the human condition in much the same way as the first Adam. If this were not the case, Jesus Christ's 40 days of temptation in the wilderness by the devil would have been meaningless and unhelpful in Christ's ability to be a merciful and faithful High Priest. If the masses in our world really knew just how merciful and faithful Christ is as High Priest, they would run for refuge under His royal priesthood.

A GREAT HIGH PRIEST

*[Christ Is Our **High Priest**] So then, since we have a great **High Priest** who has entered heaven, Jesus the Son of God, let us hold firmly to what we believe* (Hebrews 4:14).

Hebrews 4:14 tells us that Jesus Christ is not only a High Priest but a "great" one at that. Jesus Christ's greatness as a High Priest stems from two important considerations: Jesus Christ is the Son of God and He has also entered the heavens. The expression He has "entered heaven" means that Christ's priesthood is not an earthly priesthood representing a heavenly deity, but a heavenly priesthood that operates on the deity's own turf! It is no wonder He is a great High Priest.

A COMPASSIONATE HIGH PRIEST

*This **High Priest** of ours understands our weaknesses, for he faced all of the same testings we do, yet he did not sin* (Hebrews 4:15).

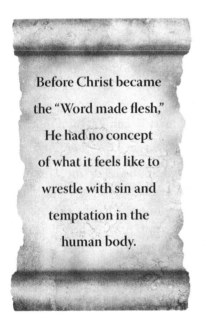

Before Christ became the "Word made flesh," He had no concept of what it feels like to wrestle with sin and temptation in the human body.

Hebrews 4:15 is one of the most humbling statements that the apostle Paul ever made to describe the character of Christ's Order of Melchizedek priesthood. Paul tells the Hebrew believers that Jesus Christ, our faithful High Priest, understands our human weaknesses because He experienced them firsthand. Even though Jesus was tested and tempted, He did not succumb to sin like the first Adam.

If you knew that you were guilty of a crime, would you want to be judged by a holier-than-thou or a compassionate judge? I think everyone would choose a compassionate judge. Paul tells us that Jesus Christ is that type of High Priest. He does not hold our sins against us longer than it takes for us to repent of them. This is why people who refuse to heed the gospel message and come under the priesthood of Jesus Christ are truly lost souls.

Chosen from among the People

*Every **high priest** is a man chosen to represent other people in their dealings with God. He presents their gifts to God and offers sacrifices for their sins* (Hebrews 5:1).

The apostle Paul uncovers another important element common to all priesthoods, whether earthly or heavenly. Paul says that every High Priest is chosen from among the people to represent them before their nation's deity. This statement explains why Christ became one of us in the mystery of the incarnation. Even though Christ's priesthood is based on His divinity, His humanity is the basis for Christ's ordination to the office of the High Priest.

Saint Paul also tells us in the same verse the primary work of Christ as our faithful High Priest. He presents the "gifts" of the people under His jurisdiction to God Most High. He also offered Himself as the sacrifice for sin to atone for the sins of the people before God. We know that Christ sacrificed Himself, once and for all, so that He doesn't have to offer sacrifices for sins every day. But if this is the case, what then is Christ's primary work as the High Priest of the New Testament Order of Melchizedek priesthood? *His primary work as our High Priest is presenting our gifts of prayer, praise, worship, tithes, and offerings to God Most High.*

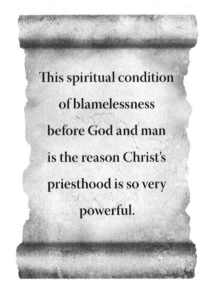

This spiritual condition of blamelessness before God and man is the reason Christ's priesthood is so very powerful.

The Honor of the High Priest

*And no one can become a **high priest** simply because he wants such an honor. He must be called by God for this work, just as Aaron* *was. That is why Christ did not honor himself by assuming he could become **High Priest**. No, he was chosen by God, who said to him, "You are my Son. Today I have become your Father"* (Hebrews 5:4-5).

The apostle Paul describes the "honor" that God has placed on the office of the High Priest. The spiritual honor that accompanies the office of the High Priest is based on one very important fact: only God can confer a person's ordination into this lofty office. Paul argues that any human being who claims to be a High Priest is a liar unless they can prove that they were ordained to that office through the direct intervention of God.

Paul argues that both Christ and Aaron did not call themselves to the office of a High Priest—God Himself conferred this lofty spiritual honor upon them. Since Jesus Christ is the High Priest of the Order of Melchizedek priesthood, which is superior to the Levitical priesthood, it follows that His priestly office carries the highest level of honor. When Christ offers our sacrifices of praise, prayer, and worship, miraculous things can break out. This explains why Christ's New Creation priesthood has an unlimited capacity for the miraculous, because the miracle ministry is not based primarily upon a person's faith. Even though having faith is important to experiencing the miraculous, the main reason God answers our prayer of faith is to uphold the honor of our High Priest because we are using His name.

Therefore, God elevated him to the place of highest honor and gave him the name above all other names, that at the name of Jesus every knee should bow, in heaven and on earth and under the earth, and every tongue confess that Jesus Christ is Lord, to the glory of God the Father (Philippians 2:9-11).

THE SOURCE OF ETERNAL SALVATION

*In this way, God qualified him as a perfect **High Priest**, and he became the source of eternal salvation for all those who obey him* (Hebrews 5:9).

The eternal priestly ministry of our Lord Jesus Christ is also vicarious because He took upon Himself the punishment for our sins. No other priesthood in human history can claim to have the power to save souls from eternal damnation. All other earthly priesthoods have wrestled with the ravaging powers of sin. Sin's terrible toll on the fabric of human relationships is evidenced worldwide.

Sin has also sentenced millions to eternal damnation in hell's unquenchable flames. Not until the advent of our Lord Jesus Christ did sin begin to lose its hold on the souls of men and women. The Christ child born through the virgin birth became God's perfect sacrificial lamb. His incorruptible blood and sinless life made Him the ideal sacrifice to atone for the sins of the world. What's more, Jesus Christ is not just the perfect sacrifice; He is also the Source of eternal salvation, which adds even more weight to Christ's New Testament order of Melchizedek priesthood.

GREATER THAN ABRAHAM

*[Melchizedek Is Greater Than Abraham] This Melchizedek was king of the city of Salem and also a **priest of God Most High**. When Abraham was returning home after winning a great battle against the kings, Melchizedek met him and blessed him. Consider then how great this Melchizedek was. Even Abraham, the great patriarch of Israel, recognized this by giving him a tenth of what he had taken in battle* (Hebrews 7:1,4).

The apostle Paul tell us that the Melchizedek who met Abram when he was returning from the slaughter of the kings from the east, was superior and greater in stature than Abram. This is one of the reasons why I believe that the Melchizedek who met Abram in the Valley of Shaveh was really the pre-incarnation appearance of Christ.

As discussed previously, here is why I make such a claim. *If the Melchizedek who met Abram was a mere mortal then it would mean that there was a man on earth who was greater and of a superior pedigree than Abraham.* If this were the case then Abraham is not qualified to be the father of many nations and the spiritual father of the New Creation. The "greater" is always more honorable and more blessed than the "lesser." Melchizedek, the king-priest of the ancient city of Salem, is therefore more suited to be the father of many nations and the spiritual father of the New Creation than Abraham. If we insist that the Melchizedek who met Abram was a mere mortal who was stationed here on earth, we must also shift our eyes from Abraham to Melchizedek as the spiritual father of the New Creation. But what is true is that Christ is greater than Abraham. This would also explain why the New Creation priesthood of our Lord Jesus Christ is the administrator over the blessing of Abraham.

HOLY AND BLAMELESS

*He is the kind of **high priest** we need because he is holy and blameless, unstained by sin. He has been set apart from sinners and has been given the **highest** place of honor in heaven* (Hebrews 7:26).

Our High Priest is both *holy and blameless*—no human or spirit being can find anything faulty in the priestly ministry of our Lord Jesus Christ. When Jesus stood in Pontius Pilate's judgment hall facing Jewish religious leaders who were accusing Him of blasphemy, Pilate went before the Sanhedrin council and said, "I find no fault in this man." Whoa! Under the critical stare of Christ's enemies, Pontius Pilate gave the verdict that Jesus Christ was blameless. This spiritual condition of blamelessness before God and man is the reason Christ's priesthood is so very powerful.

Pilate said to Him, "What is truth?" And when he had said this, he went out again to the Jews, and said to them, "I find no fault in Him at all" (John 18:38 NKJV).

THE PERFECT SACRIFICE

*Unlike those other **high priests**, he does not need to offer sacrifices every day. They did this for their own sins first and then for the sins of the people. But Jesus did this once for all when he offered himself as the sacrifice for the people's sins* (Hebrews 7:27).

Another very important aspect of Christ's eternal priesthood is the fact that Jesus Christ was God's perfect sacrifice—the offering of Himself on the cross completely paid for the sins of the whole world. As God's perfect sacrifice, Jesus Christ completely satisfied the righteous demands of the Law of God that had been broken by humankind's sin. So how does this important fact affect us today? Sin should not have dominion over us. The power to rise above the encroachment of sin is available to us under our Lord Jesus Christ's New Testament Order of Melchizedek priesthood.

THE PERFECT HIGH PRIEST

> *The law appointed **high priests** who were limited by human weakness. But after the law was given, God appointed his Son with an oath, and his Son has been made the perfect **High Priest** forever* (Hebrews 7:28).

> *But our **High Priest** offered himself to God as a single sacrifice for sins, good for all time. Then he sat down in the place of honor at God's right hand* (Hebrews 10:12).

Not only is Jesus Christ God's perfect sacrifice, He is also God's perfect High Priest. This statement has very deep and far-reaching spiritual ramifications. Even though there were some great High Priests in Israel, none were perfect. The sin nature inside them would rise occasionally and interrupt the proper flow of the life of God in the priesthood. Two examples quickly come to mind.

Even though Aaron (Moses' brother) was the first high priest over the Levitical order of priesthood, he often succumbed to the pressure of the people. When Moses was on Mount Sinai receiving the Covenant of Law, Aaron was pressured by the people's idolatrous nature to create a golden calf that they could worship instead of God. When Moses returned, he was shocked and angered at the sight of Israelites bowing to a lifeless golden calf. The high priest Eli, on the other hand, was a very passive leader and irresponsible father. His passivity and his irresponsibility as a father brought the entire priesthood into total disrepute with God and man. The Lord Jesus Christ however, is a perfect

High Priest. We never ever have to worry about the fact that Jesus Christ would ever compromise the power and integrity of His royal priesthood.

SEATED IN STATURE WITH ALL AUTHORITY

*[Christ Is Our **High Priest**] Here is the main point: We have a **High Priest** who sat down in the place of honor beside the throne of the majestic God in heaven* (Hebrews 8:1).

It is quite unfortunate that many spiritual leaders in the Body of Christ know a lot about walking in the anointing but very few truly understand the "power of spiritual stature." It is very possible to be very anointed or gifted without having character. This is because giftedness and the anointing are supernatural impartations of the Holy Spirit. Spiritual stature, on the other hand, requires that a man's life be found pleasing in God's sight. Spiritual stature is a position of influence with God that God bestows upon a man or woman to negotiate with God over the destiny of nations. America is full of very gifted and anointed preachers and businessmen, but how many of them are in a place of spiritual stature with God and man?

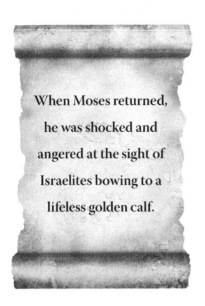

When Moses returned, he was shocked and angered at the sight of Israelites bowing to a lifeless golden calf.

Then the men got up from their meal and looked out toward Sodom. As they left, Abraham went with them to send them on their way. "Should I hide my plan from Abraham?" the LORD asked. "For Abraham will certainly become a great and mighty nation, and all the nations of the earth will be blessed through him" (Genesis 18:16-18).

God wanted to destroy Sodom, but He refused to do it without talking with Abraham about it. This is because Abraham was in a place of spiritual stature with God. God also knew that Abraham had the power to negotiate with Him over the future of Sodom. My dear friend, this biblical example shows us the difference between being anointed and living in stature. Saint Paul tells us that Christ our High Priest is seated in a place of honor before the throne of God. What a powerful position of influence in the Kingdom of God! Under Christ's New Testament order of Melchizedek priesthood, we can confidently negotiate with God for the destiny of our nations if we invoke the name of Jesus.

PRIESTLY GIFTS AND SACRIFICES

And since every high priest is required to offer gifts and sacrifices, our High Priest must make an offering, too (Hebrews 8:3).

Every high priest is required by divine law to offer both gifts and sacrifices. This was also true of pagan priesthoods. Pagan high priests would sometimes sacrifice women and infants to demon-gods in order to appeal to them for national prosperity. Under the Levitical priesthood there were numerous gifts and sacrifices that the high priest offered daily to appease the God of Israel.

For us to be effective members of the New Testament royal priesthood of Jesus Christ, we must understand what the gifts and sacrifices are that we need to present to God. When we present the appropriate gifts and sacrifices, Christ our High Priest will take them and offer them to God as sweet smelling savor. The New Testament shows us the following gifts and sacrifices that we can give God:

1. Our Bodies

    *I beseech you therefore, brethren, by the mercies of God, that ye present your bodies a living **sacrifice**, holy, acceptable unto God, which is your reasonable service* (Romans 12:1 KJV).

2. Walking in the Love of God

    *And walk in love, as Christ also hath loved us, and hath given himself for us an offering and a **sacrifice** to God for a sweet smelling savor* (Ephesians 5:2 KJV).

3. Service of Faith

    *Yea, and if I be offered upon the **sacrifice** and service of your faith, I joy, and rejoice with you all* (Philippians 2:17 KJV).

4. Sacrificial Offerings

    *But I have all, and abound: I am full, having received of Epaphroditus the things which were sent from you, an odor of a sweet smell, a **sacrifice** acceptable, wellpleasing to God* (Philippians 4:18 KJV).

5. Tithes

    ...but he whose genealogy is not derived from them received tithes from Abraham and blessed him who had the promises. Now beyond all contradiction the lesser is blessed by the better. Here mortal men receive tithes, but there he receives them, of whom it is witnessed that he lives (Hebrews 7:6-8 NKJV).

6. Praise and Worship

    But you are a chosen generation, a royal priesthood, a holy nation, His own special people, that you may proclaim the praises of Him who called you out of darkness into His marvelous light (1 Peter 2:9 NKJV).

7. Talents and Skills

    *If any man speak, let him speak as the oracles of God; if any man minister, let him do it as of the **ability** which God giveth: that God in all things may be glorified through Jesus Christ, to whom be praise and dominion for ever and ever. Amen* (1 Peter 4:11 KJV).

8. Prayer

    He said to them, "The Scriptures declare, 'My Temple will be called a house of prayer,' but you have turned it into a den of thieves!" (Matthew 21:13).

An Excellent and Superior Ministry

*But now Jesus, our **High Priest**, has been given a ministry that is far superior to the old **priest**hood, for he is the one who mediates for us a far better covenant with God, based on better promises* (Hebrews 8:6).

The New Testament Order of Melchizedek priesthood of Christ is also powerful because Jesus Christ has an *"excellent and superior ministry"* to that of any other earthly high priest. The most unique aspect of the Order of Melchizedek priesthood is that unlike the Levitical priestly Order, this eternal priestly Order is both a marketplace *and* priestly ministry. The High Priest of this eternal priestly Order is first and foremost a King who does priestly work. As a King, His influence extends beyond the boundaries of the temple, right into the marketplace. As a King-Priest, Jesus Christ has an ongoing dual influence over both the services of the temple and the activities of the marketplace. This is why Christ's priesthood has a more excellent and superior ministry than the Levitical priesthood.

In the Holy of Holies

*But only the **high priest** ever entered the Most Holy Place, and only once a year. And he always offered blood for his own sins and for the sins the people had committed in ignorance* (Hebrews 9:7).

*[Christ Is the Perfect Sacrifice] So Christ has now become the **High Priest** over all the good things that have come. He has entered that greater, more perfect Tabernacle in heaven, which was not made by human hands and is not part of this created world* (Hebrews 9:11).

Since the fall from grace of Adam and Eve in the Garden of Eden, men have tried to find their way back into the presence of God. Simply observing humankind's propensity to worship some invisible or visible being, underscores the craving for the presence of God that is hidden in the crevices of the human heart. But after sin entered the world, it created an unholy fear of the presence

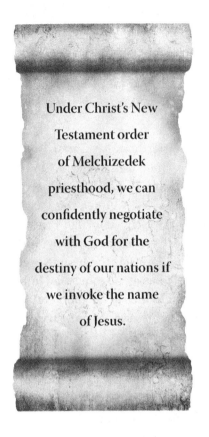

Under Christ's New Testament order of Melchizedek priesthood, we can confidently negotiate with God for the destiny of our nations if we invoke the name of Jesus.

of God. When Adam and Eve heard the voice of God traveling in their direction, they hid themselves.

Under the Levitical priesthood, entering into any room that contained the manifest presence of God was a scary experience. Even the high priest entered the Holy of Holies only once a year to make atonement for the people of Israel. But under Christ's New Creation priesthood, our High Priest lives in the Holy of Holies. Since we are also seated with Him in heavenly places, it follows then that the regenerated spirit of every born-again believer lives in the Holy of Holies. Beloved, under this New Testament order of Melchizedek priesthood, we can truly know the joy of living in God's presence.

HIS BLOOD OF ATONEMENT

*Under the old system, the **high priest** brought the blood of animals into the Holy Place as a sacrifice for sin, and the bodies of the animals were burned outside the camp. So also Jesus suffered and died outside the city gates to make his people holy by means of his own blood* (Hebrews 13:11-12).

*And since we have a great **High Priest** who rules over God's house, let us go right into the presence of God with sincere hearts fully trusting him. For our guilty consciences have been sprinkled with Christ's blood to make us clean, and our bodies have been washed with pure water* (Hebrews 10:21-22).

The apostle Paul uncovers one of the most important aspects of the royal priesthood of Jesus Christ. It is related to the power of the blood of atonement

JESUS CHRIST: OUR ROYAL HIGH PRIEST

that God has made available to every person on earth who desires forgiveness from sin and deliverance from eternal damnation. Under the Levitical system of sacrifices, the priests slaughtered bulls, goats, and sheep daily to atone for the sins of the people of Israel. Even though these blood sacrifices covered the sins of the people, the blood of bulls and goats was not powerful enough to abolish the sin nature in the worshippers.

Since the blood of bulls and goats could only *cover* the sins of the people instead of *removing* them, the worshippers' consciences were constantly burdened with guilt from past sins. This is in direct contrast to what Jesus Christ's blood has made available to members of the New Creation. The blood of Jesus doesn't just cover sin it removes the sin nature in humankind. This is why the Scripture says that *"if any man be in Christ he is a new creature: old things art passed away, behold, all things are become new"* (2 Cor. 5:17 KJV).

The inexhaustible redeeming power that God has invested in the blood of Jesus Christ is the main reason the order of Melchizedek priesthood of Christ is so very powerful. Since the blood of Christ overpowers and silences sin, it yields tremendous power over the devil. The devil's kingdom of darkness can only prevail in atmospheres that are charged with the technology of sin. The devil feeds on sin and the sin nature, because he is a slave to Sin. But the blood of Jesus Christ has complete authority over both, Sin and the devil. No wonder the overcomers overcame him (the devil) through the word of their testimony and the power of the blood of Jesus.

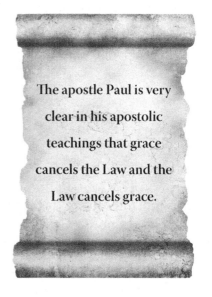

The apostle Paul is very clear in his apostolic teachings that grace cancels the Law and the Law cancels grace.

> *And they have defeated him by the blood of the Lamb and by their testimony. And they did not love their lives so much that they were afraid to die* (Revelation 12:11).

LIFE APPLICATION SECTION

Memory Verses

Now after Jesus was born in Bethlehem of Judea in the days of Herod the king, behold, wise men from the East came to Jerusalem, saying, "Where is He who has been born King of the Jews? For we have seen His star in the East and have come to worship Him" (Matthew 2:1-2 NKJV).

Reflections

What are the prophetic events that took place when Christ was born?

_____

_____

_____

_____

_____

_____

_____

Write three things that the book of Hebrews tells us about the priesthood of Christ.

_____

_____

_____

How does Christ's priesthood affect you in the Marketplace?

_____

_____

_____

_____

_____

_____

JOURNAL YOUR PERSONAL NOTES ON THIS CHAPTER

CHAPTER TEN

Tithing Under the Order of Melchizedek

O NE OF THE MOST frequently asked questions in Christendom is related to the practice of tithing in the global Church: *Is tithing for today?* This seemingly innocent question arouses some of the most passionate debates among the saints, pitting those in favor of the biblical practice of tithing against those who believe that tithing is modern-day extortion of gullible saints by modern-day Pharisees. These heartfelt debates over the practice of tithing have increased with the economic decline of many nations. Tithing debates in the blogosphere have been fueled to the point of explosion by the unrestrained and extravagant lifestyles of many of the notable proponents of the "gospel of prosperity."

I am the senior pastor of a thriving church in Texas, and I am also an itinerant minister of the gospel. My position in the Kingdom of God has given me a unique vantage point to answer the tithing question. I have looked into the eyes of many well-meaning born-again believers who told me how their life and personal economy changed for the better when they started tithing. I have heard from very sincere God-loving children who have said, "Francis my tithe is not working for me. I have been tithing for years but the windows of heaven I was promised never opened for me." And there are those who have told me that they do not believe that tithing is applicable to post-Calvary New Testament believers.

Since I have done extensive research on the subject of tithing under the Order of Melchizedek in my book titled *The Return of the Lost Key*, I will simply give an overview in this chapter. Let's begin by looking at the popular method for exacting the tithe in the global Church.

> *Bring all the tithes into the storehouse, that there may be food in My house, and try Me now in this," says the LORD of hosts. "If I will not open for you the windows of heaven and pour out for you such blessing that there will not be room enough to receive it. And I will rebuke the devourer for your sakes, so that he will not destroy the fruit of your ground, nor shall the vine fail to bear fruit for you in the field," says the LORD of hosts; "and all nations will call you blessed, for you will be a delightful land," says the LORD of hosts* (Malachi 3:10-12 NKJV).

This passage from the book of Malachi gives us several benefits of tithing under the Levitical priesthood. Please remember that the book of Malachi was never addressed to post-Calvary New Testament believers; it was written to specifically rebuke Levites who were withholding the tithe from the household of Aaron. What's more, the entire book of Malachi was written for one main purpose: to make the people of Israel (especially the Levites) remember the Law of Moses.

> *Remember to obey the Law of Moses, my servant—all the decrees and regulations that I gave him on Mount Sinai for all Israel* (Malachi 4:4).

Malachi 4:4 means that those who are anxious to *"remember to obey the Law of Moses"* need to get busy. The word "re-member" carries the meaning of "putting the different parts of the Law of Moses back together." So New Testament preachers and teachers who use Malachi 3:8-12 to exact the tithe, must not end there. They must heed the prophet Malachi's call to *remember to obey the entire Law of Moses*. They cannot have the best of both worlds (grace and Law). These spiritual leaders either believe that the New Testament Church is under grace or under the Law of Moses; but they cannot believe that the Church is under both. The apostle Paul is very clear in his apostolic teachings that *grace cancels the Law and the Law cancels grace*.

Without a shadow of doubt, there are some very powerful spiritual benefits which will begin to flow our way when we shift from the Malachi 3:8-12 tithing model to the Genesis 14:17-20 tithing model. The spiritual benefits of tithing into the priestly Order of Melchizedek are infinitely greater than the spiritual benefits of tithing into the Levitical priesthood. For the sake of our study I have listed the spiritual benefits of tithing into the Levitical priestly Order and then contrasted them with the spiritual benefits of tithing into the priestly Order of Melchizedek.

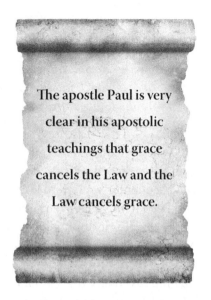

The apostle Paul is very clear in his apostolic teachings that grace cancels the Law and the Law cancels grace.

BENEFITS OF TITHING INTO THE LEVITICAL PRIESTHOOD

1. open windows of heaven
2. a poured out blessing with not enough room to receive it
3. the rebuking of the devourer by God for the people's sake
4. preservation of the fruits of the ground
5. protection from untimely harvest
6. nations shall call you blessed

Why wait outside the window, when you can work from inside the Father's house? One of the spiritual benefits promised to tithers who tithe according to Malachi 3:8-12 is that God will open the windows of heaven and pour out a blessing. The challenge I have with this promise is simply this: *if the blessing is being poured out of the windows of heaven, it means that the recipients of the blessing are operating from outside of the eternal structures of the Kingdom of Heaven.* It is tragic when post-Calvary, New Testament believers believe that they are operating from outside of the Kingdom of Heaven, which goes against everything that the Lord Jesus Christ and His apostles taught us about New Testament post-Calvary living.

Jesus replied, "I tell you the truth, unless you are born again, you cannot see the Kingdom of God."

"What do you mean?" exclaimed Nicodemus. "How can an old man go back into his mother's womb and be born again?" Jesus replied, "I assure you, no one can enter the Kingdom of God without being born of water and the Spirit" (John 3:3-5).

When Nicodemus, a notable teacher of the Law, came to Jesus in the night hours, an interesting conversation broke out between the two spiritual leaders. Nicodemus wanted to know the secret behind Jesus' spiritual power. Jesus told Nicodemus that even though he was a teacher of the Law and lived under the Levitical priesthood, he couldn't enter the Kingdom of God unless he was born of the Spirit. It sounds to me like Jesus was telling Nicodemus that he was operating from the outside of the spiritual Order that Jesus was part of. Jesus told him explicitly that he had to be born again to enter into the Kingdom of God. So here is the million dollar question: *If being born again brings us into the Kingdom of God, why do we tithe as though we are still on the outside looking in?* I rest my case.

The Scriptures say, "No eye has seen, no ear has heard, and no mind has imagined what God has prepared for those who love him" (1 Corinthians 2:9). We are no longer strangers and outsiders to the heavenly sanctuary of God. Jesus already told us that He has given us the keys of the Kingdom of Heaven" and if this is the case, then we need to be talking about *opening the doors* of the Kingdom of Heaven instead of the *windows* of Heaven.

Access to a No Limit Blessing

"Bring all the tithes into the storehouse, that there may be food in My house, and try Me now in this," says the LORD of hosts, "If I will not open for you the windows of heaven and pour out for you such blessing that there will not be room enough to receive it" (Malachi 3:10 NKJV).

One of the promises for tithing, which was bequeathed upon the people who tithed into the Levitical priesthood, was a poured out blessing that they did not have room enough to receive. Right away you can see that something is seriously wrong with this picture of promise. What we thought was a great blessing was actually a limited blessing compared to the fullness of what God has prepared for His covenant people. Anytime you are the recipient of a blessing for which you do not have enough room to receive, you have a problem on your hands. Why would God pour out a blessing for His people for which they did not have "enough room to receive" in its fullness? This is a very legitimate question, so I will give you a probable answer.

> *Now I say that the heir, as long as he is a child, does not differ at all from a slave, though he is master of all, but is under guardians and stewards until the time appointed by the father. Even so we, when we were children, were in bondage under the elements of the world. But when the fullness of the time had come, God sent forth His Son, born of a woman, born under the law, to redeem those who were under the law, that we might receive the adoption as sons* (Galatians 4:1-5 NKJV).

This passage in Galatians contains the answer to the perplexing question. Under the Covenant of Law, God never ever revealed or did anything in its fullness. Based on the teachings of the apostle Paul, everything that happened under the Old Testament Covenant of Law was but a shadow of things to come. Whatever God did under the Mosaic Covenant Dispensation, He was working toward its *fullest expression in Christ.*

The apostle Paul tells us that when Jesus was born of the virgin birth, the period called *the fullness of time* was initiated. This means that since the virgin birth of Jesus Christ, God wants to deal with His people from a *position of fullness* and not from a *position of types and shadows.* Under the Levitical priesthood, tithers were given a poured out blessing without enough room to receive it simply because God had not yet established a spiritual

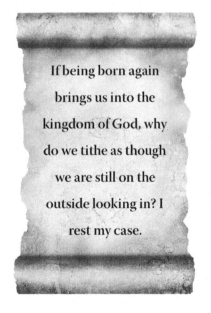

If being born again brings us into the kingdom of God, why do we tithe as though we are still on the outside looking in? I rest my case.

structure in the Old Testament that could contain the fullness of the blessing of Abraham.

When Jesus said *"It is finished"* while hanging from the cross, the Old Testament transitional period of types and shadows came to a sudden end. This marked the beginning of the day of fullness for everything God had prepared for the Seed of Abraham from before the foundation of the world. When we give a tithe based on the priestly Order of Melchizedek, our tithe has the power to infinitely increase our spiritual capacity to receive the fullness of the blessing of Abraham, which God wants to confer upon us as His dear children.

But as it is written: "Eye has not seen, nor ear heard, nor have entered into the heart of man the things which God has prepared for those who love Him" (1 Corinthians 2:9 NKJV).

Two Trees and Two Sons

And out of the ground the LORD God made every tree grow that is pleasant to the sight and good for food. The tree of life was also in the midst of the garden, and the tree of the knowledge of good and evil (Genesis 2:9).

The Old Testament is full of prophetic patterns, which when illuminated by the light of the Spirit, uncover spiritual pathways to rich and deep spiritual truths. The Scriptures give us a very detailed account of the creation and the beginning of human and animal life as we know it. We are told in the Genesis account that God planted a Garden in Eden where He placed the man whom He had created.

This was a garden of tremendous beauty and untold abundance. The most unique thing about this garden is that God planted two spiritual trees in the center— one was the Tree of Life and the other was

When Jesus said "It is finished" while hanging from the cross, the Old Testament transitional period of types and shadows came to a sudden end.

the Tree of the Knowledge of Good and Evil. These two trees have powerful prophetic symbolic representations and allude to the Old and New Testaments. The trees speak of the first and last Adam, and serve as a prophetic picture of the two priesthoods that God gave to humankind. The Tree of Life that speaks of Christ correlates with the eternal priestly Order of Melchizedek; whereas the Tree of the Knowledge of Good and Evil foreshadows the Mountain of Law which correlates with the earthly Levitical priesthood.

The Tree of the Knowledge of Good and Evil is the Mountain of Law, and the foundation for right and wrong, justice and injustice, good and evil. The Ten Commandments that Moses wrote under divine inspiration are based upon the Mountain of Law. The Mountain of Law also controls the flow of blessings and curses within the earthly structure and is the basis for reward and punishment within the earth realm. The Mountain of Law is also the foundation of the judicial systems of most law-abiding nations. The Mountain of Law can be easily manipulated by those who have been given the spiritual or civil authority to interpret its laws and ordinances.

God did not want Adam and Eve to eat of the fruit originating from the Mountain of Law. God told them very plainly that eating from the Tree of the Knowledge of Good and Evil would introduce them to the machinery of sin and death. The Mountain of Law always stirs man's individual sense of reasoning, placing him in a position where he (and not God) has to decide what is good and what is evil. This in itself is death, because spiritual death is simply separation from God in any area of our lives.

God never ever intended for humankind to eat from the Tree of the Knowledge of Good and Evil, but from the Tree of Life. God did not warn Adam and Eve against eating from the Tree of Life because it represents the incorruptible Life of Christ. God never stops people from enjoying the "Life" of His dear Son. Had Adam and Eve eaten of the Tree of Life instead of the other tree, their entire system of reasoning would have taken on the complete nature of Christ. God would have been the focal point of their reasoning, instead of self. So, here are two million-dollar questions: *Why did God base His covenant with Israel on the basis of the Mountain of Law? Why would God base the priestly Order of Aaron on the foundation of the Mountain of Law?*

> *I have discovered this principle of life—that when I want to do what is right, I inevitably do what is wrong. I love God's law*

THE ORDER OF MELCHIZEDEK

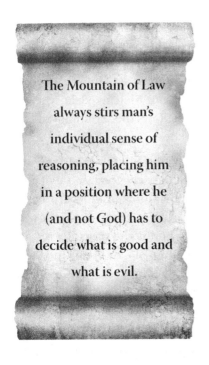

The Mountain of Law always stirs man's individual sense of reasoning, placing him in a position where he (and not God) has to decide what is good and what is evil.

with all my heart. But there is another power within me that is at war with my mind. This power makes me a slave to the sin that is still within me (Romans 7:21-23).

The answer to the first question is this: *God wanted to convincingly show the children of Israel and all the inhabitants of the earth how utterly depraved and self-absorbed humankind had become.* God had to show the children of Israel just how much they needed a Savior who could save them from themselves and from the righteous demands of the Law of God. Inherently, they knew that the Law of God is good and its demands honorable, yet they discovered that their nature was set against obeying God's holy Law even when their minds agreed with it.

Before God gave the nation of Israel the Covenant of Law, they had no idea how incapable of satisfying the righteous Law of God they were because of their fallen nature. This is why the Bible says that before the giving of the Law, there was no Sin. This statement does not in anyway mean that there was no Sin at work in the earth before the giving of the Mosaic Law. But before the Law was given, there was nothing to measure ourselves against to see whether or not we were in compliance with God's requirements.

The old system under the law of Moses was only a shadow, a dim preview of the good things to come, not the good things themselves. The sacrifices under that system were repeated again and again, year after year, but they were never able to provide perfect cleansing for those who came to worship. If they could have provided perfect cleansing, the sacrifices would have stopped, for the worshipers would have been purified once for all time, and their feelings of guilt would have disappeared (Hebrews 10:1-2).

The answer to the second question builds upon the answer to the first. The reason God built the Levitical priesthood on the basis of the Mountain of Law was to show the children of Israel that *there was no way that they could be redeemed from the power of sin and death by following the works of the Law.* After hundreds and hundreds of blood sacrifices the people who lived under the Levitical priesthood realized that the many sacrifices did little to ease their guilt-ridden conscience. The constant struggle with the machinery of sin in their lives began to breed a sense of spiritual despair and desperation among the people, which in turn made the people look forward to the coming of a future Messiah who would one day save them from sin.

Two Women and Two Sons

Tell me, you who want to live under the law, do you know what the law actually says? The Scriptures say that Abraham had two sons, one from his slave wife and one from his freeborn wife. The son of the slave wife was born in a human attempt to bring about the fulfillment of God's promise. But the son of the freeborn wife was born as God's own fulfillment of his promise. These two women serve as an illustration of God's two covenants. The first woman, Hagar, represents Mount Sinai where people received the law that enslaved them. And now Jerusalem is just like Mount Sinai in Arabia, because she and her children live in slavery to the law. But the other woman, Sarah, represents the heavenly Jerusalem. She is the free woman, and she is our mother (Galatians 4:21-26).

Abraham's two sons are important prophetic symbols within the progressive revelation of God. Paul tells us that the two sons of Abraham, Ishmael and Isaac, represent two priesthoods and two separate and distinct covenants that God made with man. This great apostle to the Church tells us that Ishmael who came out of Hagar represents the "covenant of Law" which God gave to Moses at Mount Sinai. Paul shows us that this covenant from Mount Sinai is serviced by an earthly priesthood which operates out of the temple in natural Jerusalem. We know that this priesthood is the Order of Aaron (Levitical priesthood).

Paul also tells us that natural Jerusalem (including everything in it) is in bondage with her children. So why in God's name would we want to tithe into a priesthood that Paul says is in a season of bondage with her children? This is exactly what we are doing when we teach people to tithe according to Malachi 3:8-12, which describes a tithe in accordance with the Law.

On the other hand, Paul tells us that Abraham's second son, Isaac, represents the New Testament "covenant of Grace" and spiritual Jerusalem which is the "mother of us all." The priestly Order of Melchizedek is a heavenly priesthood that operates from within the eternal structures of spiritual Jerusalem. This is the priesthood we need to be tithing into. This pattern of tithing is going to bring us into great spiritual freedom even as spiritual Jerusalem is free.

HOW THE MOSAIC GENERATION TITHED

So I want to remind you, though you already know these things, that Jesus first rescued the nation of Israel from Egypt, but later he destroyed those who did not remain faithful (Jude 5).

The Mosaic generation is the generation of Israelites from the time Moses led the children of Israel out of Egypt until the day Jesus died on the cross of Calvary. We will now look at how the Moses generation tithed.

1. *They paid a tithe according to the Law.*

   Now the law of Moses required that the priests, who are descendants of Levi, must collect a tithe from the rest of the people of Israel, who are also descendants of Abraham (Hebrews 7:5).

As you know, the entire priestly Order of Aaron was based upon the Mountain of Law. The giving and practice of tithing was done in accordance with what God had established within the Mosaic Covenant of Law. Under the Levitical priesthood, paying one's tithe was as expected and as required as paying taxes is in the United States, which is strictly enforced. Failure to pay one's taxes can have disastrous consequences. This is how paying tithes was under the Levitical priesthood.

2. Their tithe was payment for priestly services.

As for the tribe of Levi, your relatives, I will compensate them for their service in the Tabernacle. Instead of an allotment of land, I will give them the tithes from the entire land of Israel (Numbers 18:21).

Under the priestly Order of Aaron, the concept of giving the tithe did not really exist. The tithe was not "given;" it was "paid out." The difference here is critical, inviting further investigation. *Giving* involves the concept of free will and also evokes the involvement of our highest nature, while *paying* involves the concept of meeting one's financial obligations. Here is an example: My gas company is based out of Houston, Texas. Every month this company faithfully provides the energy I need to run my house. At the end of the month they send me a bill for the services rendered. I have no emotional obligation to them, but I definitely have a financial obligation to them. They provided a service that I enjoyed for a whole month; now it is time to pay. Failure do to so will result in my gas being turned off and eventually my name may end up with credit collection agencies.

Tithing under the Mosaic generation was no different from this illustration. This does not mean that tithing under the Levitical priesthood was not spiritual. It was as spiritual as the Law is spiritual—nothing more and nothing less. Tithing under the Levitical priestly Order was strictly payment for priestly services the tribes of Israel were receiving from the Levitical priesthood. Members of the tribe of Levi who were also the priests of Israel, were not allowed by divine decree to own their own land (business). God gave them no inheritance of land. Their life occupation was to serve in the office of a priest all the days of their lives.

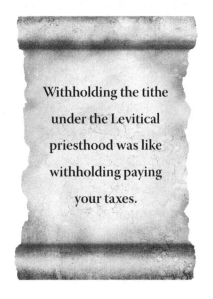

Withholding the tithe under the Levitical priesthood was like withholding paying your taxes.

To ensure that these men and their families did not starve to death because of financial lack, God gave them the tithes of the tribes of Israel. The tithes of the children of Israel were to replace the lack of land and secular wages. This is why tithing under the Order of Aaron is paid out and not given. The people had no choice but to give it. Failure to do so was tantamount to stealing or robbing a bank. This is exactly what the prophet Malachi is alluding to in Malachi 3:8 when he asks the question, "will a man rob God?" *Withholding the tithe under the Levitical priesthood was like withholding paying your taxes.* In America, people have been thrown into prison for tax evasion. This is because the US government regards such actions as robbing the government, which is a felony offense.

On the other hand, since the tithe was payment for priestly services, the people who tithed had a legal right to expect the priests to provide them with the stipulated priestly services. If the priests failed to perform their priestly assignments, they automatically forfeited their rights to the tithes of the people.

Under the priestly Order of Melchizedek, the tithe is *given* as a royal endowment of honor. It is never ever *paid out.* The High Priest after the Order of Melchizedek is both God and King, and our New Testament High Priest can never ever be on the payroll of His own Kingdom citizens. Even the mention of "paying our tithes" is an insult under this eternal priestly Order, and pastors do not have to give us priestly services in order for them to earn our tithe.

The demonic mindset that causes born-again believers to withhold their tithes originates from the Church's usage of Malachi 3:8-12 as a New Testament tithing model.

Our tithe already belongs to our faithful High Priest who is both God and King of the universe. As God and King, Christ does not need to perform for us in order to earn our tithe because everything we have and use to acquire resources belongs to Him. But out of our own *free will* we can choose to *give Him* the endowment of tithe, which already belongs to Him because He alone is worthy. Under the priestly Order of Melchizedek, the priestly services the High Priest provides for His Kingdom citizens through His earthly under-shepherds (pastors) are secondary to the fact that He is worthy of all our praise and adoration. This also means that under the priestly Order of Melchizedek, we cannot withhold the tithe from the local church where God has planted us because we feel as if the pastor is not giving us enough priestly services. This demonic mindset that causes born-again believers to withhold their tithes originates from the Church's usage of Malachi 3:8-12 as a New Testament tithing model. This inaccuracy must come to an end.

Nevertheless, I do not want to be misconstrued as supporting the spiritual neglect of the sheep by pastors of churches. This is far from what I am suggesting. It's important for pastors to do their best to feed the flock that God has placed in their care. I am saying that any member of God's New Testament Church has no spiritual grounds under the priestly Order of Melchizedek for withholding the tithe from the Church of God because he or she has been offended by the pastor.

3. *A curse as prescribed by the Mosaic Law was placed upon non-tithers.*

You are under a curse, for your whole nation has been cheating me (Malachi 3:9).

The prophet Malachi asks the question, "will a man rob God?" He then proceeds to tell the Jewish people who lived under the Covenant of Law how they had robbed God. They had robbed Him by withholding their tithes and offerings which they were required by the Law to give to the Levites in exchange for the priestly services that they were receiving. The sentence for withholding the tithes and offerings was the superimposition of a curse upon their lives. The prophet Haggai describes in great detail how this curse worked.

> *Then the LORD sent this message through the prophet Haggai: "Why are you living in luxurious houses while my house lies in ruins? This is what the LORD of Heaven's Armies says: Look at what's happening to you! You have planted much but harvest little. You eat but are not satisfied. You drink but are still thirsty. You put on clothes but cannot keep warm. Your wages disappear as though you were putting them in pockets filled with holes!* (Haggai 1:3-6).

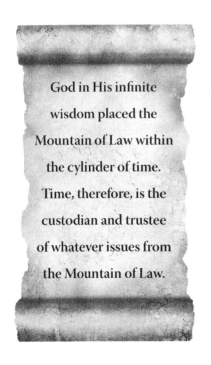

God in His infinite wisdom placed the Mountain of Law within the cylinder of time. Time, therefore, is the custodian and trustee of whatever issues from the Mountain of Law.

Here is the billion dollar question: *Who cursed these people and why did they get cursed?* The answer is simply: *they were not cursed by God but by the Mountain of Law on which the whole priesthood of Aaron was based.* Had God cursed them, the curse would have remained unbreakable because everything God decrees from eternity becomes eternal here on earth.

They were cursed by the same Law that guaranteed their blessing if they obeyed its righteous requirements. This is important because if they were cursed by not obeying the demands of the Law in the area of tithes and offerings, they could also break the curse of the Law by simply coming back into a place of obedience to the Law. The reason the curse was prescribed upon the people is because the Mountain of Law is the basis for blessings and curses. The Mountain of Law allows for the release of both good and evil, blessings and curses, life and death—all from the same stream. *God in His infinite wisdom placed the Mountain of Law within the cylinder of time. Time, therefore, is the custodian and trustee of whatever issues from the Mountain of Law.*

The time span for the flow of generational blessings was set to span a thousand generations, whereas the life span of generational curses was set to run up to the fourth generation. This is a very important fact for us to understand. God quarantined the power of whatever issues out of the Mountain of Law in the cylinder of time, to ensure that there was always *a way of escape* for those who found themselves on the wrong side of the Law of God. This means then that whatever curse falls upon us within the cylinder of time can be changed by the power of God when we make the right choices and yield to God's Word.

Then the angel showed me a river with the water of life, clear as crystal, flowing from the throne of God and of the Lamb. It flowed down the center of the main street. On each side of the river grew a tree of life, bearing twelve crops of fruit, with a fresh crop each month. The leaves were used for medicine to heal the nations. No longer will there be a curse upon anything. For the throne of God and of the Lamb will be there, and his servants will worship him (Revelation 22:1-3).

On the other hand, the priestly Order of Melchizedek operates within the eternal structures of the Kingdom of Heaven. This is the same eternal structure where the throne of God and of the Lamb reside. According to the apostle John, no curse can exist in a spiritual structure which has both the throne of God and of the Lamb. (Revelation 22:3.) This is why New Testament spiritual leaders must not threaten New Testament believers who live under the priestly Order of Melchizedek with a curse if they do not tithe. The curse of not tithing that is prescribed in Malachi 3 can never be applied to post-Calvary New Testament believers, whether they tithe or not. There is a more excellent way of exacting the tithe from New Testament believers, which I briefly describe in this writing. My book, *The Return of the Lost Key,* discusses this issue of the tithe more extensively.

Please remember that the priestly Order of Melchizedek operates out of the Tree of Life, which has *no curse in it.* This does not mean that there are no spiritual consequences for not tithing under the priestly Order of Melchizedek. *Under the priestly Order of Melchizedek, non-tithers are chastised with a diminishing capacity for manifesting the favor of God.* When our capacity for manifesting the favor of God becomes diminished, it is quite difficult to get the spiritual breakthroughs we need in reasonable time frames.

Breakthroughs that should come relatively easy into our life-stream suddenly become points of serious struggles because our ability to manifest the favor of God is constantly diminishing. If we continue to dishonor God by not giving Him His proper endowment of tithe, God will eventually stop giving us the bread and wine of the priestly Order of Melchizedek. This means that the flow of God's divine revelation and the anointing of His precious Holy Spirit may also begin to diminish. This is due to the fact that under the priestly Order of Melchizedek, the Holy Spirit is given to those who obey our faithful High Priest who is also the King of kings.

And we are His witnesses to these things, and so also is the Holy Spirit whom God has given to those who obey Him (Acts 5:32 NKJV).

4. ***They brought their tithes to the storehouse.***

"Bring all the tithes into the storehouse so there will be enough food in my Temple. If you do," says the LORD of Heaven's Armies, "I will open the windows of heaven for you. I will pour out a blessing so great you won't have enough room to take it in! Try it! Put me to the test!" (Malachi 3:10)

During the Mosaic generation, the people who were serviced by the Levitical priesthood were instructed to bring their tithes and offerings to the storehouse, which was the temple of God in natural Jerusalem. God promised to open the windows of heaven for them and pour out a blessing if they brought their tithes to His house. The bringing of tithes and offerings to the storehouse (local church) is one of the similarities between the Levitical priestly Order and the priestly Order of Melchizedek. Under both priestly Orders, one of the sacred places God identified for bringing the tithe to is the storehouse or local church.

ABRAM MEETS MELCHIZEDEK: THE KING-PRIEST

And the king of Sodom went out to meet him at the Valley of Shaveh (that is, the King's Valley), after his return from the defeat of Chedorlaomer and the kings who were with him. Then Melchizedek king of Salem brought out bread and wine; he was the priest of God Most High. And he blessed him and said: "Blessed be Abram of God Most High, Possessor of heaven and earth; and blessed be God Most High, Who has delivered your enemies into your hand." And he gave him a tithe of all (Genesis 14:17-20 NKJV).

The lofty man whom Abram met when he was returning from the slaughter of the kings was a King and Priest of God Most High. This heavenly man carried bread and wine, which he offered to the stunned Abram. Abram was so impressed with this awesome man that he gave Him a tenth of all. The man seemed to know everything about Abram. He even told Abram why he had won the fight against such a mighty foreign army with only 318 men who were trained in his own house. Melchizedek told Abram that the God of Heaven and earth had sent his warring angels ahead of Abram into the battlefield. By the time Abram got to the camp of his enemies, their fate had already been delivered into his hands.

THE TITHE OF ABRAHAM

And blessed be God Most High, who has defeated your enemies for you." Then Abram gave Melchizedek a tenth of all the goods he had recovered (Genesis 14:20).

Abram was so moved by this man's spiritual stature and divine-royalty that Abram did something that was customary to the people of the ancient world. His response to Melchizedek was inspired by his personal sense of awe and by the prevailing culture and protocol of hosting a king. The men of the ancient world did not go to a king without presenting a gift or royal endowment. As far as Abram was concerned, Melchizedek was the greatest and most glorious King he had ever met.

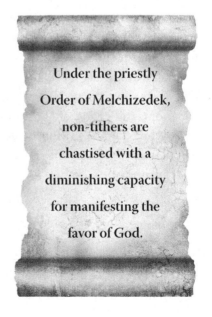

Out of his deep sense of honor and personal awe, Abram, the father of the faithful, gave his first tithe into the priestly Order of Melchizedek thereby establishing a prophetic pattern of tithing for all of his spiritual descendants. Abram did not tithe into Melchizedek because he thought Melchizedek could use the money. Abram knew that there was nothing that he owned that could pay for the services of such a great King. Abram's motivation and reason for tithing are sadly missing in much of today's tithing patterns. This is why it's

Under the priestly Order of Melchizedek, non-tithers are chastised with a diminishing capacity for manifesting the favor of God.

imperative that we rediscover the spiritual ramifications of belonging to the priestly Order of Melchizedek.

Abram had visited and entertained many other kings before he met Melchizedek the king-priest in the valley of Shaveh, but Abram knew during his encounter that this Melchizedek was the loftiest king he had ever met. *I truly believe that Abram sensed that he was standing in the presence of God when he had a face-to-face encounter with Melchizedek.* Out of a heart filled with worship, honor, and inspiration, Abram gave his endowment of tithes to the Order of Melchizedek. He gave Melchizedek the king-priest tithes of honor. The Church must rediscover this prophetic pattern of tithing that was set by our father Abraham.

Abraham gave tithes to a King and not just to a priest. Since every king has a kingdom it is safe to assume that *Abraham's tithes were used to support a "Kingdom."* Everything that is given to a king becomes part of his royal estate. This means then that the Abrahamic tithing model"is a Kingdom driven and Kingdom minded tithing model. This is why it is the highest form and level of tithing mentioned in the scriptures. Under the Levitical priesthood, tithes were given to support the priesthood (the clergy) whereas under the Order of Melchizedek, tithes are given to support and sustain the advancement of God's Kingdom on earth. Since Abraham's tithes were employed to advance a "Kingdom" it is quite redundant for us to say that there is no requirement for tithing in the New Testament. Consider this, New Testament living has a greater emphasis on advancing God's Kingdom on earth, than under the Old Testament. Since New Testament living revolves around advancing the Kingdom, the giving of "tithes of honor" will continue until the Kingdom is established. Dr Myles Munroe describes tithes as a form of "Kingdom tax" that Kingdom citizens give into the Kingdom treasury to show their allegiance with the Kingdom.

SEVEN REASONS TO GIVE TO A KING

Dr. Myles Munroe, in his best-selling book *Kingdom Principles*, lists seven reasons why citizens of a kingdom give to a reigning king. I have taken the liberty to quote him verbatim so we can gain a greater understanding as to why and how Abraham tithed into Melchizedek. Please remember that Melchizedek was both the King of Jerusalem, as well as the Priest of God Most High.

1. *Royal protocol requires that a gift must be presented when visiting a king.* This is why the queen of Sheba brought such lavish gifts to King Solomon even though he was richer than she was. It was royal protocol. He would have done the same had he visited her.

2. *The gift must be fitting for the king.* Worse than approaching a king with no gift is to bring a gift unworthy of him. An inappropriate or inadequate gift amounts to an insult to the king. It shows that the giver does not properly respect the king or his authority.

3. *The gift reveals our value or "worth-ship" of the king.* The quality of what we offer the king and the attitude with which we offer it reveal much more than our words do of the value or worthiness we attach to him.

4. *Worship demands a gift and giving is worship.* "Worth-ship" is where we get "worship." To worship the king means to ascribe worth or worthiness to Him. And as we have already seen, that always involves bringing him a gift. There is no genuine worship without gift-giving. But giving is itself an act of worship and worship is always fitting for the king. The Magi who saw His star in the east understood this, which is why they brought gifts when they came to find Him.

5. *Giving to a king attracts his favor.* Kings are attracted to people who give with a willing and grateful spirit. Like anyone else, a king likes to know he is loved and appreciated. The King of Heaven is the same way. The Giver is attracted to the giver and extends His favor. Gifts open doors to blessings, opportunities and prosperity.

6. *Giving to a king acknowledges his ownership of everything.* Remember, kings are lords; they own everything in their

domain. So giving to a king is simply returning to him what is already his. That's why in the Kingdom of Heaven we are always stewards and never owners.

7. ***Giving to a king is thanksgiving.*** One of the best ways to express gratitude is with a gift. Gratitude expressed is in itself a gift.[1]

Before Melchizedek left the scene, he blessed Abram, who was the custodian of the covenant of promise. The fact that this king-priest blessed Abram proves that he was far more powerful and loftier than Abram. Melchizedek also gave Abram the supernatural bread and wine that he had brought for him from His eternal priestly Order. Bread and wine are the eternal emblems of the priestly Order of Melchizedek. We have discussed the spiritual implications of these spiritual emblems in a previous chapter.

LIFE APPLICATION SECTION

MEMORY VERSES

This Melchizedek was king of the city of Salem and also a priest of God Most High. When Abraham was returning home after winning a great battle against the kings, Melchizedek met him and blessed him. Then Abraham took a tenth of all he had captured in battle and gave it to Melchizedek. The name Melchizedek means "king of justice," and king of Salem means "king of peace" (Hebrews 7:1-2).

REFLECTIONS

What are the main differences between the Malachi tithing model and the Abrahamic tithing model?

Explain the significance of the covenantal bread and wine that Melchizedek gave to Abram?

How does knowing the Abrahamic tithing model affect your disposition towards tithing?

How can you employ the power of tithing to unleash prosperity in your business?

JOURNAL YOUR PERSONAL NOTES ON THIS CHAPTER

CHAPTER ELEVEN

𝕿𝖍𝖊 𝕲𝖔𝖘𝖕𝖊𝖑 𝖔𝖋 𝖙𝖍𝖊 𝕶𝖎𝖓𝖌𝖉𝖔𝖒

PLEASE REMEMBER THIS IMPORTANT FACT: *no one can operate in and under the Order of Melchizedek without understanding the message of the Kingdom of God.* Transporting the gospel of the Kingdom of God is the primary mandate of those who have a ministry or business patterned after the Order of Melchizedek. If we agree that Jesus Christ is our High Priest after the Order of Melchizedek, then we need to emulate His example. Jesus Christ spoke more about the Kingdom of God than any other prophet or priest before Him.

The Order of Melchizedek is the eternal priestly agency which represents Kingdom citizens here on earth. This priestly agency has both covenantal and custodial rights to advance and spread the gospel of the Kingdom God on planet Earth. The members of the Order of Melchizedek have a divine mandate to superimpose the culture and values of the Kingdom of God over every industry of human endeavor. They have ambassadorial assignments to transform the kingdoms of this world (systems) into the Kingdoms of God and of His Christ.

Here is what legendary teacher and author T. Austin Sparks has to say about the Kingdom:

> And the Church is not an end in itself. We find in "Revelation" the end—the city is in its place of administration, and it is the

nations that are deriving the benefit. The light of the nations, the leaves for the health of the nations, the water for the life of the nations, issue from that city. The Church, then, is to be so constituted as to be God's instrument of administration and manifestation of His Kingdom.[1]

In this chapter your attention will be drawn to the greatest message that Jesus Christ ever preached—the gospel of the Kingdom. A clear-cut understanding of the gospel of the Kingdom will deliver us from being trapped in a Levitical or local church mindset. We will begin to see farther than the four walls of the church. Our vision of what is truly possible under this royal priesthood of Jesus Christ will greatly refresh us.

> *Jesus traveled throughout the region of Galilee, teaching in the synagogues and announcing the Good News about the Kingdom. And he healed every kind of disease and illness* (Matthew 4:23).

The greatest discovery in life is the discovery of purpose. The genesis of God's purpose for creating the human race can be found in the first two chapters of Genesis. The Genesis account underscores God's inherent motivation for creating a physical planet called Earth and creating spirit-children that He collectively called "Adam." God then created physical bodies made of dirt to house these spirit-beings so that they could become legal residents and guardians of the visible world. From the beginning, our physical world (earth) was designed to be a spiritual colony of the Kingdom of heaven.

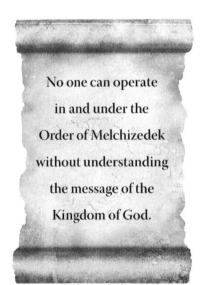

No one can operate in and under the Order of Melchizedek without understanding the message of the Kingdom of God.

Then God said, "Let Us make man in Our image, according to Our likeness; let them have dominion over the fish of the sea, over the birds of the air, and over the cattle, over all the earth and over every creeping thing that creeps on the earth." So God created man in His own image; in the image of God He created him; male and female He created them. Then God blessed them, and God said to them, "Be fruitful and multiply; fill the earth and subdue it; have dominion over the fish of the sea, over the birds of the air, and over every living thing that moves on the earth" (Genesis 1:26-28 NKJV).

The greatest discovery in life is the discovery of purpose.

PURPOSE AND ORIGINS

The Genesis passage above describes the origins of the species called humankind and also exposes the divine intent for the creation of a physical planet. Contrary to the teaching of modern science, the presence of humankind on planet Earth has nothing to with Darwin's hypothesis of evolution. Darwin's hypothesis is unscientific and has now been largely discredited by many credible scientists. Ben Stein, in his famed movie *Expelled: No Intelligence Allowed*, exposes the glaring flaws behind Darwin's hypothesis of evolution and reveals the diabolical conspiracy to silence scientists and educators who strongly disagree with Darwin's outdated and unscientific hypothesis by liberal scholars with a Godless agenda.

According to Darwin's theory of evolution, all living creatures on earth came from a random explosion of matter millions of years ago. Since this supposed random explosion of matter, humankind has evolved from an amoeba to the complex creature that we are now. Unfortunately for Darwin, whose hypothesis of evolution was born out of a desire to disavow the existence of a creator in the affairs of men, the discovery of the human genome and its vast scientific complexity has released all of the steam out of this nonsensical and unscientific hypothesis. The theory of evolution is taught in public schools as a matter of political expediency rather than as a matter of science.

Any serious student of bio-genetics, genetic engineering, or genetic mutation will quickly tell you how impossible it is for the vastly complex genetic codes and instructions that are hidden in every strand of DNA to have simply come together in perfect symmetry through a mere random explosion of matter. Scientists who have studied genetic mutation are the first ones to admit how difficult it would be for the DNA of a crocodile to mutate into the highly complex DNA found in the human genome. In 6,000 years of recorded human history we have yet to see a dog or a cat that has mutated into a highly sophisticated human being. *The truth of the matter is that humankind is a product of a purpose-driven Creator.*

This leads us to a most sobering question, *Why would the devil work so tirelessly to confuse the origins of the species called humankind?* The answer is staggeringly simple. The *purpose* of a thing is intricately connected to its *source.* The source is the manufacturer or creator of the product. This means that when we discover the manufacturer or the creator of a thing, we have discovered the source for answers relating to the purpose of the product. The purpose of a thing is always found in the mind or in the original intent of its manufacturer. When we discover the original thought in the mind of the manufacturer which inspired the creation of the product, we have discovered the inherent nature and purpose of the product. People can never truly discover their true purpose while they are still confused about their true origins.

The Manufacturer's (God) original intent for the human race is revealed in Genesis 1:26-28. *Humankind was created by God to be an ambassadorial representative of God's invisible Kingdom on the visible planet, Earth.* Said simply, we were created to rule over the world of matter on behalf of the Kingdom of God. Our purpose on earth is intricately tied to fulfilling our prophetic assignment as official representatives of the Kingdom of God. Anything short of fulfilling our ambassadorial assignment of manifesting the Kingdom of God here on earth showcases the spiritual malfunctioning of the God-product called humankind. We were created to manifest God's invisible spiritual Kingdom here on earth.

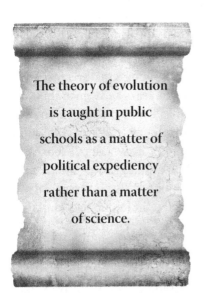

The theory of evolution is taught in public schools as a matter of political expediency rather than a matter of science.

DEFINING THE KINGDOM

But if I am casting out demons by the Spirit of God, then the Kingdom of God has arrived among you (Matthew 12:28).

In our endeavor to transform the kingdoms (systems) of this world into the Kingdoms of God and of His Christ, we must first have a clear-cut definition of the term *Kingdom*. Dr. Myles Munroe gives us a definitive meaning of this very powerful word:

> A kingdom is…The governing influence of a king over his territory, impacting it with his personal will, purpose, and intent, producing a culture, values, morals, and lifestyle that reflect the king's desires and nature for his citizens."[2]

From this definition we can quickly see what God wants to do with the seven mountains or kingdoms of Babylon on which the great whore, Babylon the Great, sits. God wants His covenant people to take the governing influence of His Kingdom and superimpose it over the spiritual and natural activities of the seven mountains of Babylon. God desires to superimpose His personal will, purpose, and intent, upon the mountains of finance, business, law, media, sports/celebration, family, and church. God wants the vehicle of human government to line up with His Kingdom agenda.

GOD'S KINGDOM: OUR INHERITANCE

Then the King will say to those on his right, "Come, you who are blessed by my Father, inherit the Kingdom prepared for you from the creation of the world" (Matthew 25:34).

We must not forget that all of God's children who are born of the Spirit have been called to inherit the Kingdom which was prepared for us from before the creation of the world! This is why we must ask God to deliver us from religion—religion is the biggest obstacle to experiencing the life of the Kingdom. More wars have been fought over religion than for political and economic reasons combined.

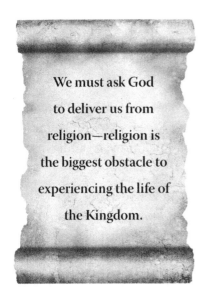

We must ask God to deliver us from religion—religion is the biggest obstacle to experiencing the life of the Kingdom.

HEAVEN ON EARTH

From the closure of the gates of the Garden of Eden to the opening of the pearly gates of the New Jerusalem, the divine manifesto remains the same. The colonization of the earth by superimposing heaven's spiritual climate and culture over our troubled planet is still God's first order of business. God has always desired for heaven and earth to become identical in culture, spiritual atmosphere, and lifestyle. The fall of Adam and Eve, the first kingdom ambassadors, was a temporary interruption in the unchangeable plan of God.

When the disciples came to Jesus and asked Him to teach them how to pray, Jesus responded in a very unreligious manner. The disciples came to Him with a religious question, but He responded by teaching them the model for governmental prayer that revolves around an ancient divine political agenda, which leads all the way back to the Garden of Eden.

Why did Jesus Christ give a political answer instead of a religious answer to a question about prayer? The answer to the question is simple but deeply profound in its spiritual ramifications. Jesus Christ did not give His disciples a religious answer because Adam and Eve did not lose a religion when they fell into sin—they lost a Kingdom. They lost the ability to superimpose the government of God's invisible Kingdom over the physical planet, Earth. They also lost their positions of headship authority over the planet. Jesus knew that all the religious praying in the world would not bring God's Kingdom Order to our troubled world unless our praying revolves around restoring the influence of the Kingdom of God over the earth realm.

So He said to them, "When you pray, say: Our Father in heaven, hallowed be Your name. Your kingdom come. Your will be done on earth as it is in heaven. Give us day by day our daily bread. And forgive us our sins, for we also forgive everyone who is indebted to us. And do not lead us into temptation, but deliver us from the evil one" (Luke 11:2-4 NKJV).

The Lord Jesus Christ is the Chief Apostle of our faith. He is the first person in the New Testament who had a bona-fide apostolic ministry. He later commissioned a second company of emerging apostles in the form of His twelve disciples. From simply observing Christ's ministry, we can conclude that true apostles are more concerned about *how* people pray than *when* they pray! On several occasions Jesus was quick to point out what was wrong with the methods of prayer that many of the Pharisees and Sadducees were employing.

Once His disciples gave Him an opportunity to teach them a more excellent way of praying, Jesus pointed out that apostolic praying is built on an ancient spiritual manifesto of the Kingdom of God born in the heart of God. This divine manifesto revolves around the restoration of a lost Kingdom and involves the manifestation of that Kingdom here on earth. *Jesus made it very clear that the engines of true apostolic praying are fueled by a driving passion to see God's will done here on earth as it is in heaven!*

Apostolic praying does not end with a feeling of goose bumps but in the establishment of the Kingdom of God on earth. God wants us to pray in such a way that the Spirit-driven culture of the Kingdom of God will begin to manifest itself here on earth. We need to find this prevailing position in prayer before we start challenging demonic principalities that are ruling and controlling the destiny of nations from the seven mountains. (See Revelation 17:9.)

A CLASH OF DEITIES

The serpent was the shrewdest of all the wild animals the LORD God had made. One day he asked the woman, "Did God really say you must not eat the fruit from any of the trees in the garden?"

"Of course we may eat fruit from the trees in the garden," the woman replied. "It's only the fruit from the tree in the middle of the garden that we are not allowed to eat. God said, 'You must not eat it or even touch it; if you do, you will die.'"

"You won't die!" the serpent replied to the woman. "God knows that your eyes will be opened as soon as you eat it, and you will be like God, knowing both good and evil" (Genesis 3:1-5).

The greatest part of the tragedy of the fall of Adam and Eve is not simply that they disobeyed God and ate fruit from the forbidden tree. The greatest part of this tragedy is that in disobeying God they (Adam and Eve) unconsciously rejected God and placed their allegiance in a demon-god, Satan. They discovered that their act of treason had superimposed the leadership of Sin and a fallen angel over their hearts and minds. They discovered with terror that by their one act of rebellion they had switched citizenry from being regent kings over God's Kingdom here on earth to being mere pawn subjects of the kingdom of darkness. Adam and Eve were also expelled from the Garden of Eden, which was where the culture and atmosphere of the Kingdom of Heaven was manifesting itself on earth.

Then Elijah stood in front of them and said, "How much longer will you waver, hobbling between two opinions? If the LORD is God, follow him! But if Baal is God, then follow him!" But the people were completely silent (1 Kings 18:21).

From the moment that Adam and Eve switched allegiances through their act of disobedience, they discovered that the kingdom of darkness is hostile and diametrically opposed to everything the Kingdom of Heaven stands for. They discovered that these demonic entities were fighting tenaciously to stop the advancement of God's Kingdom in all areas of human endeavor.

Ever since the fall of Adam and Eve, spiritual warfare has been the ongoing clash between God and all the demonic entities that fell with Lucifer. This means that once we start talking about the Kingdom of God, we are challenging every demonic entity that is opposed to the establishment of Christ's Kingdom.

KINGDOM PRAYING VERSUS RELIGIOUS PRAYING

And when you pray, do not be like the hypocrites, for they love to pray standing in the synagogues and on the street corners to be seen by men. I tell you the truth, they have received their reward in full. But when you pray, go into your room, close the door and pray to your Father, who is unseen. Then your Father, who sees what is done in secret, will reward you. And when you pray, do not keep on babbling like pagans, for they think they will be heard because of their many words (Matthew 6:5-7 NIV).

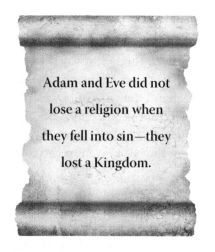

Adam and Eve did not lose a religion when they fell into sin—they lost a Kingdom.

There is one ritual shared by all religions—prayer (or meditation). Perhaps nothing exposes the universal human need for dominion and self-fulfillment like the desire to pray to a deity. In the art of prayer there is the acknowledgement of a supreme being who operates outside the limitations of our physical world. Since religion is man's failed attempt to communicate with and appease the invisible God, much of the praying in all religions seems to follow suit.

Much of the religious praying tends to be very impersonal, ritualistic, and misguided. The Pharisees for instance, made a spectacle of praying. They used prayer to draw the attention of the masses to their own perceived sense of importance. They prided themselves in dazzling the bystanders with many flattering words in prayer. In their eyes, prayer leveraged their celebrity status and advanced their political agenda among the devout populace. It is no wonder that there is very little power in much of today's religious praying.

> *And they were all amazed, insomuch that they questioned among themselves, saying, What thing is this? what new doctrine is this? for with authority commandeth he even the unclean spirits, and they do obey him* (Mark 1:27 KJV).

When Jesus Christ arrived on the scene, the citizenry had endured the powerless praying of the Pharisees and Sadducees for many years. They had come to associate praying with powerlessness. You can imagine the shock of utter relief and bedazzlement that went through the devout populace when they experienced firsthand the miraculous explosion of *Kingdom-driven prayer*.

Each time this young Jewish rabbi (Jesus) prayed, there was an immediate and noticeable answer by the Divine to His power-packed prayers.

Both the politically-driven Pharisees and the devout populace knew that they were experiencing a totally new kind of praying. They were experiencing firsthand the aura of power-packed praying. They were being introduced to a new order of praying! Nothing would ever be as it was. Christ's new order of praying had a profound effect on His own disciples who asked Him to teach them how to pray after this new order.

And he said unto them, When ye pray, say, Our Father which art in heaven, Hallowed be thy name. Thy kingdom come. Thy will be done, as in heaven, so in earth (Luke 11:2 KJV).

Jesus responded to His disciples by giving them the mechanics and key ingredients of all Kingdom-driven praying. Christ told His apprentice apostles that Kingdom-driven praying starts with Kingdom citizens acknowledging their sonship relationship with their heavenly Father. *Kingdom praying is not the spiritual territory of mere church members; it is the portion that the Father has bequeathed to the sons and daughters of the Kingdom who are advancing His Kingdom here on earth.*

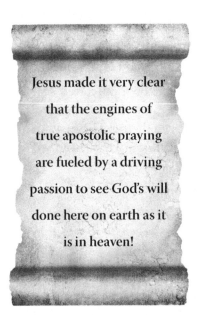

Jesus made it very clear that the engines of true apostolic praying are fueled by a driving passion to see God's will done here on earth as it is in heaven!

Without a doubt, there are many born-again believers who are heaven-bound. But being born-again does not necessarily equate to being a child of the Kingdom. Most born-again believers are trapped in a church mindset; they have very little interest in anything that is happening outside the confines of their local congregation. This is why many of them would never attend a Kingdom gathering which is not hosted by their church. Children of the Kingdom, on the other hand, have sold their souls to the task of advancing the Kingdom of God into every sphere of human endeavor. These are the people

Jesus Christ was addressing when He said, "And when ye pray...!"

I will not discuss the full scope of Kingdom-driven praying in this writing. To get the full scope on Kingdom-driven praying, please read my book, *The LORD'S PRAYER: Spiritual Technology for Manifesting the Kingdom of God on Earth*. But I do want to add another key element of Kingdom-driven praying that distinguishes it from religious praying. Kingdom-driven praying is centered on superimposing the will and culture of God and core-values of the Kingdom of heaven, onto the earth. Kingdom-driven praying causes the power and influence of the Kingdom of God to come into the visible

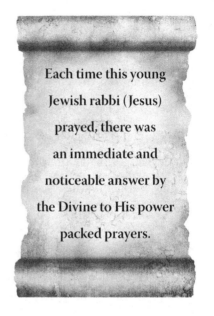

Each time this young Jewish rabbi (Jesus) prayed, there was an immediate and noticeable answer by the Divine to His power packed prayers.

realm. Kingdom-driven praying is therefore the exclusive territory of those who are of the Order of Melchizedek. This is why I said at the beginning of this chapter that it is impossible to operate in and under the Order of Melchizedek without understanding the message of the Kingdom as Christ preached it.

DREAMS OF A PARADISE LOST

At that moment their eyes were opened, and they suddenly felt shame at their nakedness. So they sewed fig leaves together to cover themselves. When the cool evening breezes were blowing, the man and his wife heard the LORD God walking about in the garden. So they hid from the LORD God among the trees. So the LORD God banished them from the Garden of Eden, and he sent Adam out to cultivate the ground from which he had been made. After sending them out, the LORD God stationed mighty cherubim to the east of the Garden of Eden. And he placed a flaming sword that flashed back and forth to guard the way to the tree of life (Genesis 3:7-8,23-24).

Kingdom-driven praying causes the power and influence of the Kingdom of God to come into the visible realm.

The fall of Adam and Eve, the first regent kings on behalf of God's government over the colony called Earth, forced God to evict them from the governor's mansion. God could no longer trust them with the stewardship of Eden's paradise. They were driven out of this supernatural garden of abundance and were subjected to a life of endless toiling and sweating outside God's paradise.

Lucifer, an unemployed cherub who had been cast out of heaven, became the de facto king of this world! I believe it was during this time when the kingdoms (systems) of finance, business, law, sports, media, family, and church fell into the hands of demonic powers. This explains why God warned the first couple that if they lost their ambassadorial position over the earthly colony they would have to "toil and sweat" for all their daily needs. The devil will not allow God's people easy access to the mountains of finance, business, media, law, sports/celebration, family, and church, without intense warfare.

THE MINDSET OF THE KINGDOM

Seek the Kingdom of God above all else, and live righteously, and he will give you everything you need (Matthew 6:33).

And saying, Repent ye: for the kingdom of heaven is at hand (Matthew 3:2 KJV).

These two Scripture passages in Matthew set the tone for the kind of prevailing mindset God wants His people in the earth to have—a mindset that is set on assimilating and advancing God's will and Kingdom agenda. This prevailing Kingdom mindset is not an option for those who are serious about supporting God's eternal mandate to make the kingdoms, or systems, of this world become the kingdoms of God and His Christ. Without this mindset God can never fully use us in His eternal plan of conquest. We cannot challenge the ancient spirit called Babylon the Great that sits on the seven mountains if we do not have an unshakeable mindset to advance God's Kingdom.

THE RETURN OF THE GOVERNOR

There is so much more I want to tell you, but you can't bear it now. When the Spirit of truth comes, he will guide you into all truth. He will not speak on his own but will tell you what he has heard. He will tell you about the future (John 16:12-13).

On the day of Pentecost all the believers were meeting together in one place. Suddenly, there was a sound from heaven like the roaring of a mighty windstorm, and it filled the house where they were sitting. Then, what looked like flames or tongues of fire appeared and settled on each of them. And everyone present was filled with the Holy Spirit and began speaking in other languages, as the Holy Spirit gave them this ability (Acts 2:1-4).

There was more information about the Kingdom of God that Jesus wanted to impart to His apprentice apostles, but He was held back by their limited spiritual capacity to understand the message of the Kingdom. The disciples' natural minds couldn't comprehend in fullness matters related to the Kingdom of God because such things are spiritually discerned. To answer this obvious dilemma, Jesus Christ made a startling announcement. He told His disciples that when He got back to Heaven, He was going to send the Holy Spirit to our sinful planet. The Holy Spirit would become the primary ambassador and governor general of the Kingdom of Heaven here on earth.

During the era of the monarchs, whenever a kingdom established a colony in a distant land, the crown king or queen would send out an official representative of the kingdom to the new colony. This high ranking official was usually called the royal governor or governor general. The presence of the royal governor in the new colony signified that the kingdom of the monarch he represented had also arrived in an official capacity in the new colony.

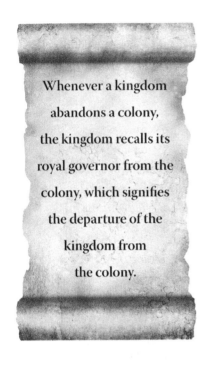

Whenever a kingdom abandons a colony, the kingdom recalls its royal governor from the colony, which signifies the departure of the kingdom from the colony.

Whenever a kingdom abandons a colony, the kingdom recalls its royal governor from the colony, which signifies the departure of the kingdom from the colony. When Adam and Eve sinned and committed high treason against the Kingdom of Heaven, Heaven recalled its Royal Governor (the Holy Spirit) from our sin-ravaged planet.

Over 4,000 years later, the Royal Governor of the Kingdom of Heaven returned to our troubled planet in a very spectacular way—on the day of Pentecost. Even though the Holy Spirit had manifested Himself in the earthly realm in spurts throughout the Old Testament, the day of Pentecost marked a new era in God's plan of restoration and conquest. The day of Pentecost marked the return of the Royal Governor on a permanent basis. The return of the Royal Governor signified the return of the Kingdom and its agenda in full force. This is why it is impossible for us to fail to subdue the human systems of finance, business, law, media, sports/celebration, family, and church if we are led by the Holy Spirit. The Holy Spirit has never failed to accomplish any Kingdom assignment that God has ever placed in His care.

THE MESSAGE OF THE KINGDOM

Then the seventh angel blew his trumpet, and there were loud voices shouting in heaven: "The world has now become the Kingdom of our Lord and of his Christ, and he will reign forever and ever" (Revelation 11:15).

Perhaps no other scriptural passage captures the spirit of the gospel of the Kingdom like this powerful passage from the book of Revelation. In a nutshell, the message of the Kingdom is wrapped up in this understanding: *God is committed to transforming the kingdoms of this world into the Kingdom of God and His Christ.* The good news is that God has not completely forsaken our sin-troubled planet. On the contrary, God so loved the world that He gave His only begotten Son that whosoever believes in Him should not perish. (See John 3:16.) Through the sacrificial offering of His dear Son, God plans to invade Earth with His peace, righteousness, joy, and prosperity. The Kingdom that Adam and Eve lost through rebellion is returning to us in its full glory.

THE PRICELESS NATURE OF THE KINGDOM

The Kingdom of Heaven is like a treasure that a man discovered hidden in a field. In his excitement, he hid it again and sold everything he owned to get enough money to buy the field (Matthew 13:44).

The greatest asset that we can ever own and invest our lives into is the Kingdom of heaven. When Adam and Eve sinned, they did not lose a religion; they lost a Kingdom. This is why man's greatest and deepest need is to rediscover the Kingdom. In rediscovering the Kingdom, most answers people seek concerning their inherent purpose for living will be answered. Our purpose for living and our ability to live a fulfilling life is intricately connected to rediscovering our place in the Kingdom of God. This fact by itself makes the Kingdom a priceless treasure indeed.

In a nutshell, the message of the Kingdom is wrapped up in this understanding: God is committed to transforming the kingdoms of this world into the Kingdom of God and His Christ.

It is very important for us to be awed and captivated by the incredible value of the Kingdom of God before attempting to climb and subdue the seven mountains of Babylon. If we are not captivated by the awesome beauty of taking our place in God's Kingdom, we will be tempted to sell out to the king of Sodom—the world system. (See Genesis 14:21.)

I have seen many great men and women of God become corrupted after they achieved a measurable level of success and fame in any of the seven mountains of Babylon. (See Revelation 17:9.) Some fell into sexual sin, while others were overtaken with greed. Some became drunk with power. Why does this happen often among God's covenant people? The answer is simple: *they were not totally sold out to the Kingdom of Heaven.* Somewhere in their hearts they believed that there were some things in this world more precious than inheriting the Kingdom. In reality, nothing is farther from the truth. This is why I believe that church leaders must teach their people how to operate in and under the Order of Melchizedek.

ADVANCING THE KINGDOM

In Chapter One, I made a statement that may have upset those who believe that the Kingdom can be advanced through a political process. I will quickly explain how the Kingdom is advanced by Kingdom citizens who are politicians without subjecting God's higher government to a man-driven political process. Joseph and Daniel are perfect examples of how the Kingdom of God is advanced in the corridors of human government. Both men became great movers and shakers on behalf of the Kingdom in the political structures that they were part of through public demonstrations of the power of the Kingdom of God. I suggest that you prayerfully read Daniel chapter two.

After Daniel finished reconstructing and interpreting the dream that God had given King Nebuchadnezzar, the Babylonian king was so overwhelmed by this public demonstration of the power of God that he got off his throne and bowed before Daniel! I can almost hear the gasp of surprise that must have been voiced by King Nebuchadnezzar's shocked cabinet. They could hardly believe what they were seeing. The king of the greatest earthly kingdom of its era had just bowed before an ambassador of the Kingdom of God. After this public demonstration of power, King Nebuchadnezzar made Daniel the principal ruler of the whole of Babylon! He even promoted other Kingdom citizens (Shadrach, Meshach, and Abednego) to key positions of leadership within the Babylonian empire! My dear friend this is how the Kingdom of God is advanced. It has never been advanced through a political process.

But this kind of public demonstration of the power of the Kingdom of God that Joseph and Daniel exhibited in the corridors of human government has been lost on many of today's Kingdom citizens. The primary reason for this is the proliferation of the user friendly gospel in today's church (especially in the American church). This user friendly gospel is designed to please men instead of God. This gospel promises gullible saints covenant blessings without covenant obedience. This type of gospel is very toxic to the advancement of the Kingdom because the Kingdom can only be advanced effectively through the lives of Kingdom citizens who have crucified self and are sold out to Christ. *God will never entrust the awesome power of His Kingdom to half-hearted, in-love-with-the-world saints.* The spiritual consequences of this user friendly gospel, especially over the American church, will plague us for many years to come. This is why God is calling for a time of great persecution and suffering in the United States, to purify the section of the Church that has become toxic to Kingdom advancement.

Joseph and Daniel are perfect examples of how the Kingdom of God is advanced in the corridors of human government!

LIFE APPLICATION SECTION

MEMORY VERSES

Then God said, "Let Us make man in Our image, according to Our likeness; let them have dominion over the fish of the sea, over the birds of the air, and over the cattle, over all the earth and over every creeping thing that creeps on the earth." So God created man in His own image; in the image of God He created him; male and female He created them. Then God blessed them, and God said to them, "Be fruitful and multiply; fill the earth and subdue it; have dominion over the fish of the sea, over the birds of the air, and over every living thing that moves on the earth" (Genesis 1:26-28 NKJV).

REFLECTIONS

What was Jesus Christ's most important message?

_____

_____

_____

_____

_____

THE GOSPEL OF THE KINGDOM

Why did God create man, and what Kingdom mandate did God place
on humankind?

_____

_____

_____

_____

_____

_____

How can you advance the Kingdom of God in the Marketplace?

_____

_____

_____

_____

_____

_____

JOURNAL YOUR PERSONAL NOTES ON THIS CHAPTER

CHAPTER TWELVE

The Kingdom in the Marketplace

U NLIKE THE LEVITICAL PRIESTLY ORDER which was completely one dimensional, Christ's Order of Melchizedek priesthood is both a marketplace *and* priestly ministry. This is because the High Priest of this eternal priestly order is first and foremost a King, who does priestly work. As a King, Jesus Christ's influence extends beyond the boundaries of the temple, into every corner of the marketplace. Every king owns everything that is within his kingdom. As a King-Priest, Jesus Christ has an ongoing dual influence over both the services of the temple and the activities of the marketplace.

DEFINING THE MARKETPLACE

Since we will be discussing in great detail how the Order of Melchizedek priesthood impacts the ambassadorial assignments of Kingdom citizens in the marketplace, I believe that it would be prudent to give clear definition to the term "marketplace." I know that in recent years the global Church has begun to awaken to its Kingdom assignment to the marketplace. As such, the term marketplace is being thrown around quite flippantly. As is often the case, much has been lost in translation by our failure to clearly understand what was on the mind of God, when He coined the word *marketplace.*

So here is the million dollar question: What is the meaning of the term "marketplace" in light of the holy Scriptures? Definition: *The marketplace involves every activity under the sun which transpires outside the temple of God (local church).* This just about covers 90 percent of most of our daily activities. This means that people spend more time in the marketplace than they do in the church. This is why the devil has no qualms about people attending church regularly if they do not know how to live in victory in the marketplace.

The high priest under the Levitical priesthood and his staff of priests were not expected to engage in any form of secular business activity outside the normal activities of servicing the spiritual needs of the people of Israel. Moses made it clear that God did not want the Levites to be involved in any form of secular business activity. God wanted them to focus their energy on servicing the spiritual needs of the people of Israel and those of the temple of God. To ensure that this was the case, God gave the tithes of the eleven tribes of Israel to the tribe of Levi as an everlasting inheritance.

> *As for the tribe of Levi, your relatives, I will compensate them for their service in the Tabernacle. Instead of an allotment of land, I will give them the tithes from the entire land of Israel* (Numbers 18:21).

Understanding Christ's Order of Melchizedek priesthood will not only revolutionize how the Church exacts the tithe, but it will also introduce the global Church to many creative ways of wealth creation outside the normal practice of giving tithes and offerings. Unlike the Levitical priestly order, the priesthood (members of the clergy) under the priestly Order of Melchizedek do not have to depend entirely on the tithes and offerings of the people in the church to sustain the work of the ministry. Under the Order of Melchizedek, the tithes and offerings of the people are just one of the many streams of income that God has made available to the New Testament Church.

Under the priestly Order of Melchizedek, senior pastors or founding apostles of churches can be just as involved in business as they are in ministering to the spiritual needs of the people in their church. Under this eternal priestly order, spiritual leaders can lead a church while managing a profitable business in the marketplace. This dual involvement in ecclesiastical and marketplace ministry increases the scope and spiritual reach of the ministries of senior leaders under the Order of Melchizedek.

Under the Order of Melchizedek, senior pastors or apostolic founders of churches are not limited to reaching only the people who step inside the four walls of the church. The majority of lost souls are found in the marketplace. The apostle Paul is a classic example of this powerful synergy of marketplace and priestly ministry. The apostle Paul reached far more people with the gospel because his ministry was never limited to the people who stepped inside the four walls of the church. Many of Paul's converts came from his business dealings in the marketplace.

> *Then Paul left Athens and went to Corinth. There he became acquainted with a Jew named Aquila, born in Pontus, who had recently arrived from Italy with his wife, Priscilla. They had left Italy when Claudius Caesar deported all Jews from Rome. Paul lived and worked with them, for they were tentmakers just as he was. Each Sabbath found Paul at the synagogue, trying to convince the Jews and Greeks alike* (Acts 18:1-4).

Unfortunately many pastors in the Body of Christ are not aware that New Testament ministry is supposed to function after the Order of Melchizedek, so they are leading their churches under an Old Testament Levitical priestly mindset. I know this because many pastors are obsessed with tithes and offerings as the only method for raising money to fund the vision of their church. Many pastors who are trapped in this Levitical mindset stress themselves into a panic whenever they see that the tithes and offerings of the church are running low. This Levitical mindset has robbed many of these able pastors of entrepreneurial endeavors that could have effectively financed their vision in the Kingdom of God.

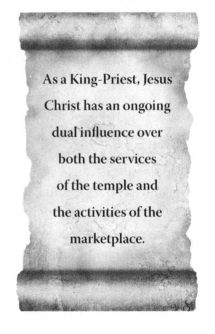

As a King-Priest, Jesus Christ has an ongoing dual influence over both the services of the temple and the activities of the marketplace.

The following quote (also cited in Chapter Seven but worth repeating) underscores just how widespread and deeply rooted this Levitical mindset really is in many of the leaders in the Body of Christ.

I was excited to attend my first pastoral roundtable, but that excitement turned quickly to frustration. After the laughs sub-sided, one pastor said, "You do not make money young man; you raise money. You have to get before your church and challenge them to give more. Teach your church to give." "Amen," the others responded.

They went on to share with me fifty ways to handle an offering. I learned how to take an offering, receive an offering, and pull an offering. I have heard these methods echoed throughout the last twenty years.

Thus, everything I've learned from the church and in formal training about wealth-building can be summed up in two familiar words: Tithes and Offerings. That was the extent of the wealth knowledge I learned for many years.[1]

I can empathize with the author's frustration at the lack of creativity in the area of wealth creation in many of the senior leaders of the global Church. My main objective for including this chapter on Kingdom-minded marketplace min-istry is to confer spiritual honor and add credibility to the Kingdom assignments of brothers and sisters in Christ who have a primary call to the marketplace.

The most tragic side effect of having senior leaders in the global Church who are trapped in a Levitical mindset is simply that there is very little spiri-tual honor and credibility placed on the lives of believers who are laboring for Christ in the marketplace. I was saved and raised in a church that was led by a pastor who believed this way. I was an active member of the church's youth ministry, and also worked for an accounting firm at the time. This pastor con-stantly referred to himself and those full-time staff at his church as being in "full-time ministry." His continual use of this phrase made it quite clear that those of us who spent a majority of our time in secular employment were not as spiritual as those who were on his ministerial staff in the local church.

Since many of us in the youth group were really hungry for the Lord and wanted desperately to please Him, we started competing for who would be the first one to abandon the secular for the spiritual. We quickly developed a critical spirit against brothers and sisters who seemed to be too entrepreneurial. We accused them of being too business minded, saying that they were no longer heavenly minded. Even though God had given me a very good job at an accounting firm, I dreaded going to work. In my mind my secular employment was visible proof that I was not yet a member of the highly spiritual who were serving God in full-time ministry.

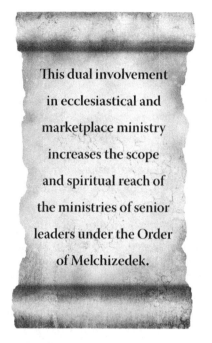

This dual involvement in ecclesiastical and marketplace ministry increases the scope and spiritual reach of the ministries of senior leaders under the Order of Melchizedek.

As you can imagine, the day I went into the so-called "full-time ministry," I was the happiest person on earth. Yet I was also broke. While I am convinced that there are some among us whose primary Kingdom assignment is to serve God in the local church, saying that Kingdom citizens who are serving God in the marketplace are not in full-time ministry is wrong. It is erroneous and devaluing to fellow Kingdom citizens whose primary prophetic assignment is to minister to the masses of lost souls who patronize the marketplace. This is why I love the Order of Melchizedek priesthood. It is the only priestly order that does not create a chasm between the marketplace and the priestly. It does not foster erroneous distinctions between the clergy and the rest of the Body of Christ. Christ's Order of Melchizedek priesthood places spiritual honor and credibility on the Kingdom assignments of believers who are anointed by God to minister in the marketplace.

Here is another fine quote from *Rich Church Poor Church*:

> *Therefore, Pharaoh should find an intelligent and wise man and put him in charge of the entire land of Egypt. Then Pharaoh should appoint supervisors over the land and let them collect one-fifth of all the crops during the seven good years. Have them gather all the food produced in the good years that are just ahead and bring it to Pharaoh's storehouses. Store it away, and guard it so there will be food in the cities. That way there will be enough to eat when the seven years of famine come to the land of Egypt. Otherwise this famine will destroy the land* (Genesis 41:33-36).

Much of the Body of Christ is dreaming when they should be receiving wisdom and knowledge to make their dreams a reality. Pharaoh recognized that Joseph manifested a type of wisdom not seen in any Egyptian. As it reads,

And Pharaoh said unto Joseph, Forasmuch as God hath shewed thee all this, there is none so discreet and wise as thou art (Genesis 41:39 KJV).

Unfortunately, in some circles the word of wisdom and knowledge has become mystical. Too often God's wisdom and knowledge has been trivialized. We've reduced the "word of knowledge" to nothing more than a televangelist pinpointing bodily defects in an audience or a word to sow a financial seed to receive some "miracle harvest."

Like Joseph, believers need to use the gift of wisdom outside the church service, and in the marketplace. The Bible teaches that God, through the gift of wisdom will give us plans, strategies, organizational designs, the ability to unravel complex equations and other resources required for building wealth. The knowledge and wisdom essential for wealth generation doesn't come through passivity – it's given by God. We are to pursue it and seek it. As we take the initiative to petition God, He supplies the resource. God's supply of knowledge and wisdom is abundant.[2]

One of the most powerful consequences of rediscovering the Order of Melchizedek lies in the kind of spiritual revolution it will bring to the global Church. When the masses of believers sitting in church pews discover that serving God in the marketplace is just as spiritual as serving God in His temple, there will be an incredible spiritual revival like we have never seen before in the marketplace. Imagine telling a medical doctor that God will show up in the operating room in the same way that He will show up during a church service. Imagine telling a sports star that God desires to manifest Himself through them in the world of sports. Imagine telling a business person that God will show up in the boardroom while he or she is negotiating a lucrative business deal. Imagine telling the masses of born-again believers who have secular vocations that they can prophesy, cast out devils, and heal the sick while they are fulfilling their Kingdom assignments in the marketplace. The possibilities are endless.

> And whatsoever ye do in word or **deed,** do all in the name of the Lord Jesus, giving thanks to God and the Father by him (Colossians 3:17 KJV).

If you can imagine these scenarios happening on a daily basis, then you are beginning to understand just how powerful and influential Christ's Order of Melchizedek priesthood really is. I truly believe that the final frontier to be subdued by God's covenant people on the earth is the marketplace. This is why the Kingdom battle lines have shifted significantly from inside the four walls of the church to the boardrooms and offices of the marketplace.

> During the reigns of those kings, the God of heaven will set up a kingdom that will never be destroyed or conquered. It will crush all these kingdoms into nothingness, and it will stand forever. That is the meaning of the rock cut from the mountain, though not by human hands, that crushed to pieces the statue of iron, bronze, clay, silver, and gold. The great God was showing the king what will happen in the future. The dream is true, and its meaning is certain (Daniel 2:44-45).

God wants to expand the reach of His glorious Kingdom from the pews of the church to the peripherals of the marketplace. The prophet Daniel tells us in his apocalyptic vision that the Stone (Christ) cut without the help of human hands in King Nebuchadnezzar's dream is the Kingdom of God and of His Christ. Daniel tells us that this Kingdom will crush and replace every other spiritual and human kingdom. Daniel tells us that Christ's Kingdom will cover and fill the whole earth—there will be no sphere of human endeavor where Christ's Kingdom influence will not be felt. But

In my mind my secular employment was visible proof that I was not yet a member of the highly spiritual who were serving God in full-time ministry.

Daniel's prophetic decree is only plausible if we agree that God's plan of conquest includes invading every sphere of human enterprise with His glory.

GOD'S KINGDOM AGENDA

Then the seventh angel sounded: And there were loud voices in heaven, saying, "The kingdoms of this world have become the kingdoms of our Lord and of His Christ, and He shall reign forever and ever!" (Revelation 11:15 NKJV)

God has a very powerful and unchanging divine agenda to bring entire nations into complete alignment with His divine Kingdom order. Making the kingdoms (systems) of this world into the Kingdoms (systems) of God and His Christ is God's primary agenda. God is determined to see the spiritual, social, and economic structures of nations line up with His divine will and purpose. The scripture from Revelation shows us that there is an angelic agency within the Kingdom of God whose primary assignment in the Kingdom is to help the children of the Kingdom shift the course of nations into divine alignment with God's prophetic purposes.

The phrase *the kingdoms of this world* in Revelation 11:15 alludes to the seven spiritual systems that control the internal and external affairs of nations. These seven spiritual systems represent the seven spiritual kingdoms that control the future and daily activities of nations through demonic Babylonian technology. These seven spiritual systems are the seven spiritual mountains of Revelation 17:9 on which the spiritual demonic kingdom (Babylon the Great) sits.

The angel who shouted with a loud voice that the kingdoms of this world have become the Kingdoms of God and of His Christ, reveals that the seven spiritual systems have been set for conquest. The spiritual and physical infrastructure which Babylon the Great has built for herself around these seven spiritual systems shall be brought into complete subjection to God's Kingdom order.

Imagine a world where the systems of finance, business, law, media, sports/celebration, family, and church have been brought into complete divine alignment with God's Kingdom agenda. For the most part, these seven systems have been in subjection to demonic powers making it quite difficult for God's people to effectively advance the Kingdom of God here on earth. This is why church leaders cannot remain ignorant as to what God has made available for the members of their church under Christ's Order of Melchizedek priesthood. There is a raging war between the kingdoms of this world and the Kingdom of God, and the frontlines of this prophetic war are found in the marketplace.

THE BATTLE GROUND

*And it came to pass, as we went to prayer, a certain damsel possessed with a spirit of divination met us, which brought her masters much gain by soothsaying: The same followed Paul and us, and cried, saying, These men are the servants of the most high God, which shew unto us the way of salvation. And this did she many days. But Paul, being grieved, turned and said to the spirit, I command thee in the name of Jesus Christ to come out of her. And he came out the same hour. And when her masters saw that the hope of their gains was gone, they caught Paul and Silas, and drew them into the **marketplace** unto the rulers, And brought them to the magistrates, saying, These men, being Jews, do exceedingly trouble our city* (Acts 16:16-20 KJV).

For the most part, the Church knows how to deal with demonic powers when these spirits are in the spirit world. But many Kingdom citizens do not know how these demonic powers tangibly manifest themselves. The answer: demonic powers always manifest themselves in the marketplace. The spiritual attacks against the Body of Christ and spiritual resistance to the Kingdom of God are not coming from the demonic world (underworld), they are coming from the marketplace. If the people who come to our churches do not know how to live in victory and dominion in the marketplace, they pose no real threat to the kingdom of darkness. Sadly, many born-again believers live defeated and marginalized lives in the marketplace.

The apostle Paul and his apostolic team were challenged by a spirit of divination in the marketplace on their way to prayer (a church activity). This particular passage from the book of Acts underscores why many church prayer meetings are so poorly attended. This passage shows us that there are demonic powers that the devil has stationed in the marketplace with diabolical assignments to intercept Kingdom citizens on their way to prayer. Many pastors will

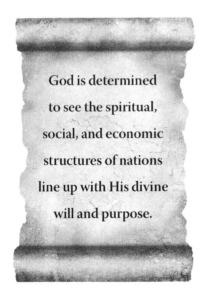

God is determined to see the spiritual, social, and economic structures of nations line up with His divine will and purpose.

tell you that the number one excuse they hear as to why their people did not show up for prayer is, "Something happened at my job; at the last minute my boss asked me to work overtime!" This is why I call the marketplace the ultimate battle ground. Thank God for the Order of Melchizedek. *This priestly and marketplace priesthood is the only hope Kingdom citizens have for living in complete victory in the marketplace.*

The Order of Melchizedek and The Mountain of Business

Before I conclude this chapter on the Kingdom of God and the marketplace, I want to answer a question that most business leaders have asked me. "Dr Myles, how can the Order of Melchizedek change the bottom line and profitability of my vehicle of commerce (business) in the twenty-first century?" I know that most successful serial entrepreneurs have climbed to the top of the "Business Mountain" by being pragmatists. I definitely understand the "roots and origins" of their question. They want to know how restoring an ancient order like the Order of Melchizedek in their 21st Century business can impact the growth and profitability of their business in a very competitive marketplace.

> *And I know that whatever God does is final. Nothing can be added to it or taken from it. God's purpose is that people should fear him. What is happening now has happened before, and what will happen in the future has happened before, because God makes the same things happen over and over again* (Ecclesiastes 3:14-15).

The above passage shows us why governing principles, patterns or blueprints that God established in the past for successful Kingdom living affect us in the present time. King Solomon tells us that God in his infinite genius requires the "past from the present" because the principles and blueprints for business and personal success that God established in Abraham eons ago do affect the business success of every Kingdom business person who call themself the seed of Abraham. Since it is the Order of Melchizedek (Genesis 14) that introduced Abraham, the world's first Kingdom businessman, to real Kingdom wealth and radically changed how he ran his business, God will require that the past is repeated in the present. When that "past" (Kingdom businessmen and women coming under the Order of Melchizedek) is repeated in the present time we will experience the same radical change in personal character as well as supernatural increase in the profitability of our businesses.

One of my favorite definitions of the Order of Melchizedek is that it is Jesus Christ putting on flesh and walking among us! This means that if you were transported through a time machine to the days of old when Jesus Christ walked the earth, you would be meeting the Divine-man who was the Savior of the world, but you would also be meeting a Man who was the embodiment of an eternal Order that has the power to save and transform the marketplace. With this understanding I will give you bullet points based on Luke 5:1-9 on how the Order of Melchizedek can transform businessmen and their vehicles of commerce in real time. These bullet points represent blueprints for transforming any struggling business into a very profitable Kingdom enterprise.

One day as Jesus was preaching on the shore of the Sea of Galilee, great crowds pressed in on him to listen to the word of God (Luke 5:1).

- The first business in creation is Kingdom Business and its primary product is the Word of God.

He noticed two empty boats at the water's edge, for the fishermen had left them and were washing their nets (Luke 5:2).

- Jesus Christ, the CEO of the number one business in creation (Kingdom business), is searching for business men and women who will allow their businesses (vehicle of commerce) to become distribution centers for His number one product, the Word of God.

Stepping into one of the boats, Jesus asked Simon, its owner, to push it out into the water. So he sat in the boat and taught the crowds from there (Luke 5:3).

- When a king sits down; his royal government goes into active session. When Peter gave the chief seat in his fledgling business to the great King who was also the head of an eternal order (the Order of Melchizedek), his business immediately became a Kingdom business. God makes Himself personally responsible for blessing a business that exists solely or primarily to advance His Kingdom.

When he had finished speaking, he said to Simon, "Now go out where it is deeper, and let down your nets to catch some fish" (Luke 5:4).

- When Christ's voice had become the governing voice in Peter's fishing business, God gave Peter and his business partners a new business strategy for growing their business and increasing their profitability and market share.

"Master," Simon replied, "we worked hard all last night and didn't catch a thing. But if you say so, I'll let the nets down again" (Luke 5:5).

- The Order of Melchizedek (Jesus Christ) restored the engines of total obedience to God in Peter's fishing business, by restoring obedience in the heart of the CEO (Peter).

And this time their nets were so full of fish they began to tear! (Luke 5:6).

- The Order of Melchizedek (Jesus Christ) released a spirit of supernatural profit in Peter's fishing business, taking Peter's business from operating in the red to operating in the black.

A shout for help brought their partners in the other boat, and soon both boats were filled with fish and on the verge of sinking (Luke 5:7).

- The Order of Melchizedek (Jesus Christ) brought the fishing industry out of a severe economic recession that had arrested the entire industry.

When Simon Peter realized what had happened, he fell to his knees before Jesus and said, "Oh, Lord, please leave me—I'm too much of a sinner to be around you" (Luke 5:8).

- The Order of Melchizedek (Jesus Christ) restored the engines of righteousness in Peter's vehicle of commerce and the fear of the Lord in Peter's heart.

For he was awestruck by the number of fish they had caught, as were the others with him (Luke 5:9).

- The Order of Melchizedek (Jesus Christ) brought Peter's fishing business into an endless season of cash flow. Peter came to understand that Jesus Christ represented the richest eternal Order in the whole of creation, the Order of Melchizedek.

LIFE APPLICATION SECTION

MEMORY VERSES

Therefore, Pharaoh should find an intelligent and wise man and put him in charge of the entire land of Egypt. Then Pharaoh should appoint supervisors over the land and let them collect one-fifth of all the crops during the seven good years. Have them gather all the food produced in the good years that are just ahead and bring it to Pharaoh's storehouses. Store it away, and guard it so there will be food in the cities. That way there will be enough to eat when the seven years of famine come to the land of Egypt. Otherwise this famine will destroy the land (Genesis 41:33-36).

REFLECTIONS

How do you know when a church is trapped in a Levitical mindset?

Why is the Order of Melchizedek conducive for the proliferation of marketplace ministry?

JOURNAL YOUR PERSONAL NOTES ON THIS CHAPTER

CHAPTER THIRTEEN

The Manifest Sons of God

T HE ROOTS AND ORIGINS OF GOD'S purpose for creating the human race are found in the first two chapters of the book of Genesis. God wanted His spirit-children to become legal residents and guardians of the visible planet called Earth. This physical world that we live in was designed to be a spiritual colony of the Kingdom of heaven.

GOD'S ORIGINAL IDEA

Then God said, "Let us make human beings in our image, to be like us. They will reign over the fish in the sea, the birds in the sky, the livestock, all the wild animals on the earth, and the small animals that scurry along the ground." So God created human beings in his own image. In the image of God he created them; male and female he created them. Then God blessed them and said, "Be fruitful and multiply. Fill the earth and govern it. Reign over the fish in the sea, the birds in the sky, and all the animals that scurry along the ground" (Genesis 1:26-28).

Genesis 1:26-28 uncovers God's greatest idea, and gives us insight into God's original idea and enduring intent for creating humankind. God never gives up on an original idea because God will not allow His Word to return to Him unfulfilled. God's Word will always prosper in the accomplishment of whatever God intended it to do. Please remember that God knows the end from the beginning; this is why there is no chance of failure for any of His original ideas.

So what is God's original idea? To have spirit-children who can manage and govern the affairs of His invisible Kingdom here on earth.

THE MANIFEST SONS OF GOD

For the earnest expectation of the creation eagerly waits for the revealing of the sons of God. For the creation was subjected to futility, not willingly, but because of Him who subjected it in hope; because the creation itself also will be delivered from the bondage of corruption into the glorious liberty of the children of God. For we know that the whole creation groans and labors with birth pangs together until now (Romans 8:19-22 NKJV).

When we fast forward to the New Testament, we discover that God has not given up on His original idea. Even though the fall from grace of Adam and Eve created a short delay in the fulfillment of this divine mandate, God never ever gave up on the idea of having Spirit-led children on earth who can forcefully advance and execute His Kingdom agenda here on earth.

What's more, the apostle Paul in his epistle to the Romans tells us that God went a step farther and placed a deep groaning in all of creation for the manifestation of the true sons of God here on earth. The apostle Paul tells us that all of creation will be delivered from the technology of sin and death through the ministry of the manifest sons of God. The ministry of the manifest sons of God will overturn the Adamic curse that was placed upon the whole of creation when Adam and Eve sinned and fell from dominion. What a powerful end-time ministry the sons of the Kingdom have been given!

THE NEW CREATION

So we have stopped evaluating others from a human point of view. At one time we thought of Christ merely from a human point of view. How differently we know him now! This means that anyone who belongs to Christ has become a new person. The old life is gone; a new life has begun! (2 Corinthians 5:16-17)

Therefore, from now on, we regard no one according to the flesh. Even though we have known Christ according to the flesh, yet now we know Him thus no longer. Therefore, if anyone is in Christ, he is a new creation; old things have passed away; behold, all things have become new (2 Corinthians 5:16-17 NKJV).

It is quite clear that Christ came to the earth for the primary purpose of restoring humankind to God's original idea for the human race. After the first Adam fell into sin and became a puppet of the devil, God had to find a way to legally restore the broken covenant of fellowship. The apostle Paul tells us that when any person is *in Christ* he or she becomes a *new creation*. When a person becomes a new creation, God cancels the power of past sins and iniquities from their lives. The person truly becomes a brand-new person from the inside out. Said plainly the "new creation" is the spiritual identity of the manifest sons of God for which all of creation is waiting.

JESUS WAS BORN, CHRIST WAS GIVEN

*Without question, this is the **great mystery** of our faith: Christ was revealed in a human body and vindicated by the Spirit. He was seen by angels and announced to the nations. He was believed in throughout the world and taken to heaven in glory* (1 Timothy 3:16).

One of the most important mysteries of God is the mystery of the incarnation. Saint Paul tells us that the incarnation of Christ (God) into the human body is a *"great mystery."* Unfortunately, many ecclesiastical leaders and believers do not understand this great mystery. Many

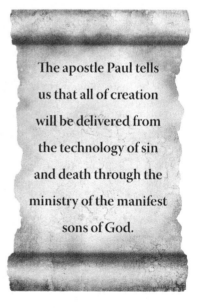

The apostle Paul tells us that all of creation will be delivered from the technology of sin and death through the ministry of the manifest sons of God.

believers do not understand why the Word became flesh. After the fall of Adam and Eve in the Garden of Eden, humankind became shrouded completely in sin. The fall of Adam and Eve was so drastic that sin invaded every fiber of man's triune being. Man's spirit lost the life of God, his soul also became a prisoner of sin while death attached itself to man's body. Sin in the human nature spread like a malignant cancer to every fiber of man's being.

A total overhaul of man's entire nature was required. Humankind needed a brand-new spirit, soul, and body. What's more, sin had destroyed humankind's God-given capacity to become like God and represent Him fully. When Christ (the eternal Word and Image of God) saw the utter depravity of humankind's condition, He knew that the only way humankind could ever become like God was if He became one of us. Thus the Word became flesh through the virgin birth and God became one of us.

> *For a child is born to us, a son is given to us. The government will rest on his shoulders. And he will be called: Wonderful Counselor, Mighty God, Everlasting Father, Prince of Peace* (Isaiah 9:6).

> *Therefore, from now on, we regard no one according to the flesh. Even though we have known Christ according to the flesh, yet now we know Him thus no longer. Therefore, if anyone is in Christ, he is a new creation; old things have passed away; behold, all things have become new* (2 Corinthians 5:16-17 NKJV).

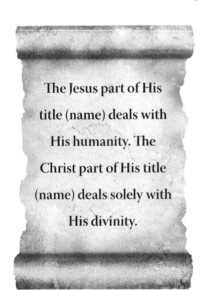

The Jesus part of His title (name) deals with His humanity. The Christ part of His title (name) deals solely with His divinity.

These Scriptures are probably two of the most misunderstood passages in the Bible. We can never appreciate who Christ and Jesus really are if we remain ignorant as to what really transpired in both the incarnation and the resurrection. So I will spend some time uncovering these two great mysteries and see how they affect us today as we endeavor to enter into the ministry of the Order of Melchizedek.

In Isaiah 9:6, the prophet Isaiah makes two very important prophetic statements that we need to understand if we want to know Christ the hope of glory. The prophet tells us that *"a Child was born to us"* and that *"a Son was given to us."* Herein lies the entire mystery of Christ's incarnation. The Child who was born is Jesus of Nazareth. The Son who was given to us is Christ (the eternal Word and Image of God.) (See John 1:1.)

Interestingly enough, the angel who appeared to Joseph in a dream made it quite clear that Jesus of Nazareth was the Child who was to be born; whereas the apostle John informs us that Christ was the Son of God who was given (gifted) to us. Take a look at these two Scriptures and see if they match up with what the prophet Isaiah told us in Isaiah 9:6:

> When the Church is obsessed with talking about Jesus of Nazareth (Christ's humanity), it also has a tendency to treat members of the Body of Christ on the basis of race (humanity).

As he considered this, an angel of the Lord appeared to him in a dream. "Joseph, son of David," the angel said, "do not be afraid to take Mary as your wife. For the child within her was conceived by the Holy Spirit. And she will have a son, and you are to name him Jesus, for he will save his people from their sins" (Matthew 1:20-21).

For God loved the world so much that he gave his one and only Son, so that everyone who believes in him will not perish but have eternal life (John 3:16).

So the Word became human and made his home among us. He was full of unfailing love and faithfulness. And we have seen his glory, the glory of the Father's one and only Son (John 1:14).

The Bible makes important distinctions between Jesus Christ's humanity and His divinity. The Jesus part of His title (name) deals with His humanity. The Christ part of His title (name) deals solely with His divinity. He saves us through His humanity, but He glorifies us into Christ-like sonship through His divinity. He redeems us from sin through His humanity, but He exalts us to reign with Him through His divinity. His ministry to us in His humanity had limitations on it, but His ministry to us in His divinity will last throughout eternity. We can never truly appreciate why the Church needs to enter into the Order of Melchizedek if we fail to appreciate Jesus Christ's dichotomy.

> *Therefore, from now on, we regard no one according to the flesh. Even though we have known Christ according to the flesh, yet now we know Him thus no longer. Therefore, if anyone is in Christ, he is a new creation; old things have passed away; behold, all things have become new* (2 Corinthians 5:16-17 NKJV).

As I mentioned, Second Corinthians 5:16-17 is one of the most misunderstood scriptural passages. I will explain. Saint Paul tells us that after Jesus Christ's crucifixion and resurrection, it is now illegal for New Testament born-again believers to know Christ after the flesh. Said simply, Paul did not want the Church to be so obsessed with Jesus of Nazareth (Christ's humanity) that it failed to comprehend the depth, width, and height of Christ's divinity. Paul tells us that there was a time when they (Jewish believers) knew Christ after the flesh, but that time had come and gone. Paul goes on to say that, from now on, we regard no one according to the flesh (including Jesus Christ).

Kingdom citizens are not allowed to know Christ after the flesh. What is Saint Paul talking about? Is he inferring that we are to ignore what Jesus Christ did for us in His humanity? By no means. So what does he mean? Paul is saying that once we are born-again, we must not obsess about Christ's humanity. Instead, we must strive tenaciously to know Christ and Him crucified. We must strive to know the mystery that is Christ, who is all and in all. We must strive to know Christ who is the express image of the invisible God. We must strive to know why Christ in us is the hope of glory! I am in no way diminishing what Jesus Christ accomplished for us in His humanity; it is the only reason why I stand forgiven of all my sins. It's the reason I am saved and heaven-bound. But if we fail to transition from what Christ did for us in His humanity to embrace who He has become in us in His divinity, then we will fall short of what Christ really came for.

The apostle Paul knew firsthand the dangers that exist in a body of believers who are obsessed with Christ's humanity but have little revelation of His divinity. When the Church is obsessed with talking about Jesus of Nazareth (Christ's humanity), it also has a tendency to treat members of the Body of Christ on the basis of race (humanity). This is why every Sunday morning in the United States of America, there is a tragic indictment on the Body of Christ. When Sunday morning comes, brothers and sisters who "think white" will drive by every church that they think is Black or Hispanic, until they find a "white church." Brothers and sisters who "think black" will drive by every church that they think is White or Hispanic, until they get to a "black church." Even secular politicians know that Sunday morning is the most segregated time of the week in America. How tragic!

Perhaps this is the reason why the Lord does not want His children to know Him or know each other after the flesh. How much damage has been done to the cause of Christ in the earth by born-again believers who either "think white" or "think black"? So what must the Church do? A dear man of God, friend, and mentor, Bishop Robert Smith, says it like this, "The Church must preach and present Jesus of Nazareth to the world while preaching and presenting Christ to the Church." Jesus saves the world from sin, while Christ glorifies the New Creation (the Church) into the glorious liberty of the sons of God.

You may be wondering what all of this has to do with the Order of Melchizedek. The Order of Melchizedek is the eternal priestly ministry of Christ. Please remember that Christ (the Word) existed before God created Jesus of Nazareth (His humanity) through the mystery of the incarnation. Since the Order of Melchizedek is an eternal priesthood, it therefore falls under the spiritual jurisdiction of Christ (the eternal Word, who was in the beginning with God, see John 1:1). As such, the Order of Melchizedek priesthood is based primarily upon Christ's divinity and not on His humanity which happened much later. As a matter of fact, Jesus of Nazareth did not fully enter into the office of the High Priest of Christ's eternal priesthood until after He rose from the dead. After Jesus Christ rose from the dead, His humanity was completely shrouded by His divinity by the spirit of the resurrection. He became both Lord *and* Christ. Since Christ's eternal priesthood is based primarily upon His divinity, the resurrection welded Christ's humanity into His divinity. Nevertheless Christ's humanity is a mitigating factor in how His priesthood is executed under the New Testament. We cannot enter into the fullness of what God has made available to us under the Order of Melchizedek until we begin to appreciate who Christ really is—to us and in us.

THE ONE NEW MAN

For He Himself is our peace, who has made both one, and has broken down the middle wall of separation, having abolished in His flesh the enmity, that is, the law of commandments contained in ordinances, so as to create in Himself one new man from the two, thus making peace (Ephesians 2:14-15 NKJV).

And have put on the new man, which is renewed in knowledge after the image of him that created him: Where there is neither Greek nor Jew, circumcision nor uncircumcision, Barbarian, Scythian, bond nor free: but Christ is all, and in all (Colossians 3:10-11 KJV).

We have already established the fact that the New Creation is the spiritual identity of Kingdom citizens or what the Bible calls the manifest sons of God. The apostle Paul goes a step further in identifying or decoding the spiritual DNA of the new creation. Saint Paul calls this new nature the *one new man* and explains that God has abolished the cultural divisions of race, gender, and pedigree in the lives of those who are members of the new creation.

In our Christ-like nature as the one new man, we have become renewed in the knowledge of Christ, who is the express image of the invisible God and firstborn of all creation. Saint Paul also tells us that in our new nature as the one new man, there is neither Greek nor Jew. There is neither circumcision nor uncircumcision. There is neither Barbarian nor Scythian. There is neither bond nor free. This means that the ministry of those who are of the Order of Melchizedek can never be restricted by race, gender, pedigree, religious or social status.

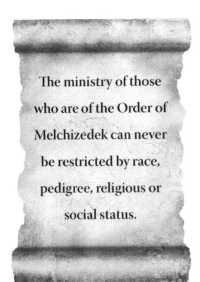

The ministry of those who are of the Order of Melchizedek can never be restricted by race, pedigree, religious or social status.

UNVEILING THE MYSTERY

And He Himself gave some to be apostles, some prophets, some evangelists, and some pastors and teachers, for the equipping of the saints for the work of ministry, for the edifying of the body of Christ, till we all come to the unity of the faith and of the knowledge of the Son of God, to a perfect man, to the measure of the stature of the fullness of Christ (Ephesians 4:11-13 NKJV).

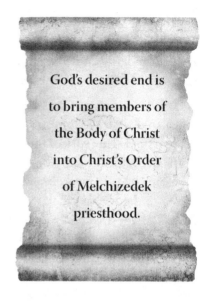

God's desired end is to bring members of the Body of Christ into Christ's Order of Melchizedek priesthood.

There has been a lot of talk in the Body of Christ in recent years about the restoration of the ministry of the apostle to the church. Serious debates have ensued, pitting those who believe that God is restoring apostles against those who believe that apostles are not for today. The truth lies somewhere in the middle. It is true that God is re-emphasizing the importance of apostles in today's global Church, but He is not "restoring them" because they never ceased to exist. There have always been apostles, prophets, teachers, evangelists, and pastors in every generation since the day of Pentecost, whether we acknowledged them or not. But God is definitely restoring the global Church's understanding of apostleship and apostolic ministry. As such, apostles are emerging across the globe from the shadows of man-made religious tradition.

God's Word tells us that these ascension gifts of Christ were leased to the Body of Christ for a very distinct period of time. Saint Paul tells us that these five-fold ministry gifts would last till we all [the Church] come into the knowledge of the Son of God and unto the full measure of the stature of Christ. Until God's eternal purpose is fulfilled, these ascension gifts can never be lost to the Church, even though they can go unrecognized to the detriment of the Body of Christ.

The apostle Paul identifies the primary mission of these ascension gifts, which is to perfect the Saints for the work of the ministry. To understand the full measure of the stature of Christ as well as identify the ministry Paul is referring to, we need to examine who Christ is in Heaven today. We also need to understand Christ's present-day ministry. We will quickly discover that the full measure of the stature of Christ points to Christ's exalted position of honor on the right hand of God as the High Priest after the Order of Melchizedek.

To understand Christ's present-day ministry we must ask, *What is Christ doing today while He is seated on the right hand of the throne of God?* Paul tells us that Christ is waiting for His enemies to be placed under His footstool and the last enemy is death. Christ is also interceding to bring many sons unto glory.

It follows then that the "work of the ministry" that Saint Paul is referring to in Ephesians 4:12 is the ministry that involves placing all of Christ's enemies under His footstool. The work of the ministry also involves bringing many sons (born-again believers) into the glory of Christ-likeness. When you thoroughly examine Ephesians 4:11-13, you discover the fact that the five-fold ministry gifts are not an end in themselves; they are simply the means to a desired end in the plan of God. God's desired end is to bring members of the Body of Christ into Christ's Order of Melchizedek priesthood. When this happens, the Body of Christ will reign on earth as a functional Kingdom of kings and priests unto our God.

THE MINISTRY OF THE MANIFEST SONS OF GOD

And they sang a new song, saying: "You are worthy to take the scroll, and to open its seals; for You were slain, and have redeemed us to God by Your blood out of every tribe and tongue and people and nation, and have made us kings and priests to our God; and we shall reign on the earth" (Revelation 5:9-10 NKJV).

Revelation 5:9-10 should remove any doubts whatsoever as to what is God's primary intention for bringing Christ to the earth. I love the book of Revelation because it is a prophetic picture of the end before there was ever a beginning. While the book of Genesis is the book of beginnings, the book of Revelation is the book of endings. John the apostle was transported into the portals of eternity by the power of the Holy Spirit when he wrote the book of Revelation. During this time of the heavenly vision, John was given a panoramic view of God's eternal plans and purposes.

When the apostle John looked into the future of the perfected Church, he discovered something very powerful. He saw by the Spirit that the perfected Church of the future is a functional Kingdom of kings and priests unto God. He discovered prophetic songs have already been written in the realms of eternity to celebrate this glorious development of the Body of Christ. The only priesthood that God ever gave to His people that includes both kings and priests in the nomenclature of the priesthood is the Order of Melchizedek.

This means that when Ephesians 4:11 ministry gifts have done their job in helping perfect the saints for the work of the ministry, the Church as a whole will enter into Christ's Order of Melchizedek priesthood. The Church as Christ's Body will know how to function effectively as kings and priests unto God. The Church will know how to reign with Christ here on earth without losing the ability to minister to the Lord in heartfelt worship. From this perspective it is easy to see why the Order of Melchizedek is the highest ministry of the new creation. It is also easy to see why it is patterned after Christ Himself, who is the spiritual head of our priestly Order.

LIFE APPLICATION SECTION

Memory Verses

For the earnest expectation of the creation eagerly waits for the revealing of the sons of God. For the creation was subjected to futility, not willingly, but because of Him who subjected it in hope; because the creation itself also will be delivered from the bondage of corruption into the glorious liberty of the children of God. For we know that the whole creation groans and labors with birth pangs together until now (Romans 8:19-22 NKJV).

Reflections

Why is the rest of creation waiting for the manifestation of the Sons of God?

Explain this statement, "The Order of Melchizedek is the primary ministry of the true Sons of God."

JOURNAL YOUR PERSONAL NOTES ON THIS CHAPTER

CHAPTER FOURTEEN

The Power of the Order of Melchizedek

B EFORE I GET INTO this chapter's focus, the power of the Order of Melchizedek, I'd like to re-examine the spiritual ramifications of the apostle Peter's summation that we (New Testament believers) are a royal priesthood.

A ROYAL PRIESTHOOD

But you are a chosen generation, a royal priesthood, a holy nation, His own special people, that you may proclaim the praises of Him who called you out of darkness into His marvelous light (1 Peter 2:9 NKJV).

The apostle Peter was writing to the followers of Christ who were scattered in the regions of Galatia, Bithynia, and Asia Minor. He made one of the most profound announcements ever made by a New Testament apostle. He told the believers in Christ that they were a *"royal priesthood."* What makes this announcement even more remarkable is the fact that Peter was writing to a primarily Jewish audience, because he was an apostle to the Jews. Preaching the gospel of the Kingdom to his fellow Jews was Peter's primary apostolic assignment.

Instead, they saw that God had given me the responsibility of preaching the gospel to the Gentiles, just as he had given Peter the responsibility of preaching to the Jews. For the same God who worked through Peter as the apostle to the Jews also worked through me as the apostle to the Gentiles (Galatians 2:7-8).

In his epistle to the Galatians, Paul made it quite clear that he was an apostle to the Gentiles, while Peter was an apostle to the Jews. Bearing this important consideration in mind, let us re-examine Peter's important summation, *"But you are a chosen generation, a royal priesthood...."*

A JEWISH MINDSET

Since the apostle Peter was telling fellow Jewish believers in Yeshua that they had become a royal priesthood, it will help to view Saint Peter's summation from a Jewish mindset. At the time Peter wrote his first epistle, the Jewish people had spent more than 3,000 years of their natural history under the Levitical order of priesthood. Since the believers Peter was addressing were Jewish, they knew from the testimony of written and cultural history that only the tribe of Levi could serve in the office of the priesthood. Other tribes in Israel had to come through the ministry of the Levites to access the presence of God. They were also aware of the spiritual consequences of pretending to be a priest under the Mosaic Covenant of Law.

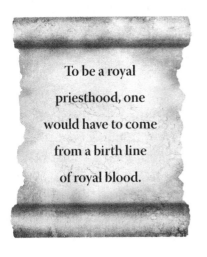

To be a royal priesthood, one would have to come from a birth line of royal blood.

Also bear in mind that when the apostle Peter wrote this particular epistle, the Levitical temple in natural Jerusalem had not yet been destroyed by the Romans. Highly dedicated Levites were still offering bulls and sacrifices to the God of Israel. The Jewish believers whom Peter was writing to also knew that even though the Levites were priests under the old order, they were not of royal blood. They knew that the priesthood Peter was referring to was not the Levitical priesthood. But Peter makes it quite clear that these believers were now the chosen ones of God. Peter told them that God had chosen them to be in a higher and loftier priesthood than that of the Levites. Peter's words were very powerful to the Jewish believers who could hardly believe the enormity of what Peter was saying and implying.

An Important Question

The apostle Peter's summation that we (New Testament believers) who believe in Christ Jesus are a royal priesthood demands that we answer a very important question. *If Saint Peter was not referring to the Levitical priesthood, what royal priesthood was he talking about?* To arrive at an accurate answer, we must use deductive reasoning by rightly dividing the Word of God.

Let us first break down the phrase that the apostle Peter used in his epistle to Jewish believers who were scattered in Asia Minor. Saint Peter says that we are a royal priesthood. To be a royal priesthood, one would have to come from a birth line of royal blood. Since every priesthood derives its nature from its high priest, we need to find a high priest who is either a king or is of royal blood. This deduction quickly leads us to Jesus Christ, who is both a King and of royal blood. We also know from Paul's epistle to the Hebrews that Jesus Christ is both a King and a High Priest after the Order of Melchizedek. It follows therefore, that the royal priestly order that the apostle Peter was alluding to is the priestly Order of Melchizedek.

There are those who will point out that Saint Peter was referring to the New Creation priesthood of Jesus. But this position is like picking needles out of a haystack, because the New Creation priesthood of Jesus Christ is the Order of Melchizedek priesthood. They are one and the same. There are only two priesthoods that God established for His creation, the Levitical priesthood and the Order of Melchizedek. The Levitical priesthood was earthly and transitional, but the Order of Melchizedek priesthood is heavenly and eternal. So the New Creation priesthood of Jesus Christ is synonymous with the Order of Melchizedek priesthood.

Having established the prophetic identity of the royal priesthood that Saint Peter was referring to, we can now examine the incredible power of the New Testament Order of Melchizedek priesthood. In order to do so, we will examine the ministry of Jesus Christ and that of His apostles.

THE TESTIMONY OF DANIEL

We must bear in mind that even though the Lord Jesus Christ came to fulfill the Law, He also came to establish a new order of priesthood. The entrance of God's promised Messiah onto the world stage signaled the end of the Levitical order of priesthood and the beginning of the New Creation order of priesthood. The prophet Daniel beautifully described this important event in his apocalyptic vision.

> And he [Jesus] shall confirm the covenant with many for one week: and in the midst of the week [at His death] he shall cause the [Levitical order] **sacrifice** and the oblation to cease... (Daniel 9:27 KJV Emphasis added by author).

Jesus Christ definitely confirmed the covenant that God had established with Abraham. We also know that Jesus Christ gave the ultimate sacrifice of Himself on the cross after three and a half years (the middle of Daniel's prophetic week) of His earthly ministry. Saint Paul is very clear in his epistle to the Hebrews that by this ultimate sacrifice of Himself, Jesus Christ abolished or caused the daily sacrifices and oblations in the Levitical temple to cease. So observing the ministry of Jesus Christ shows us the awesome power of this priestly Order of Melchizedek.

A NEW SHERIFF IN TOWN

> Then Jesus went to Capernaum, a town in Galilee, and taught there in the synagogue every Sabbath day. There, too, the people were amazed at his teaching, for he spoke with authority. Once when he was in the synagogue, a man possessed by a demon— an evil spirit—began shouting at Jesus, "Go away! Why are you interfering with us, Jesus of Nazareth? Have you come to destroy us? I know who you are—the Holy One sent from God!" Jesus cut him short. "Be quiet! Come out of the man," he ordered. At that, the demon threw the man to the floor as the crowd watched; then it came out of him without hurting him further. Amazed,

> *the people exclaimed, "What authority and power this man's words possess! Even evil spirits obey him, and they flee at his command!"* (Luke 4:31-36)

There are several important features that allude to the power of this New Testament Order of Melchizedek priesthood that quickly rise to the surface when we dissect the passage of Scripture in Luke 4. In this information and technology era we live in, the more features or applications a product has, the more valuable it is. The Order of Melchizedek has some very exciting features that we need to be aware of, including:

- teaching with great authority
- great power for exposing hidden demonic activity
- great power for casting out devils
- supernatural grace for creative thinking in business
- supernatural authority to control the virtual world
- supernatural grace for healing the masses
- power for supernatural multiplication
- great power over death agencies
- supernatural grace for transforming cities and nations
- powerful interception technology
- supernatural grace for empowering women
- power over generational or family curses
- supernatural grace to rise above sexual perversity
- supernatural grace to live in the favor of His presence
- supernatural grace to suffer on behalf of the Kingdom

TEACHING WITH GREAT AUTHORITY

One of the features that underscores the power of the New Creation Order of Melchizedek priesthood is the order of teaching that is available to Kingdom citizens. Before the advent of Christ, the people of Israel had lived under the

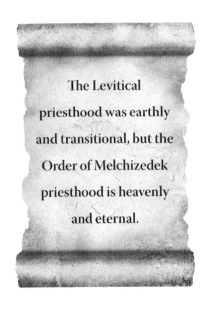

The Levitical priesthood was earthly and transitional, but the Order of Melchizedek priesthood is heavenly and eternal.

teaching ministry of many of the Levites, so they were not strangers to the teaching ministry of a Levitical priest. But when the people in the synagogue sat under the teaching ministry of Jesus Christ, they were completely dazzled by the unmistakable spiritual authority in His body of teaching.

The apostolic teaching ministry of this new Jewish Rabbi (Jesus of Nazareth) mesmerized the political, business, and religious community in Israel. People were literally on the edge of their seats each time Jesus opened his mouth to speak. We can liken it to listening to Billy Graham or T.D Jakes. The people could sense that Jesus knew what He was talking about. There was a liveliness to His teaching style that was markedly absent in the teaching ministries of the Old Testament Levites. Jesus Christ's teaching style made the Word of God come alive! I want you to know that this kind of life-giving teaching style is the rightful inheritance of every member of the New Creation Order of Melchizedek priesthood. Church services can never be boring if the senior pastor is operating under the Order of Melchizedek. Boring church services are a great embarrassment under this Order of Melchizedek. Times of personal or corporate Bible study must never be dry and dull. We have a covenant right to the life-giving teaching ministry of the Order of Melchizedek.

> Jesus came and told his disciples, "I have been given all authority in heaven and on earth. Therefore, go and make disciples of all the nations, baptizing them in the name of the Father and the Son and the Holy Spirit. Teach these new disciples to obey all the commands I have given you. And be sure of this: I am with you always, even to the end of the age" (Matthew 28:18-20).

Matthew 28:18-20 explores some of the important components of the Great Commission. Jesus told His apprentice apostles that the order of teaching under the New Creation order of priesthood is so powerful it can transform nations and superimpose the culture of the Kingdom over the affairs of these nations. Imagine how powerful a teaching ministry has to be to transform an entire nation from a "goat nation" to a "sheep nation." This is definitely not the teaching ministry we find in many of today's New Testament churches. This is sad and deeply regrettable. There is a lot of teaching coming out of the church world, but very little of it has the power to reform an entire nation.

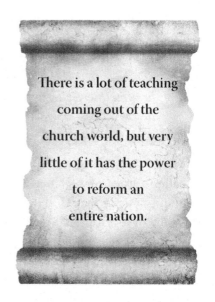

There is a lot of teaching coming out of the church world, but very little of it has the power to reform an entire nation.

He called them together, along with others employed in similar trades, and addressed them as follows: "Gentlemen, you know that our wealth comes from this business. But as you have seen and heard, this man Paul has persuaded many people that handmade gods aren't really gods at all. And he's done this not only here in Ephesus but throughout the entire province!" (Acts 19:25-26)

The apostle Paul demonstrated just how powerful the teaching ministry of the Order of Melchizedek is. Paul's teaching ministry was so powerful that it transformed a whole province in Asia. When Paul came to Ephesus, this mega metropolitan city was rife with financial corruption, idolatry, prostitution, and all kinds of witchcraft. After two years of Paul's apostolic teaching, thousands of Ephesians stopped worshipping worthless idols and began to serve the living God. What a teaching ministry! I truly believe that as we get closer to the millennial reign of Christ's Kingdom here on earth, we are going to see the complete restoration of this kind of teaching ministry that is patterned after the Order of Melchizedek. Church services all over the world will be jam-packed with people who are spiritually hungry for this type of life-giving teaching ministry.

POWER TO EXPOSE HIDDEN DEMONIC ACTIVITY

Once when he was in the synagogue, a man possessed by a demon—an evil spirit—began shouting at Jesus, "Go away! Why are you interfering with us, Jesus of Nazareth? Have you come to destroy us? I know who you are—the Holy One sent from God!" (Luke 4:33-34).

Another important feature that exposes the awesome power of this New Creation Order of Melchizedek priesthood, is the power to expose hidden demonic activity that God has given those who operate under the auspices of this new order of priesthood. For thousands of years, demons were having a free reign in the lives of the people of Israel, even among those who went to the synagogue regularly. These demonic spirits were both hidden and unrestrained in their spiritual operations in the synagogue. But what these demonic powers had been doing in secret was suddenly exposed publicly, the moment that Jesus Christ stepped through the door.

When Jesus Christ arrived, demonic spirits that had been operating undercover in the life of one of the men who attended the synagogue regularly began to expose themselves. This heated spiritual confrontation between Jesus Christ (who represented a new order of priesthood) and the demonic powers brought no small stir in the synagogue. Devout worshippers who witnessed this spiritual confrontation were completely amazed and petrified. They knew that demons existed, but they had never met a priest (rabbi) who had complete authority over demonic powers. They were amazed to see and hear just how terrified of Jesus Christ these devils were. At this point, if anyone had been sleeping through the boring, powerless preaching of the Pharisees who were in charge of the synagogue, I'm sure they became wide awake when all of this was going down.

I believe that when many New Testament believers and church leaders come to understand how to operate effectively under the Order of Melchizedek, there will be no place in the church for the devil to hide! When New Testament churches enter into this Order of Melchizedek priesthood, all undercover demonic activity will be exposed. Much like a retreating cockroach, demons will be scampering for a hiding place within the church, but to no avail. The people in our churches will stop moving around with what Dr. Kimberly Daniels calls "undercover bondage."

POWER TO CAST OUT DEVILS

Jesus cut him short. "Be quiet! Come out of the man," he ordered. At that, the demon threw the man to the floor as the crowd watched; then it came out of him without hurting him further. Amazed, the people exclaimed, "What authority and power this man's words possess! Even evil spirits obey him, and they flee at his command!" (Luke 4:35-36).

There were many testimonies of physical healing recorded under the Old Testament Levitical order of priesthood. But very few of those testimonies had to do with demons being cast out of people. The ministry of deliverance from demons is uniquely of a New Testament order. This powerful ministry is one of the operations of the Spirit that set Jesus Christ apart from any other spiritual historical figure up to that point. Under His new order of priesthood, Jesus Christ demonstrated His unlimited power and lordship over the demonic realm like no other spiritual leader in human history had ever done.

It follows then, that the ministry of deliverance is one of the most powerful governmental expressions of the priesthood of the Order of Melchizedek. Those of us who identify ourselves with this royal priestly Order of Melchizedek must never be afraid to confront demonic powers head on. Jesus Christ has given us the spiritual authority to cast devils out of people and bind them over our God-given domicile. Jesus told His apprentice apostles that every time that they were casting out devils by the Spirit of God, they were announcing the return and supremacy of the Kingdom of God here on earth. Church leaders who do not embrace the

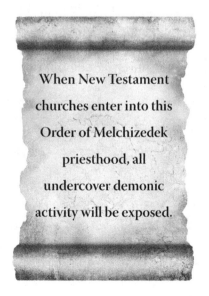

When New Testament churches enter into this Order of Melchizedek priesthood, all undercover demonic activity will be exposed.

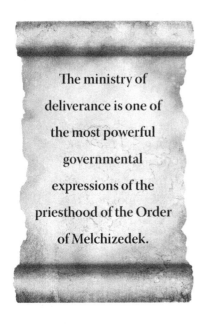

The ministry of deliverance is one of the most powerful governmental expressions of the priesthood of the Order of Melchizedek.

ministry of deliverance are missing out on a great God-given opportunity to announce the arrival of Christ's Kingdom here on earth.

God gave Paul the power to perform unusual miracles. When handkerchiefs or aprons that had merely touched his skin were placed on sick people, they were healed of their diseases, and evil spirits were expelled (Acts 19:11-12).

The apostle Paul demonstrated effectively the power of the New Creation order of Melchizedek priesthood over the demonic realm. People who were in serious need of deliverance came to Paul to get a reprieve from the demonic oppression that had enshrouded them. Since there were too many of them, Paul devised a spiritual technology for administering deliverance to the masses in a short amount of time. He gave handkerchiefs and aprons to the people, and when these anointed handkerchiefs and aprons were placed on those who were sick and demonically oppressed, deliverance was instant. I truly believe that this aspect of the Order of Melchizedek priesthood is rapidly being restored to the global Church.

POWER TO HEAL THE MASSES

The apostles were performing many miraculous signs and wonders among the people. And all the believers were meeting regularly at the Temple in the area known as Solomon's Colonnade. But no one else dared to join them, even though all the people had high regard for them. Yet more and more people believed and were brought to the Lord—crowds of both men and women. As a result of the apostles' work, sick people were brought out into the streets on beds and mats so that Peter's shadow might fall across some of them as he went by. Crowds came from the villages around Jerusalem, bringing their sick and those possessed by evil spirits, and they were all healed (Acts 5:12-16).

One of the most exciting aspects of this New Testament Order of Melchizedek priesthood has to do with the power to heal that God has invested in this royal priestly order. We know from reading the Bible that there were several people who were healed from different ailments under the Levitical order of priesthood, but those numbers pale significantly when we compare them to the vast number of people who have been miraculously healed under the New Testament order of priesthood.

If the names and testimonies of the people who have been healed by the power of God from the inception of Christ's ministry to the present day were all recorded in one book, I believe it would be the largest single book in human history. We would probably need several acres of land just to accommodate the monstrosity of such a book. This proves that the Order of Melchizedek priesthood is the most powerful priestly order that God ever made available to humankind. The late healing evangelist Kathryn Khulman believed that there is coming a day when every sick saint will be healed by the power of God. Wow, what a day that will be! I believe that churches that are built or patterned after the Order of Melchizedek will be churches where miraculous healings are commonplace. I also believe that there is coming a day when cancer will not be a disease that oppresses the Church of the living God.

THE POWER OF MULTIPLICATION

And he entered into one of the ships, which was Simon's, and prayed him that he would thrust out a little from the land. And he sat down, and taught the people out of the ship. Now when he had left speaking, he said unto Simon, Launch out into the deep, and let down your nets for a draught. And Simon answering said unto him, Master, we have toiled all the night, and have taken nothing: nevertheless at thy word I will let down the net. And when they had this done, they inclosed a great multitude of fishes: and their net brake. And they beckoned unto their partners, which were in the other ship, that they should come and help them. And they came, and filled both the ships, so that they began to sink. When Simon Peter saw it, he fell down at Jesus' knees, saying, Depart from me; for I am a sinful man, O Lord. For he was astonished, and all that were with him, at the draught of the fishes which they had taken (Luke 5:3-9 KJV).

Peter's introduction to the New Creation Order of Melchizedek priesthood never ceases to fascinate me. When Jesus saw Simon Peter's fishing boat near the banks of the sea, He asked Peter and his fishing crew for permission to use their boat as a platform for preaching to the masses. Peter and his crew readily agreed, unaware of just how life transforming this one decision would prove to be.

After Jesus finished preaching to the masses, He turned to Peter and his fishing crew and gave them a simple instruction. He told them to launch out into the deep. Peter tried to reason with Jesus because he did not know the awesome power of the spiritual order that Christ was operating under. Peter and his fishing crew did not know that the man who was instructing them to launch out into the deep was a King-Priest and God Most High. Peter did not know that the One who created fish was going to bless them with a load of fish for lending Him their boat, their vehicle of commerce.

Reluctantly, Peter and his fishing crew complied with what Jesus had instructed them to do. They cast their nets into the deep waters of the sea. Within a short while, they had a net-breaking harvest of all kinds of fish. The divine supply of fish that Peter and his crew received that day from simply lending their fishing boat to Jesus Christ was astronomical. Peter was so overwhelmed by the spirit of abundance that was displayed by this powerful Rabbi (Jesus) that he began to repent of his sins.

My dear friends, the power of multiplication or the spirit of increase that is available to all Kingdom citizens is staggering. When the global Church comes to understand how to function under this eternal Order of Melchizedek, the spirit of lack over the Body of Christ will be shattered into a million pieces. Many churches that are patterned after the Order of Melchizedek are going to be land owners, investors, and business owners in the communities where they are located. Gone are the days when the Church is despised and marginalized by the world because it is poor or economically challenged!

Jesus soon saw a huge crowd of people coming to look for him. Turning to Philip, he asked, "Where can we buy bread to feed all these people?" He was testing Philip, for he already knew what he was going to do. Philip replied, "Even if we worked for months, we wouldn't have enough money to feed them!" Then Andrew, Simon Peter's brother, spoke up. "There's a young boy here with five barley loaves and two fish. But what good is that with this huge crowd?"

"Tell everyone to sit down," Jesus said. So they all sat down on the grassy slopes. (The men alone numbered about 5,000.) Then Jesus took the loaves, gave thanks to God, and distributed them to the people. Afterward he did the same with the fish. And they all ate as much as they wanted (John 6:5-11).

Perhaps no other New Testament account displays the incredible power for multiplication that is found in the New Creation Order of Melchizedek priesthood like the supernatural feeding of the five thousand. Many Bible-believing scholars tell us that if they were to conduct an accurate count of the women and children who were also there, Jesus probably fed about 15,000 people on five loaves of bread and two fish. This passage should cure the unbelief of those who struggle to believe in the concept of a God of abundance.

Jesus tested Philip by asking him whether they had enough to feed the hungry multitudes. Philip's response was very cynical. Philip informed Jesus just how impossible and expensive it would be to try to feed this enormous crowd. Philip's business mind could not see any conceivable way to feed so many people. Just like Peter and his fishing crew, Philip had also greatly underestimated the awesome power of this new priestly order that Jesus Christ was establishing on earth.

The late healing evangelist Kathryn Khulman believed that there is coming a day when every sick saint will be healed by the power of God.

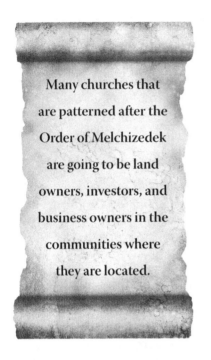

Many churches that are patterned after the Order of Melchizedek are going to be land owners, investors, and business owners in the communities where they are located.

I am sure Philip must have shaken his head in disbelief when Andrew showed up with a boy who had five loaves of bread and two small fish. How can five loaves of bread and two small fish make a difference among so many? Jesus, unfazed by Philip's attitude, told His disciples to sit the people in groups of 50. When they were seated, Jesus lifted the little boy's lunch to God and gave thanks. What happened next was an astounding miracle.

God supernaturally multiplied the little boy's five loaves and two fish. These loaves of bread and fish were multiplying while the disciples were serving the people. By the time the last person was served there were twelve baskets left over. Wow! So why is there so much lack and poverty in the Body of Christ? I truly believe that one of the reasons for this is that many New Testament churches and businesses are not patterning themselves after the Order of Melchizedek. Lack and poverty is not our portion under this New Creation priesthood.

POWER OVER DEATH

Soon afterward Jesus went with his disciples to the village of Nain, and a large crowd followed him. A funeral procession was coming out as he approached the village gate. The young man who had died was a widow's only son, and a large crowd from the village was with her. When the Lord saw her, his heart over-flowed with compassion. "Don't cry!" he said. Then he walked over to the coffin and touched it, and the bearers stopped. "Young man," he said, "I tell you, get up." Then the dead boy sat up and began to talk! And Jesus gave him back to his mother (Luke 7:11-15).

Since the spiritual fall of Adam and Eve in the Garden of Eden, men and women of all ages have been terrorized by death angels. There is no place in the world where people do not have to wrestle with the technology of death. The technology of death has claimed the lives of kings, nobles, superstars, and ordinary citizens alike, leaving a trail of sorrow and heartache in its wake.

The fear of death terrorizes and intimidates both the weak and the strong. To demonstrate the power of the new order of priesthood that Jesus was establishing on earth, God set up a demonstration. When Jesus Christ and His disciples were coming toward the City of Nain, they intercepted a big funeral procession. At the heart of this funeral procession was a widow with a very broken heart. She was the mother of the boy who had died.

Jesus stopped the funeral procession and made no apologies for the interruption. He then moved closer to the casket. He commanded the spirit of the dead boy to return into his lifeless body. Immediately the dead boy jumped out of the coffin, alive and well. I would not be surprised if the pall bearers ran for their lives in fright. Who can blame them? How often does a dead body jump out of a coffin?

My dear brothers and sisters in Christ, we must not underestimate the power of this New Testament Order of Melchizedek priesthood that we all belong to. God has given us the power to conquer death. There have been more people raised from the dead since the inception of Jesus Christ's ministry than at any other time in human history. I truly believe that many Kingdom citizens will be used by God to raise people from the dead in these last days. Nations are beginning to shake under the pressure of the miraculous through God's ecclesia.

> There was a believer in Joppa named Tabitha (which in Greek is Dorcas). She was always doing kind things for others and helping the poor. About this time she became ill and died. Her body was washed for burial and laid in an upstairs room. But the believers had heard that Peter was nearby at Lydda, so they sent two men to beg him, "Please come as soon as possible!" So Peter returned with them; and as soon as he arrived, they took him to the upstairs room. The room was filled with widows who were weeping and showing him the coats and other clothes Dorcas had made for them. But Peter asked them all to leave the room; then he knelt and prayed. Turning to the body he said,

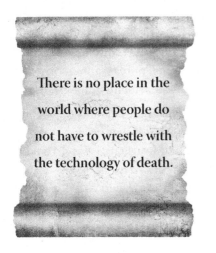

There is no place in the world where people do not have to wrestle with the technology of death.

"Get up, Tabitha." And she opened her eyes! When she saw Peter, she sat up! He gave her his hand and helped her up. Then he called in the widows and all the believers, and he presented her to them alive. The news spread through the whole town, and many believed in the Lord (Acts 9:36-42).

The Apostle Peter was also aware of this supernatural dimension for raising the dead that is tied to the power God has invested in the New Creation Order of priesthood. When Peter arrived in Joppa, they told him that there was a very special sister named Dorcas who had died. All the widows that this sister had helped while she was alive interceded for her. They compelled Peter to ask God to intervene. Many may have told these poor widows to shut up and call for the mortician, but Peter knew firsthand the power of the Order of Melchizedek priesthood that he was under.

Peter locked himself in the same room where Dorcas' dead body lay in wait. After a short time of prayer, Peter did what he had seen Jesus do to the son of the widow of Nain. He commanded Dorcas' spirit to return to her lifeless body. He addressed her like she was in a deep sleep. Immediately she opened her eyes and sat up. News of this miracle spread like wildfire in Joppa and the cities round about. Many people who heard what God had done gave their hearts to Christ. I am not suggesting that when churches begin to operate under the Order of Melchizedek that people will not die. But my argument is that not everyone who dies in our churches was meant to stay dead. We ought to be raising a few of them from the dead.

WOMAN, THOU ART LOOSED

One Sabbath day as Jesus was teaching in a synagogue, he saw a woman who had been crippled by an evil spirit. She had been bent double for eighteen years and was unable to stand up straight. When Jesus saw her, he called her over and said, "Dear woman, you are healed of your sickness!" Then he touched her, and instantly she could stand straight. How she praised God! But the leader in charge of the synagogue was indignant that Jesus had healed her on the Sabbath day. "There are six days of the week for working," he said to the crowd. "Come on those days to be healed, not on the Sabbath." But the Lord replied, "You hypocrites! Each of you works on the Sabbath day! Don't you untie your ox or your donkey from its stall on the Sabbath and lead it out for water? This dear woman, a daughter of Abraham, has been held in bondage by Satan for eighteen years. Isn't it right that she be released, even on the Sabbath?" (Luke 13:10-16).

Under the Levitical priestly system and religious structure, women played a very marginal role in the priesthood. Women's opinions and contributions to the priesthood were never treated seriously, if they were considered at all. For the most part, the predominant role of women under the Levitical priesthood was that of housewife. There is nothing wrong with a woman being a housewife but God has other equally important ministerial assignments in the Kingdom for His daughters.

Under the Levitical priesthood, women couldn't preach, teach, or prophesy in the temple or synagogue. Under the Levitical priesthood, married women could be divorced by their husbands for the flimsiest of reasons. All a man had to do under the Levitical order to get rid of his wife was send her away with a bill of divorcement. What's more, divorced women under the Levitical priesthood had no property rights, so they could not share in any assets from the dissolved marriage.

When Jesus Christ began His earthly ministry, He demonstrated through His actions that He had come to establish a new order of priesthood. One of Jesus Christ's most dramatic demonstrations of the new order of priesthood that He came to establish on earth was evidenced by a new order of honor that He personally placed upon the women He encountered. No other Jewish Rabbi had ever esteemed women as much as He did. His special care for women and the tenderness with which He treated them was unrivaled.

When Jesus came into the synagogue on the Sabbath day, there was a woman in the service who was bent over. She had been afflicted by a spirit of infirmity

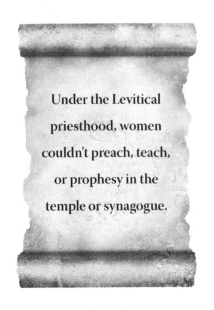

Under the Levitical priesthood, women couldn't preach, teach, or prophesy in the temple or synagogue.

for eighteen years. The Levitical religious system that she was under said that she could not be healed on the Sabbath. But Jesus healed her on the Sabbath day and used her to demonstrate that there was a new order of priesthood in town. This new order of priesthood placed more value on people than on preserving religious ritual and protocol.

In Scripture a woman is a prophetic representation of the Church. Notice that Jesus called this woman who had been bound for eighteen years by the devil a "daughter of Abraham." The Church is the seed of Abraham through Jesus Christ. The Church is made up of spiritual sons and daughters of Abraham. This woman is a prophetic representation of that section of the Church that has been bound by the devil because of religious tradition and bigotry. For many years, women in the Church have had to fight tooth and nail for a fair share of what Christ bequeathed to them under the New Creation order of priesthood. God is showing us through this Scripture passage that God is going to use apostolic and prophetic men who have a ministry patterned after the Order of Melchizedek to loose the daughters of Zion from demonic and religious bondage. This is why every woman in the Body of Christ (whether they know it or not) is waiting eagerly for church leaders in God's ecclesia to enter into this Order of Melchizedek.

> *And the scribes and Pharisees brought unto him a woman taken in adultery; and when they had set her in the midst, they say unto him, Master, this woman was taken in adultery, in the very act. Now Moses in the law commanded us, that such should be stoned: but what sayest thou? This they said, tempting him that they might have to accuse him. But Jesus stooped down, and with his finger wrote on the ground, as though he heard them not. So when they continued asking him, he lifted up himself,*

and said unto them, He that is without sin among you, let him first cast a stone at her. And again he stooped down, and wrote on the ground. And they which heard it, being convicted by their own conscience, went out one by one, beginning at the eldest, even unto the last: and Jesus was left alone, and the woman standing in the midst. When Jesus had lifted up himself, and saw none but the woman, he said unto her, Woman, where are those thine accusers? hath no man condemned thee? She said, No man, Lord. And Jesus said unto her, Neither do I condemn thee: go, and sin no more (John 8:3-11 KJV).

John 8:3-11 is further evidence that the New Creation order of Melchizedek priesthood is the only priesthood that has the power to deliver women from the demonic machinery that is designed to rob them of their life's purpose and self-worth. Some Pharisees brought a woman who was caught in adultery to Jesus, to see what kind of punishment He would prescribe for her. These Pharisees were the religious leaders of the Levitical order of priesthood. I am quite sure that the woman they brought to Jesus was terrified thinking about what would happen to her. She was convinced she would be stoned to death. The Pharisees did not bring to trial the man she was caught in adultery with. How's that for justice?

I need to point out that any religious structure or system which does not give women the same level of access to the priesthood as their male counterparts is not patterned after the Order of Melchizedek. Such a religious structure is patterned after the Levitical order of priesthood, which is diametrically different from the New Testament order of priesthood. Jesus Christ did not defend this woman's sin before her accusers; He simply defended her right to access the grace and forgiveness that God was making available to every person under the sun through the new order of priesthood that Christ came to establish on earth.

When it was all said and done, Jesus delivered this woman from the demonic machinery that was bent on killing her. He delivered her from a religious order that was using her as bait to advance its own political agenda. He delivered her from a life of sin and gave her grace to start a new life in the Lord. He delivered her from "death to destiny." What is clear from the two passages of scripture that we have thus far examined is that the Order of Melchizedek is the only priesthood that can bring liberty to the daughters of Zion for Kingdom advancement.

POWER TO TAKE THE CITY

The woman left her water jar beside the well and ran back to the village, telling everyone, "Come and see a man who told me everything I ever did! Could he possibly be the Messiah?" So the people came streaming from the village to see him (John 4:28-30).

Many Samaritans from the village believed in Jesus because the woman had said, "He told me everything I ever did!" When they came out to see him, they begged him to stay in their village. So he stayed for two days, long enough for many more to hear his message and believe. Then they said to the woman, "Now we believe, not just because of what you told us, but because we have heard him ourselves. Now we know that he is indeed the Savior of the world" (John 4:39-42).

It seems to me that God has a special affection for cities. This is even more obvious when Jesus cried over the city of Jerusalem for missing its appointed time of visitation. So it should not surprise us that under Jesus' new order of priesthood, there is a strong divine emphasis on transforming cities and nations with the gospel of the Kingdom.

One sunny day, Jesus took His disciples along a path that went through Samaria. Jesus stopped to rest when He got to the piece of ground that Jacob had given to his son, Joseph. He sent all of His disciples into the city of Samaria to get food, while He sat at Jacob's well. After His disciples left, a woman from Samaria came to draw water from the well. What ensued was a supernatural encounter with God that changed the life of this Samaritan woman.

When Jesus was finished talking with her, she was charged up in the Holy Ghost. Her spirit and soul were on fire. She had encountered a new and powerful order of priesthood. For the first time in her life she felt forgiven, free, and powerful. She was so inspired that she left the water pot behind and ran into Samaria. When she arrived inside the city gates, she started preaching up a storm. Her powerful apostolic preaching about the Messiah shook the city and brought it to its knees. The entire City responded to her powerful preaching and went looking for Jesus.

When the people of the city of Samaria found Jesus seated by Jacob's well, they became even more dumbfounded when they heard Him for themselves. They knew after they listened to Him speak that He was truly the Christ sent by God. The Bible tells us that the entire city turned to the Lord. *Imagine this, one supernatural encounter with the priestly order of Melchizedek and a broken-down, five-times divorced woman became a Billy Graham.* She was so transformed that her powerful preaching resulted in the spiritual conversion of an entire city! Wow! Under this Order of Melchizedek, God is giving His Church the power to transform and take back cities. Gone are the days of church as usual. Churches and businesses must now be built with the purpose of transforming the city that the church is stationed in.

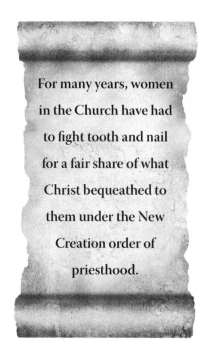

For many years, women in the Church have had to fight tooth and nail for a fair share of what Christ bequeathed to them under the New Creation order of priesthood.

The Power of Supernatural Interception

After Abram returned from his victory over Kedorlaomer and all his allies, the king of Sodom went out to meet him in the valley of Shaveh (that is, the King's Valley). And Melchizedek, the king of Salem and a priest of God Most High, brought Abram some bread and wine. Melchizedek blessed Abram with this blessing: "Blessed be Abram by God Most High, Creator of heaven and earth. And blessed be God Most High, who has defeated your enemies for you." Then Abram gave Melchizedek a tenth of all the goods he had recovered. The king of Sodom said to Abram, "Give back my people who were captured. But you may keep for yourself all the goods you have recovered." Abram replied to the king of Sodom, "I solemnly swear to the LORD, God Most High, Creator of heaven and earth, that I will not take so much as a single thread or sandal thong from what belongs to you. Otherwise you might say, 'I am the one who made Abram rich'" (Genesis 14:17-23).

Perhaps there is nothing that underscores the awesome power of the priestly Order of Melchizedek like its power of interception. Before concluding this chapter, I will examine in great detail this important aspect of this new order of priesthood. I'll begin by defining the word, *intercept:*

- To take, seize, or halt someone or something on the way from one place to another. To cut off, someone or something from an intended destination.

- To see or overhear a message or transmission meant for another (e.g., intercepting an enemy's battle plan).

- To stop the travel or check the passage of someone or something.

- To destroy or disperse enemy aircraft or a missile or missiles in the air on the way to a target.

Gone are the days of church as usual. Churches must now be built with the purpose of transforming the city that the church is stationed in.

It does not take a rocket scientist to realize just how powerful the word *intercept* is. How many of us would be eternally grateful if the police intercepted a serial killer when he was attempting to enter our house while we were sleeping? How many of the people who died in the September 11, 2001, terrorist attacks in New York would have been saved had the FBI or CIA intercepted the terrorist plot? You get the picture. Interception is a very real blessing, especially when it originates from the realm of the supernatural.

As mentioned previously, Abram was returning from the slaughter of the kings from the East when Melchizedek, the king-priest, intercepted him. Moments before the king of Sodom got to Abram, Christ (who is the Melchizedek of God) stepped out of eternity and into the portals of time and space. This Melchizedek, the priest of God Most High, intercepted Abram to protect him from the seductive and corrupting influence of the king of Sodom.

This amazing power for supernatural interception which is an intricate part of the Order of Melchizedek, is not restricted to the Old Testament. Turning to the New Testament we quickly discover one of the most powerful occasions of divine interception. We already know that our Lord Jesus Christ is the High Priest after the Order of Melchizedek. Part of His earthly ministry was designed to establish this royal priestly Order of Melchizedek here on earth.

> *"Simon, Simon, Satan has asked to sift each of you like wheat. But I have pleaded in prayer for you, Simon, that your faith should not fail. So when you have repented and turned to me again, strengthen your brothers." Peter said, "Lord, I am ready to go to prison with you, and even to die with you." But Jesus said, "Peter, let me tell you something. Before the rooster crows tomorrow morning, you will deny three times that you even know me"* (Luke 22:31-34).

One day, Jesus turned to one of His disciples by the name of Simon Peter. Jesus told Peter that He had intercepted a satanic transmission concerning him. Jesus told Peter that the devil had put together a diabolical plan to destroy him, but that he was not to worry. Jesus had already prayed for him to go through this demonically engineered trial and come out as pure as gold. This apostolic prayer that Jesus had released into the spirit world about Simon Peter's deliverance had placed a "restraining order" on the effectiveness of the enemy's diabolical agenda.

Simon Peter tried to argue with Jesus that he would never deny Him no matter what happened in his life. Jesus simply told him that before the rooster crowed, Peter would have denied the Lord three times. True to Jesus' prophetic predictions, Peter denied the Lord three times after Jesus was arrested by Jewish religious leaders. Peter was emotionally and spiritually distraught over what he had done, but Peter's fall from grace would have been much more devastating had Jesus not intercepted the enemy's diabolical agenda.

I have been saved for many years, and I can tell you for a fact that since then, God has intercepted demonic agendas against me that would have destroyed me completely on many occasions. The Order of Melchizedek priesthood is full of divine interceptions.

POWER OVER GENERATIONAL CURSES

For this Melchisedec, king of Salem, priest of the most high God, who met Abraham returning from the slaughter of the kings, and blessed him; To whom also Abraham gave a tenth part of all; first being by interpretation King of righteousness, and after that also King of Salem, which is, King of peace; Without father, without mother, without descent, having neither beginning of days, nor end of life; but made like unto the Son of God; abideth a priest continually (Hebrews 7:1-3).

As mentioned in Chapter Seven, Christ's eternal priestly order is based primarily upon His divinity and not His humanity. Christ has no earthly genealogy that can compromise His eternal priestly order. His heavenly priesthood can never be compromised by demonic influences and tendencies that have established a strong pathway through the human genome. In the miracle of the incarnation, God borrowed the womb of Mary to give birth to the Christ child but He never allowed Christ to share Mary's corrupted bloodline. This means that when we come under this priestly Order of Melchizedek, every generational curse that has been pursuing us through our bloodline abruptly ends. What a powerful priestly order! Most of the ministries who teach on breaking generational curses do not have a clear-cut revelation on the Order of Melchizedek, and that is why they have a limited level of success in breaking generational curses over people's lives.

GRACE TO RISE ABOVE GENERATIONAL SEXUAL PERVERSITY

And [Peter] solemnly and earnestly witnessed (testified) and admonished (exhorted) with much more continuous speaking and warned (reproved, advised, encouraged) them, saying, Be *saved from this crooked (**perverse,** wicked, unjust) generation* (Acts 2:40 AMP).

Peter the apostle in his first post-resurrection sermon on the day of Pentecost, makes a very interesting observation: every generation has its own share of perversity. Without a shadow of doubt, the greatest and most destructive perversity of our generation comes in the form of sexual perversity. We live in a culture that worships the sex goddess and sexualizes everything. Sexual perversity is obvious in every form of media.

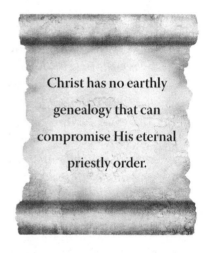

Christ has no earthly genealogy that can compromise His eternal priestly order.

In recent years, the Church has suffered the shame and pain caused by the sexual sin of some very prominent church leaders. These spiritual leaders fell into the trap of the sexual perversity of our generation. In Texas, for instance, the media gave us front row seats in one of the most bizarre and embarrassing sexual scandals involving a prominent church leader. This man was the bishop of a 3,000 member church, which was a gathering point for some of the biggest names in the so-called "Christian ministry circuit." When this high profile bishop was arrested by the Dallas police for raping about 15 women, it sent shock waves in the church world. One of the women the bishop sexually molested was a 16-year-old girl who attended his own church! This man is now serving a 20-40 year sentence at a correctional facility in Texas. His church is now a shell of its former glory. Many of the people in his church have walked away from the Lord because of these shocking revelations about their esteemed bishop.

I have already mentioned the fact that the country of Sodom is the birth place of the worst sexual perversity that you have ever seen. The king of Sodom (Satan) is the principality that is responsible for promoting sexual perversity in any generation. The good news is that since we are the seed of Abraham, we can rest assured that we can also rise above the sexual perversity in our generation if we bring ourselves under Christ's Order of

Melchizedek priesthood. Melchizedek's priesthood gave Abram the power to rise above sexual temptation which is induced by the Sodomic-demonic system. Christ's Order of Melchizedek priesthood gives us the grace to rise above the sexual perversity in our generation.

GRACE FOR CREATIVE THINKING IN BUSINESS

"The next seven years will be a period of great prosperity throughout the land of Egypt. But afterward there will be seven years of famine so great that all the prosperity will be forgotten in Egypt. Famine will destroy the land. This famine will be so severe that even the memory of the good years will be erased. As for having two similar dreams, it means that these events have been decreed by God, and he will soon make them happen. Therefore, Pharaoh should find an intelligent and wise man and put him in charge of the entire land of Egypt. Then Pharaoh should appoint supervisors over the land and let them collect one-fifth of all the crops during the seven good years. Have them gather all the food produced in the good years that are just ahead and bring it to Pharaoh's storehouses. Store it away, and guard it so there will be food in the cities. That way there will be enough to eat when the seven years of famine come to the land of Egypt. Otherwise this famine will destroy the land" (Genesis 41:29-36).

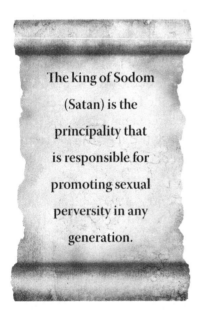

The king of Sodom (Satan) is the principality that is responsible for promoting sexual perversity in any generation.

One of the most powerful features of Christ's Order of Melchizedek priesthood is how it gives Kingdom citizens supernatural grace for creative thinking in business. This should excite Kingdom business men and women concerning what is possible for them under this royal order of priesthood. God testified concerning Abraham saying that He knew that Abraham would command his children to follow His ways. Since God's testimony is always true, we have to assume that Abraham introduced Isaac and his other descendants to the heavenly Order of Melchizedek priesthood. So it would be quite safe to assume that all the patriarchs from Abraham to Joseph knew about Christ's Order of Melchizedek priesthood. Taken in this light, all the lives of the patriarchs take on a whole new meaning.

When Joseph stood before Pharaoh, it did not take Pharaoh long to figure out that Joseph was of a different and higher spiritual order from any of the magicians of Egypt. His creative business acumen was unrivaled by any of his peers. In the face of the greatest economic turbulence that the world had ever seen, Joseph's creative business sense steered the economy of Egypt into greater prosperity. Joseph's creativity also saved the lives of multiplied millions in other nations of the world.

I prophesy to you that as the Church rediscovers Christ's Order of Melchizedek priesthood, God is going to raise men and women in His Church whose creative business acumen will dazzle nations. For the most part, the world has shunned the Church, regarding it as a de facto religious entity and not as a resource center for creative business ideas—but those days are over!

GRACE TO LIVE IN THE FAVOR OF HIS PRESENCE

So then, since we have a great High Priest who has entered heaven, Jesus the Son of God, let us hold firmly to what we believe. This High Priest of ours understands our weaknesses, for he faced all of the same testings we do, yet he did not sin. So let us come boldly to the throne of our gracious God. There we will receive his mercy, and we will find grace to help us when we need it most (Hebrews 4:14-16).

Without a doubt the greatest benefit of coming under Christ's New Testament Order of Melchizedek priesthood, is the benefit of living in the favor of God's presence. Humankind was created to live in the presence of God. When you place a fish on the ground, it starts gasping for air, but the moment you place that same fish in water, its genius will emerge instantly. Why? Because fish were created to flourish in an environment filled with water.

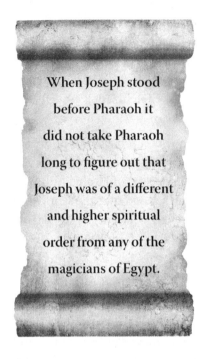

When Joseph stood before Pharaoh it did not take Pharaoh long to figure out that Joseph was of a different and higher spiritual order from any of the magicians of Egypt.

In the same fashion, God created humankind to live and thrive in His presence. But the fall of Adam and Eve into willful sin drove the entire human race out of the presence of God!

Since then men and women have been trying unsuccessfully to fill the spiritual void left in their soul by the absence of the presence of God. Human experiments to fill this void have been a dismal failure. While there was an inherent desire by all humankind to have a meaningful relationship with God, sin made the passage impossible. What's more, under the Levitical priesthood, approaching the presence of God was a terrifying experience. Under the Old Testament, men and women who made the mistake of getting too close to the presence of God were killed instantly by the glory of God.

But the death and resurrection of Jesus Christ changed the spiritual technology for approaching the presence of God. Christ's New Testament Order of Melchizedek priesthood removed fear from the process of entering into His presence. Christ's priesthood transformed the throne of God into the throne of grace. We are now charged by Scripture to enter the throne of grace boldly. We never have to fear that God's glory will strike us down if we come too close to the presence of the living God, especially if we are stained by sin.

Supernatural Grace to Suffer for the Kingdom

I will probably get attacked by "theological escapists" for saying what I am about to say. One of the most important aspects of Christ's Order of Melchizedek priesthood is the supernatural grace that is given to all Kingdom citizens to suffer triumphantly on behalf of Christ's Kingdom. Oops, I said it!

Some proponents of the faith message will criticize me for even suggesting that God can allow the faithful to suffer emotionally and physically in defense of the gospel. There is a section of the Church in North America that believes that financial prosperity is the epitome of the blessing of God. This crowd fails to see how God can be glorified by His people suffering for the advancement of the Kingdom. Surely, God is glorified by His people walking on streets paved with gold? This seems to be the governing mindset of those opposed to the gospel of suffering. Check this out:

> *"...except that the Holy Spirit tells me in city after city that jail and suffering lie ahead. But my life is worth nothing to me unless I use it for finishing the work assigned me by the Lord Jesus— the work of telling others the Good News about the wonderful grace of God. And now I know that none of you to whom I have preached the Kingdom will ever see me again"* (Acts 20:23-25).

Paul, the apostle who is responsible for introducing the New Testament Church to the Order of Melchizedek, understood that this order of priesthood can empower believers to triumph under incredible odds. He gladly accepted both the suffering and the opportunity to suffer in the future for the purpose of advancing the Kingdom of God here on earth. In some parts of the world like China, India and Sudan where Kingdom citizens (born-again believers) have accepted this supernatural grace to suffer for the advancement of the Kingdom, the Kingdom is experiencing explosive growth! I am not advocating suffering for the sake of suffering that is religion. But if the Church in North America does not include and embrace the gospel

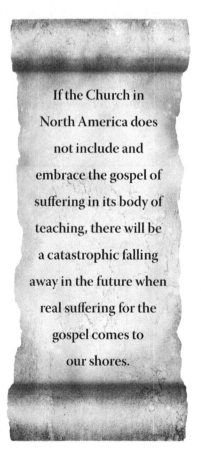

If the Church in North America does not include and embrace the gospel of suffering in its body of teaching, there will be a catastrophic falling away in the future when real suffering for the gospel comes to our shores.

of suffering in its body of teaching, there will be a catastrophic falling away in the future when real suffering for the gospel comes to our shores. The majority of these "user friendly saints" will rather curse God than shed their blood resisting sin. (Hebrews 12:4.) When the portals of hell open up to receive these backslidden, Christ denying saints, their blood will be laid on the shoulders of the prophets of the user friendly gospel. (Isaiah 12:9.)

I close this chapter by leaving you with some food for thought. Joseph would never have become the most powerful man in Egypt had he not been willing to suffer for the advancement of the Kingdom. Daniel would never have become the most powerful man in the Persian Empire had he not been willing to suffer for the Kingdom of God in the lions den. Queen Esther would never have saved the Jews from total annihilation, had she not been willing to lay her life on the line. Jesus Christ would never have redeemed all mankind from eternal damnation had He not been willing to suffer on behalf of advancing the Kingdom of God. Think on these things! Christ's Order of Melchizedek priesthood will restore the supernatural grace to suffer to the Body of Christ *and a timid, self-absorbed church, will suddenly becoming a governing force in the earth!* Militant Islam will be no match for a heart transforming, loving, peaceful and righteous army of God that is not afraid to die in the service of Christ!

LIFE APPLICATION SECTION

MEMORY VERSE

But you are a chosen generation, a royal priesthood, a holy nation, His own special people, that you may proclaim the praises of Him who called you out of darkness into His marvelous light (1 Peter 2:9 NKJV).

REFLECTIONS

Why did Peter the apostle describe Christ's priesthood as a royal priesthood?

Write three spiritual features that underscore the awesome power of the Order of Melchizedek.

What do you understand by the phrase, "the gospel of suffering?"

JOURNAL YOUR PERSONAL NOTES ON THIS CHAPTER

CHAPTER FIFTEEN

The Fathering Dimension

L IFE'S GREATEST TRAGEDY is that many nations, corporations, families and even churches are led by orphans. How many nations, corporations, families, and even churches are led by a man or woman who never knew their father? How many nations, corporations, families, and even churches are led by a man or woman who has never experienced the constant and unwavering companionship of a loving, caring, and responsible father? How many nations, corporations, families, and even churches are led by a man or woman who endured the devastating pain of seeing their father walk out on them? How many nations, corporations, families, and even churches are led by a man or woman who came home from school to hear their tear-drenched mom say, "Dad has left us! He's not coming back home."

How many of them went and looked at their reflection in the mirror wondering what was so wrong about them that caused Dad to walk away? How many of these heartbroken youngsters ran to their mother and said, "Mama, please tell Dad that if he comes back home, I will be a good boy or girl!" How many of these children ran to their front porch at the sound of every passing car that sounded like Dad's, only to discover that he was not the one in the driver's seat?

> *Look, I am sending you the prophet Elijah before the great and dreadful day of the LORD arrives. His preaching will turn the*

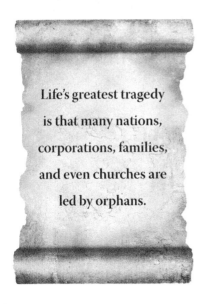

Life's greatest tragedy is that many nations, corporations, families, and even churches are led by orphans.

hearts of fathers to their children, and the hearts of children to their fathers. Otherwise I will come and strike the land with a curse (Malachi 4:5-6).

Malachi 4:5-6 is, in my opinion, one of the most profound Scripture passages in the whole of the Bible. This one verse captures the heartbeat of Kingdom living. It captures the very heartbeat of God. What is even more striking about this Scripture passage is that it is a forerunner to Christ's Order of Melchizedek priesthood. It is also the last verse in the Old Testament. Just imagine: the last thing that God talked about and mandated Himself to in the entire Old Testament involves the supernatural infusion of a fathering spirit into the earth.

After God promised to visit the earth with this "Elijah spirit" (fathering spirit), He closes the Old Testament canon of Scripture. Bible scholars tell us that the period between this final verse in Malachi and the appearance of the prophet John the Baptist is about 400 years. This period is also known as the "400-year period of prophetic silence." The truth of the matter is that while God may have been silent on the earthly side of things, in the realm of the Spirit, He was working behind the scenes to supernaturally infuse this powerful fathering spirit into our troubled world. But on the earthly side of things, Malachi 4:5-6 was deeply entrenched into every Jewish mind. There was a growing expectation in the spirits of the people of Israel about the infusion of the Elijah spirit that would turn the hearts of the fathers toward their children.

> *So if you sinful people know how to give good gifts to your children, how much more will your heavenly **Father** give the Holy Spirit to those who ask him* (Luke 11:13).

So it is in a spiritual atmosphere charged with the promise of Malachi 4:5-6 that God chooses to introduce Jesus Christ and John the Baptist to the world. Between them, these two prophetic figures represent the return of the fathering spirit and the fulfillment of Malachi 4:5-6. For a season, God uses the prophet John the Baptist to blaze a new trail to prepare the people of Israel for Christ's new order of priesthood that would overturn the hold that the "orphan spirit" has over our generation. What becomes adamantly clear when you investigate the earthly ministry of Jesus Christ is the emphasis that Christ placed on fathering. Jesus had no qualms about boasting about His heavenly Father! Every chance He got He talked about His heavenly Father and what kind of person He is. Jesus made it very clear through His actions that the primary assignment of His new order of priesthood was to restore a proper image of His heavenly Father in the hearts and minds of a generation of orphans.

THE BIRTH OF THE ORPHAN SPIRIT

One of the primary assignments of those who are of the Order of Melchizedek is to join the heavenly Father in His quest to destroy and overturn the orphan spirit that has tormented God's creation for untold generations. In order to do this we must understand the genesis (the root) of the orphan spirit. The Bible tells us that angels are called the "sons of God" by virtue of the fact that God created them. Said simply, God is the Father of the angelic order. The angels are the first sons of God, even though they were not created in the image of God, like humans were. They were, however, created in the likeness of God. Lucifer, one of heaven's most glamorous angels, was one of those "sons of God."

> Now there was a day when the sons of God [angels] came to present themselves before the LORD, and Satan came also among them (Job 1:6 KJV).

The Bible tells us that this anointed cherubim angel (Satan) became filled with the desire to break away from the Father's family and do his own thing. He managed to convince one third of the "sons of God" (angels) to break away from the Father's family and the business of the Kingdom. These rebellious angels were banished from the Father's presence forever. They collectively became the first "orphan spirits." Wherever these orphan spirits show up, relationships and family institutions begin to disintegrate. When Lucifer (the chief orphan spirit) showed up in the Garden of Eden it was with the diabolical intent of deceiving

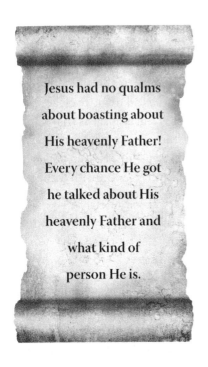

Jesus had no qualms about boasting about His heavenly Father! Every chance He got he talked about His heavenly Father and what kind of person He is.

the earthly sons of God (Adam and Eve) to break away from the heavenly Father's family and the business of the Kingdom.

Now the serpent was more subtil than any beast of the field which the LORD God had made. And he said unto the woman, Yea hath God said, Ye shall not eat of every tree in the garden? (Genesis 3:1 KJV)

Against God's better judgment, Adam and Eve gave heed to the devil (the principal orphan spirit) and the rest is history. They broke away from the Father's family and were expelled from their exalted positions as Kingdom ambassadors in the business of the Kingdom. Since then, humankind has been terrorized by the destructive power of the orphan spirit in the matrix of interpersonal relationships.

THE SYMPTOMS OF AN ORPHAN SPIRIT

A father of the fatherless, and a judge of the widows, is God in his holy habitation. God setteth the solitary in families: he bringeth out those which are bound with chains: but the rebellious dwell in a dry land (Psalm 68:5-6 KJV).

The following is a summary list of some of the symptoms of an orphan spirit:

- compulsive drive to succeed at all costs
- compulsive eating disorders
- obsession with self
- inaccurate perception of the value of self and of others
- compulsive sex drive at the expense of others

- insecurity, usually accompanied by a desire to control others

- lingering depression

- fear of intimacy

- inability to handle rejection properly

- emotional attachment disorders

- unhealthy view of father or authority figures, especially the heavenly Father

- unrelenting critical spirit

- uncontrollable outbursts of rage and violence

This list is by no means exhaustive but it does display the importance of understanding Christ's Order of Melchizedek priesthood. The Order of Melchizedek will introduce the Church to one of the most powerful fathering dimensions known to man. Melchizedek's priesthood fathered Abram into a living covenant with God until he was transformed internally. Melchizedek's priesthood fathered "Abram" into "Abraham." Men and women of God who have priestly or marketplace ministries that are patterned after the Order of Melchizedek take the issue of fathering the next generation very seriously. They are not satisfied with simply being popular, silver-tongued preachers or business leaders. They want to be known as "fathers" or "mothers" in the Kingdom.

THE HARD CHOICE:
EXALTED FATHER OR FATHER OF MANY NATIONS

Before Melchizedek's priesthood intercepted "Abraham" he was known simply as "Abram." The name "Abram" means "exalted father." Since names foreshadowed the inherent nature and character of a person in ancient biblical times, the Abram who was intercepted by Melchizedek's priesthood was all about himself. The name suggests that everything that he had done up to that point was defined primarily by how it benefited him rather than how it affected the second generation of sons and daughters in the Kingdom.

One of life's biggest tragedies is that the Body of Christ is full of "exalted fathers." The ministry of these exalted fathers largely revolves around their personal gift and charisma. The ministry of many of these exalted fathers in the Body of Christ will never grow beyond their generation. Every person who attends their church is seen as a "potential financial partner" instead of a spiritual son or daughter in need of an "inheritance" that only fathers and mothers in the Kingdom can bequeath. For the most part, these exalted fathers are leaders of great churches or corporations, patronized by hundreds and thousands of born-again spiritual orphans in desperate need of a true father or mother in the Kingdom. Instead what many of these desperate spiritual orphans get Sunday after Sunday in some churches is a silver-tongued preacher who can mesmerize the crowd but has no heart for the messy work of true spiritual parenting.

Some time later, the LORD spoke to Abram in a vision and said to him, "Do not be afraid, Abram, for I will protect you, and your reward will be great." But Abram replied, "O Sovereign Lord, what good are all your blessings when I don't even have a son? Since you've given me no children, Eliezer of Damascus, a servant in my household, will inherit all my wealth. You have given me no descendants of my own, so one of my servants will be my heir." Then the LORD said to him, "No, your servant will not be your heir, for you will have a son of your own who will be your heir." Then the LORD took Abram outside and said to him, "Look up into the sky and count the stars if you can. That's how many descendants you will have!" (Genesis 15:1-5)

One of the biggest tragedies is that the Body of Christ is full of "exalted fathers." The ministry of these exalted fathers largely revolves around their personal gift and charisma.

Immediately after encountering the power of Melchizedek's priesthood Abram's name was changed to Abraham which means "father of many nations." Abram went through a radical change of heart. He discovered that internally he had gone through a holy and radical spiritual reconfiguration. God had surgically removed the heart of an "exalted father" and replaced it with the heart of a "father of many nations." His new heart mirrored the heart of a true and selfless spiritual father. The self-absorbed, self-serving and self-centered heart of an exalted father had been supernaturally annihilated! He knew that things would never be as they once were. *It is my deepest prayer that the Holy Spirit will use the words of this book to surgically transform every exalted father in the Body of Christ into a father of many nations.* When these "exalted fathers" in the Body of Christ become "Abrahams" the spiritual dynamics of the entire Body of Christ will shift dramatically and every orphan spirit will be driven out of the lives of Kingdom citizens.

"Son what was the first prayer that Abraham prayed after being intercepted by Melchizedek's priesthood?" the Lord asked me. I did not know. The Holy Spirit then took me to Genesis 15:1-5 and suddenly I saw it. For the first time in Abram's journey with God, he made a passionate cry to God for a son (the second generation). "Son whenever a person has truly been changed by My Spirit, the change in their heart always shows up in how they pray," the Holy Spirit said to me. The "fathering dimension" in Melchizedek's priesthood had lodged itself in Abraham's heart. He was no longer interested in being the "exalted father" he desperately wanted to become the "father of many nations (sons)." Translated into today's language, here is the essence of Abraham's prayer. "Lord, all the riches and fame that you have given me will mean nothing in the end if I do not have sons and daughters who can carry on my legacy and continue the business of the Kingdom." How many exalted fathers in the Body of Christ are going to lose everything that they have worked for in the economy of the Kingdom if they do not become "fathers of many nations" before the Lord retires them?

> *"If you had really known me, you would know who my Father is. From now on, you do know him and have seen him!" Philip said, "Lord, show us the Father, and we will be satisfied." Jesus replied, "Have I been with you all this time, Philip, and yet you still don't know who I am? Anyone who has seen me has seen the Father! So why are you asking me to show him to you?"* (John 14:7-9)

How many spiritual leaders in the Body of Christ can truly fit in the shoes of John 14:7-9? Jesus Christ who is our eternal Melchizedek told His disciples that He was the physical embodiment of the heavenly Father. The genuine life-changing love and affection that was oozing out of Him towards them was how

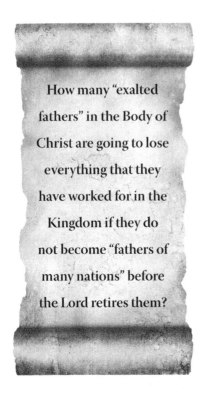

How many "exalted fathers" in the Body of Christ are going to lose everything that they have worked for in the Kingdom if they do not become "fathers of many nations" before the Lord retires them?

the heavenly Father felt about His earthly sons and daughters! "If you have known and seen me, you have known and seen My Father," Jesus told His disciples! To which Philip quickly responded, "Lord show us the Father!"

Then the Holy Spirit said to me, "Son there is a generation of Philips in the Body of Christ, who are crying for God's leaders to show them the Father!" This generation of sons and daughters has heard every sermon there is to hear and yet their hearts are still emotionally empty. *This is because the greatest cry of every* generation since the fall of Adam is not for more spell-binding sermons; it is for "fathering!" Melchizedek's priesthood specializes in releasing the "fathering spirit" that every generation desperately needs. This is why Melchizedek's priesthood is currently intercepting "exalted fathers" (Abrams) all over the world to become divine solutions to this ageless need for fathering in our generation, both in the Church and in the marketplace.

John 14:7-9 and 1 Corinthians 4:15 should quickly dispel the arguments of those who say that born again believers do not need spiritual fathers or mothers because they already have a relationship with the heavenly Father. Many of the proponents of this belief system will take offence to my usage of the term "spiritual orphans" in describing many members of the Body of Christ. My usage of this expression is not meant to imply that born again believers have been abandoned by the heavenly Father. The heavenly Father is a loving and caring Father who will never abandon His children. But there has been gross abandonment of sons and daughters of the Kingdom, by men and women that the heavenly Father appointed to represent Him physically on the earthly plane. This gross lack of fathering by spiritual leaders so appointed has become the feeding ground of orphan spirits within the Church.

THE CURSE OF FATHERLESSNESS: MALACHI 4:6

Malachi 4:6 tells us that the primary intent of God is to intercept the "orphan spirit" over our generation, and replace it with a "fathering spirit" so that the curse of fatherlessness would not destroy the land. This passage shows us that the greatest threat to the earth is not global warming but an unrestrained orphan spirit. Imagine an orphaned man as the head of a family unit, let alone the president of a nation. How many women have been emotionally traumatized and scarred for life because they married a man with an orphan spirit who was emotionally retarded?

Consider that Adolf Hitler's father died in 1903 when Adolf was 14 years old. His mother died four years later when Adolf Hitler was 18 years old. Does this surprise us that this orphan grew up to become one of the most dangerous human beings in history? Millions died worldwide, especially Jews, before this "spiritual orphan" committed suicide.

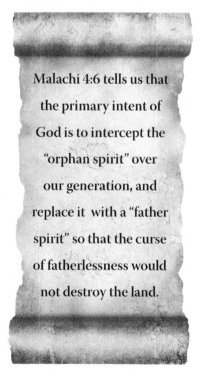

On June 25, 2009, I was on a preaching engagement in Bloomfield, Connecticut, when I received a call that sent shivers of sorrow through my spine. The call was from my dear friend, Dr. GE Bradshaw, who said, "Dr Myles, have you heard? Michael Jackson just died!" I could hardly believe my ears. I grew up listening to Michael Jackson and the Jackson Five. When the autopsy of the death of this mega icon was carried out, it was not the medical autopsy that moved me; it was the historical autopsy of his death that broke my heart. For all of his musical genius, Michael Jackson was a highly driven, self-made orphan who carried deep-seated "father pain" that he tried to medicate with prescription drugs. In all of his deeply personal interviews, he constantly went back to the sorrow of a lost childhood. When I

Malachi 4:6 tells us that the primary intent of God is to intercept the "orphan spirit" over our generation, and replace it with a "father spirit" so that the curse of fatherlessness would not destroy the land.

looked into his eyes as he bared his soul to Oprah, I saw the silent scream of an orphaned child desperate for the unconditional love and acceptance of a true father. Michael died without breaking free of the orphan spirit, but this does not have to be the case for many of the spiritual orphans who are sitting in the pews of our churches Sunday after Sunday!

THE ORDER OF MELCHIZEDEK AND THE FATHERING SPIRIT

For even if you had ten thousand others to teach you about Christ, you have only one spiritual father. For I became your father in Christ Jesus when I preached the Good News to you (1 Corinthians 4:15).

Perhaps no other New Testament apostle understood Christ's Order of Melchizedek priesthood like the apostle Paul. Paul knew that the Order of Melchizedek is a powerful fathering dimension. In First Corinthians 4:15, Saint Paul makes it clear that one true spiritual father is more valuable than ten thousand teachers in Christ. This is a deeply profound statement coming from the mouth of one of the most profound teachers of the Word in human history. Paul was a great teacher to the Gentiles and yet he knew that his great apostolic teaching was no match for a true "fathering spirit."

Like Jesus, Paul knew that all the great teaching in the world could never replace the need for true spiritual and natural fathering to a generation of orphans. It is not the lack of teaching that is destroying the world; it is the lack of fathering. Financial markets and entire communities are imploding because they are being led by men or women who are controlled by unhealed "father pain." Since the Order of Melchizedek is an agency of supernatural interception, God wants to intercept and reverse the devastation caused by the orphan spirit by releasing an unstoppable

> Saint Paul makes it clear that one true spiritual father is more valuable than ten thousand teachers in Christ.

fathering spirit in the earth. This supernatural infusion of the fathering spirit is especially needed in the marketplace. It is desperately needed in the corridors of human government and in the boardrooms of large corporations, whose decisions affect the destinies of millions of people worldwide.

God wants to raise apostolic men and women in the global Church and in the marketplace who will take responsibility for fathering this generation of orphans into the Father's Kingdom. These mature fathering type of ministers will not be afraid to break bread and wine with this generation of orphans. These mature ministers will also not be afraid to stand on behalf of Christ between the king of Sodom and their sons and daughters in the Kingdom. Like Jesus, these mature ministers will not be afraid to show their own scars to every doubting and wavering Thomas in the Kingdom, if they know that such an act will bring healing to their sons and daughters in the Kingdom.

PRAYING LIKE A SON

When you pray, don't be like the hypocrites who love to pray publicly on street corners and in the synagogues where everyone can see them. I tell you the truth, that is all the reward they will ever get. But when you pray, go away by yourself, shut the door behind you, and pray to your Father in private. Then your Father, who sees everything, will reward you. When you pray, don't babble on and on as people of other religions do. They think their prayers are answered merely by repeating their words again and again. Don't be like them, for your Father knows exactly what you need even before you ask him! Pray like this: Our Father in heaven, may your name be kept holy (Matthew 6:5-9).

One of the most potent spiritual weapons for restraining demonic powers and communicating with God is prayer. Prayer is also one of the most critical elements for living under Christ's Order of Melchizedek priesthood. But like everything else that the orphan spirit touches, prayer itself has become one of the greatest casualties of the orphan spirit. When Jesus Christ prayed, He prayed like a Son. His praying was defined by His relationship with the Father and energized by the knowledge of His Father's unconditional love.

But when many of us pray, we pray with the mentality of an orphan. Men and women who are bound by an orphan spirit use prayer as leverage to earn God's attention and hopefully secure His love. When Christ arrived on the scene, He was greeted by the hypocritical praying of the Pharisees and Sadducees who were using prayer to showcase their perceived sense of importance. They would stand on public corners and then pray prayers that were written by some of the best speech writers in Israel. But their orphaned prayers lacked authenticity and spiritual power. Jesus warned His disciples against such methods of praying. He knew that such praying was driven by an orphan spirit.

Thankfully Jesus went further in His teaching on prayer and showed His disciples how to pray to the Father under His new order of priesthood. He showed them that praying under the New Testament Order of Melchizedek priesthood is centered on knowing the Father, the Father's will, and the Father's Kingdom. Jesus showed them that prayer under the Order of Melchizedek is of the highest order and governmental in its ultimate expression. It is the kind of prayer that causes the Kingdom of God to become an established entity on the earth. But this kind of militant, governmental prayer can never be prayed by people who approach the heavenly Father with the mentality of an orphan.

THE IMAGE OF A LOVING FATHER

*For the **Father** loves the Son and shows him everything he is doing. In fact, the **Father** will show him how to do even greater works than healing this man. Then you will truly be astonished* (John 5:20).

One of the greatest desires of the human spirit is the desire to experience the unconditional love and acceptance of a true father, especially our heavenly Father. The devil also knows this important fact, so he has employed many evil spirits with diabolical assignments to disrupt and distort the relationship between natural fathers and their offspring. In so doing, the devil has managed to transpose the negative feelings and perceptions that this generation of orphans has about their natural fathers onto the Father God.

This explains why millions of people in our world struggle with accepting the concept of a loving heavenly Father. The devil has managed to convince many people that God is like their natural father who walked out on them. They think that He has no desire to be bothered with them. The image of a loving heavenly Father is a heavy burden to bear in the mind fractured by an orphan spirit. But Jesus Christ made it adamantly clear that His new order of priesthood would heal and repair the distorted view of this generation of orphans concerning the heavenly Father.

> God never buys into our egoistical nature. God is a God of purpose, and His purpose never bows down to service our ego or our greed.

Preachers of the gospel (in the church and in the marketplace) who do not want to be bothered with the responsibility of fathering this generation are not operating under Christ's Order of Melchizedek priesthood. It is my deepest prayer that this book will find its way into the hands of men and women of God who will take personal responsibility for fathering and mothering this generation of orphans.

THE FATHER'S KINGDOM

*Then the righteous will shine like the sun in their **Father's** Kingdom. Anyone with ears to hear should listen and understand!* (Matthew 13:43).

In the first chapter of this book, I clearly defined the Order of Melchizedek. I will quickly restate that definition here. *The Order of Melchizedek is an eternal spiritual order of kings and priests who have both covenantal and custodial rights to advance and teach the gospel of the Kingdom until the kingdoms of this world have become the Kingdoms of God and of His Christ.* The most exciting aspect about advancing the gospel of the Kingdom has to do with the fact that the Kingdom we are advancing is our Father's Kingdom. If we think that we are called to advance the Kingdom of God we may end up doing it religiously but if we realize that we are called to advance our Father's Kingdom, it changes the spiritual and internal dynamics of how we do it. Even the way we give ourselves and our resources to the Kingdom will also change dramatically. This is why it is impossible to be an effective member of Christ's New Testament Order of Melchizedek priesthood without knowing our heavenly Father intimately.

CHRIST'S PERSPECTIVE ON ETERNAL LIFE

These words spake Jesus, and lifted up his eyes to heaven, and said, Father, the hour is come; glorify thy Son, that thy Son also may glorify thee: As thou hast given him power over all flesh, that he should give eternal life to as many as thou hast given him. And this is life eternal, that they might know thee the only true God, and Jesus Christ, whom thou hast sent (John 17:1-3 KJV).

When I got saved, I was told by my Pentecostal pastor at the time that I now had eternal life. "What is eternal life?" I asked. "It is life without end," came the reply. But after I became a student of the Bible, it dawned on me that there had to be something more to eternal life than simply "life without end." I also discovered that even people in hell are going to live forever. Then one day I stumbled upon John 17:1-3. I came face-to-face with how Christ defined eternal life. To my surprise Jesus Christ did not define eternal life in the terms of "timelessness." In Christ's perspective, eternal life is knowing the Father (God) and Jesus Christ (the Son) whom He (the Father) sent intimately. So under Christ's New Testament Order of Melchizedek priesthood, our approach to eternal life and eternity will be redefined in the context of our dynamic relationship with our heavenly Father, who loved us so much that He was willing to sacrifice His only Son to redeem us to Himself.

JOSEPH, PHARAOH, AND THE EGYPTIAN MARKETPLACE

In recent years there has been a lot of talk in the global Church about the "Joseph anointing." I have met several godly business men and women who believe that God has called them to be a "Joseph to their generation." This is truly exciting, because Joseph is a biblical prototype of how a Kingdom business person operates in the marketplace. Unfortunately many preachers and business persons who are excited about the return of the Joseph anointing to the Church and the marketplace, do not fully understand who Joseph really was.

To understand who Joseph was in the scope of God's Kingdom economy, we must ask ourselves several key questions. These questions are answered in great detail in my book, *The Joseph Project: God the Father in the Marketplace.* But here I will list some of the inclusive questions:

- What priestly Order was Joseph operating under when he was in Egypt?
- Why did God give Joseph incredible favor with Pharaoh?
- What position did Joseph hold in Egypt?
- Why did God give Joseph such massive global influence?
- Why is God raising a "Corporate Joseph" in the earth today?

To explain who Joseph was and the intricate connection between the Order of Melchizedek and the Fathering Dimension, I will answer these probing questions.

What Priestly Order Was Joseph Operating Under when He Was in Egypt?

Without a doubt, Joseph was operating under the Order of Melchizedek priesthood when he was stationed in Egypt. This is why Joseph could flow seamlessly in the priestly and marketplace (kingly) anointing. Joseph was as comfortable interpreting a prophetic dream as he was at interpreting a business plan. (See Genesis 41:25-33.) Pharaoh saw this uncanny ability in Joseph and quickly promoted him.

But the Bible also tells us that God testified that He knew that Abraham was able to command his sons to walk in the revelation that God had given him during his spiritual excursion. (Please read Genesis 18:17-19.) Joseph knew that he was operating under the highest priestly order in the entire universe. This is why he was not intimidated to stand in front of Pharaoh, who was treated like a god in Egypt. Marketplace ministers who feel like they are called to be "Josephs" to this generation would be well-advised to understand the Order of

Melchizedek if they really desire to become like Joseph of old. Many of the so-called Christian business men and women are quickly intimidated when they stand in front of renowned movers and shakers of this fallen world! This is why they become easy preys for the king of Sodom (the devil).

WHY DID GOD GIVE JOSEPH INCREDIBLE FAVOR WITH PHARAOH?

This second question underscores the most misunderstood aspect of Joseph's life. This misunderstanding has produced spiritual casualties among many so-called Christian or Kingdom business men and women. They are preachers who teach that God gave Joseph favor with Pharaoh so that Joseph could profit from the economy of Egypt. They conclude that without the favor that God gave him with Pharaoh, Joseph would never have become a powerful and rich man in Egypt. Regrettably, whenever our hearts have not yet been delivered from greed every revelation that God gives to us is quickly reduced to dollars and cents. This is why the concept of Joseph having favor with Pharaoh for the purpose of exacting profit appeals to many of the so-called Christian business men and women.

Armed with this distorted view of Joseph, many marketplace ministers enter the marketplace with a driving passion to discover their "Pharaoh" and obtain their perceived "share of favor" so that they can profit financially from such relationships. Once they become rich after profiting, and sometimes pocketing millions of dollars from their network of relationships in the marketplace, these so-called Christian business men and women quickly conclude that they are walking in the Joseph anointing. But spiritually they leave the marketplace pretty much unchanged.

Turning Joseph into a rich or powerful person in Egypt was the last thing that God had in mind. God never buys into our egotistical nature. God is a God of purpose and His purpose never bows down to service our ego or our greed. There was a much higher purpose for the favor that God gave Joseph in Pharaoh's eyes. The money and power that Joseph ended up with in Egypt was simply a byproduct of "fulfilling a much higher purpose." It behooves us to discern this higher purpose.

WHAT POSITION DID JOSEPH HOLD IN EGYPT?

To discern and understand this higher purpose that compelled God to place Joseph in one of the loftiest positions in Egypt, we must first answer the question, "What position did Joseph hold in Egypt?" The answer to this question lies at the heart of understanding who Joseph really was before God. When many of those who call themselves "Josephs," including those who teach on the subject, are asked this question, they quickly refer to Genesis 41:40-41. This passage reads as follows:

> *Thou shalt be over my house, and according unto thy word shall all my people be ruled: only in the throne will I be greater than thou. And Pharaoh said unto Joseph, See, I have set thee over all the land of Egypt* (Genesis 41:40-41 KJV).

"Joseph was the second most powerful person in Egypt," I have heard many say after I asked them the question. But was Joseph really the second in command in Egypt? It is not enough to know what position a person holds in the realms of men. To truly discern the spiritual stature that God has given a man or woman in the Kingdom, we need to hear what God says about them. Ultimately, who people are to God trumps whatever title or rank they hold in the natural. In the natural order of things, Joseph was second in command in the land of Egypt—or was he? Did Joseph believe that he was second in command in the land of Egypt, or did God show him his actual position in Egypt in light of who he was in the Kingdom? Like the old folks used to say, let the holy Book speak for itself.

> *And God sent me before you to preserve you a posterity in the earth, and to save your lives by a great deliverance. So now it was not you that sent me hither, but God: and he hath made me a father to Pharaoh, and lord of all his house, and a ruler throughout all the land of Egypt* (Genesis 45:7-8 KJV).

When Joseph revealed himself to his brothers, he told them the position that God had given him in Egypt. When you discover what God told Joseph, you will instantly become overwhelmed by the awesome position that God gave him in Egypt. Joseph tells his brothers that "God has made me a father to Pharaoh!" Wow! Are you catching this? Joseph was not second in command in Egypt; he was *the* most powerful man in all of Egypt—powerful enough to spiritually father Pharaoh and his entire senate!

Suddenly everything becomes crystal clear. We have unmasked God's higher purpose for giving Joseph the favor that he had with Pharaoh. The favor was not given for the purpose of helping Joseph profit financially from the Egyptian economy. The supernatural favor was given to help him provide spiritual fathering into the life of Egypt's greatest orphan—Pharaoh himself! By fathering Pharaoh, Joseph was able to saturate the highest orders of government in Egypt with a fathering spirit from the Kingdom of God. Through this powerful fathering spirit, Joseph was able to effectively father every system of industry in the land of Egypt. Even the banking and real estate laws of Egypt were established by Joseph. Instead of looking for favor for profit, real "Josephs" must look for divine opportunities to father many of the orphans who are in positions of great influence in the marketplace.

Why Did God Give Joseph Such Massive Global Influence?

Now therefore be not grieved, nor angry with yourselves, that ye sold me hither: for God did send me before you to preserve life. For these two years hath the famine been in the land: and yet there are five years, in the which there shall neither be earing nor harvest. And God sent me before you to preserve you a posterity in the earth, and to save your lives by a great deliverance (Genesis 45:5-7 KJV).

We finally get to the point where we can now effectively answer the final piece of this puzzle. Why did God give Joseph such massive global influence? The answer is four fold and deeply profound.

First, God gave Joseph massive global influence because he belonged to the highest spiritual order of priesthood any human being could ever belong to—the Order of Melchizedek. Since he belonged to the loftiest priestly order in all of creation, how could he ever be second in rank to a man (Pharaoh) who was under a demonic system? This is why it is critical that the Body of Christ understand the Order of Melchizedek. When it does, the Church will never ever accept second place to any demonic system, because it is of a higher order of priesthood.

Second, God gave Joseph massive global influence because He could trust him with the level of favor that He had given him. God knew that Joseph was not going to allow his favor with the movers and shakers of Egypt to get to his heart or his head. I wonder how many Kingdom business men and women can pass this test.

Third, God gave Joseph massive global influence because he knew that Joseph had been delivered from greed. God knew that Joseph was not going to allow his desire to profit financially from his high profile connections to take priority over the need to father a generation of orphans in the marketplace. Even though God prospered Joseph financially, the money was simply a byproduct of his willingness to father Pharaoh and his senators. If present day "Josephs" can allow God to circumcise their hearts of the cancer of greed so they can become spiritual fathers to orphans in the marketplace, God will supernaturally give them more influence and money than they had ever imagined possible.

Fourth, God gave Joseph massive global influence because God could trust him completely to use his lofty position to provide for the advancement of the Kingdom. God could trust him not to use his massive influence to exact personal vendettas. Joseph had the power to destroy his brothers who had sold him into slavery, but instead he chose to bless them because he recognized that they were fellow Kingdom citizens. Joseph told his brothers that God had raised him up to "preserve their lives" (Genesis 45:7). Joseph told his brothers that God had raised him up to preserve Abraham's inheritance in the nations of the earth.

Today the Church is being held hostage by orphan millionaires and billionaires who claim to be "Josephs," but are not. True "Josephs" have no desire to use their financial power to manipulate God's leaders in the Kingdom. It is my prayer that all men and women who are called to be "Josephs" would be transformed by this revelation on the Order of Melchizedek.

Why Is God Raising a "Corporate Joseph" in the Earth Today?

Finally, God is raising a "Corporate Joseph" in the earth today, because the spiritual and natural consequences of generations of greed driven decisions are about to come to bear on the economies of many nations. The economies of most nations have been pillaged into bankruptcy by many power brokers in both the boardrooms of mega corporations and in the corridors of government. When the real estate bubble burst in the United States, it exposed just how deeply entrenched this culture of unrestrained greed really was. The sudden collapse of the American real estate market plunged the rest of the country into a deep and long recession. This has created a "famine" in the land that has politicians pointing fingers at each other.

The interconnectedness of the global market to the fledging US economy has sent spasms of financial and economic pain into every economy on earth. This has caused the "famine" caused by the greed of American politicians and business men to spread throughout the nations. Some nations are in complete dire distress. The unemployment rate in Zimbabwe, for instance, stands at a whopping 90%! In the United States, the unemployment rate has reached 10% with no immediate end in sight to the worsening economic recession.

In order to deliver the Body of Christ from being destroyed by the consequences of the greed of worldly men and women, God has established a counter strategy. God's counter strategy to the growing pockets of "famine" in the nations of the world is to raise a "Corporate Joseph" who will preserve the saints and sustain the ongoing work of advancing the Kingdom of God. But this "Corporate Joseph" will not rise in fullness until the global Church rediscovers the Order of Melchizedek.

The Return of the Lost Culture of Honor

He lifts the poor from the dust and the needy from the garbage dump. He sets them among princes, placing them in seats of honor. For all the earth is the LORD's, and he has set the world in order (1 Samuel 2:8).

There is nothing more powerful and life-giving than the bestowment of honor upon those to whom honor is due. The primary Being who deserves

to be honored by all of His creation is God. Honor is one of the most important principles of the Kingdom of God. It is the cornerstone of kingdom living;
without it kingdoms go into a state of decline. No spiritual culture can ever be
referred to as a "Kingdom culture" which does not have this principle of honor
deeply imbedded in it. Honor quickly establishes itself as a divine life-giving
principle whenever it is instituted into any relationship. Marriages, govern-
ments, friendships, covenants, and business relationships flourish whenever
the principle of honor is engrafted into them.

> *Honor your father and your mother, that your days may be long
> upon the land which the LORD your God is giving you* (Exodus
> 20:12 NKJV).

> *Jesus replied, "And why do you break the command of God for
> the sake of your tradition? For God said, 'Honour your father
> and mother' and 'Anyone who curses his father or mother must
> be put to death.' But you say that if a man says to his father or
> mother, 'Whatever help you might otherwise have received from
> me is a gift devoted to God'"* (Matthew 15:3-5 NIV).

   In the synoptic gospels, Jesus Christ went as far as establishing the spiritual
connection between honor and "material prosperity and long life." Jesus made
it very clear that children who honor their parents are guaranteed a long and
prosperous life. Children who did not honor their parents were deserving of
death. Whoa! What an incredible promise from the mouth of God! It is the
reason I honor my natural and spiritual parents. Many of us who live in morally
liberal nations like the United States of America discover that the principle of
honor is foreign to our culture. The culture war between Judaic-Christian values and secular liberalism has taken its toll. We live in a nation where insulting
governing authorities and undermining spiritual leaders is commonplace (in
the church and in the marketplace). It is quite difficult to show people (including Kingdom citizens) the critical importance of the principle of honor to the
survival of any civilization.

   The establishment of the principle of honor in any church or business
will instantly result in raising the productivity and profitability levels of the
organization. In any corporation, the establishment of this principle of honor
can stop the embezzlement of company funds by transforming employees

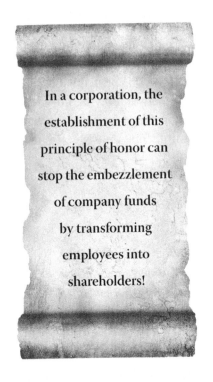

In a corporation, the establishment of this principle of honor can stop the embezzlement of company funds by transforming employees into shareholders!

into shareholders. This principle of honor is so powerful it incites God to honor those who honor Him. But the principle of honor can never flourish in an atmosphere saturated with the orphan spirit. The fathering dimension under the Order of Melchizedek will restore the principle of honor in many strategic Kingdom relationships by displacing the orphan spirit with the Father's love.

Whoso keepeth the fig-tree shall eat the fruit thereof; And he that regardeth his master shall be honored (Proverbs 27:18 ASV).

Abraham lived in a kingdom culture that understood the critical importance of bestowing honor on governing authorities and upon those to whom honor is due. Abraham understood that the quickest way to unleash the favor and blessing of a king (CEO) is to approach him or her from a position of heartfelt honor. *The principle of honor was the governing principle behind Abraham's motivation for tithing into Melchizedek, the King-Priest.* This principle of honor is sadly missing in many relationships in the Body of Christ.

I really believe that God will use this book to restore the principle of honor which is a necessary ingredient in any fathering (mentoring) relationship. What would motivate a rookie basketball or football player to use his signing-bonus-money to build a magnificent home for his single mother? The answer is honor. Honor is truly the greatest and highest motivator for giving to those in authority over us, who have served us well. Under this Order of Melchizedek God will supernaturally restore the broken channels of honor between spiritual parents and their spiritual sons and daughters in the Kingdom!

God bless you!

LIFE APPLICATION SECTION

MEMORY VERSE

And God sent me before you to preserve you a posterity in the earth, and to save your lives by a great deliverance. So now it was not you that sent me hither, but God: and he hath made me a father to Pharaoh, and lord of all his house, and a ruler throughout all the land of Egypt (Genesis 45:7-8 KJV).

REFLECTIONS

What is an orphan spirit?

Write a brief thesis on Malachi 4:5-6.

What position did Joseph hold in Egypt and why?

What is the difference between an "exalted father" and a "father of many nations"?

Briefly describe how the principle of honor can transform the corporate culture of any business organization.

JOURNAL YOUR PERSONAL NOTES ON THIS CHAPTER

CHAPTER SIXTEEN

𝔄 𝔓𝔯𝔦𝔢𝔰𝔱 𝔬𝔫 𝔥𝔦𝔰 𝔗𝔥𝔯𝔬𝔫𝔢

O NE OF THE CRITICAL issues of the last days is how the global church can come into its God-given financial inheritance. One of the mountains that must come into total subjection to allow the church to express its kingly and priestly ministry in its totality is the Mountain of Finance. This mountain must bow to the authority of Christ through His universal Church. The writer of the book Ecclesiastes tells us that money is the answer to all things. Money is the answer to so many things that we need within the realms of men. But the Bible is not silent on this important subject, which is a critical factor in advancing the gospel of the Kingdom. For several decades the church has been bombarded by the messages from well-meaning televangelists who promise it the supernatural wealth transfer which for the most part has not been made manifest in the life of many believers. The proverbial disconnect between the promise, the vision and the provision has caused many believers and ministries to come into a place of frustration and disempowerment. For the longest, I sought the Holy Spirit as to why the Church was failing to enter into the promised supernatural transfer of wealth from the hands of the wicked to the just.

THE PHONE CALL

It was not until the Holy Spirit began to reveal to me the mystery of the Melchizedek priesthood that the answer to the much-anticipated supernatural wealth transfer came into view. The veil over this proverbial promise of wealth transfer began to break when I was ministering in South Carolina for a dear friend, Bishop Larry Jackson. I received a call from a Pastor in Hartford, Connecticut who had read my book on the Order of Melchizedek. He told me that the Holy Spirit told him to tell me that He wanted me to read the sixth chapter of the book of Zechariah and I will discover answers to questions that were lodged in my mind.

What I read in the sixth chapter of Zechariah caused a powder keg of faith and hope to explode inside my spirit. What I discovered in the sixth chapter of the book of Zechariah was a spearhead revelation that took the mystery out of the fulfillment of the promise of the supernatural transfer of wealth. The mystery of the supernatural wealth transfer that the body of Christ has been waiting on was finally revealed. I discovered that the whole process of the supernatural transfer of wealth from the hands of the wicked to the hands of the righteous is predicated on the body of Christ understanding and entering into the Melchizedek priesthood of Jesus Christ.

THE PROPHETIC VISION

And again I lifted up my eyes and saw, and behold, four chariots came out from between two mountains; and the mountains were mountains of firm, immovable bronze. The first chariot had red or bay horses, the second chariot had black horses, The third chariot had white horses, and the fourth chariot had dappled, active, and strong horses. Then I said to the angel who talked with me, What are these, my lord? And the angel answered me, These are the four winds or spirits of the heavens, which go forth from presenting themselves before the Lord of all the earth (Zechariah 6:1-5 Amplified).

In the sixth chapter of the book of Zechariah, the prophet of God is given a very powerful prophetic vision. In this prophetic vision the prophet sees four Chariots of fire coming from between two mountains from the heavenly realms. The first chariot was made up of red horses, the second chariot had black horses, the third chariot had white horses and the fourth Chariot was made up of horses with mixed colors. The prophet was so moved by the prophetic vision that he asked the angel of the Lord who was standing next to him a question. "What are these my Lord?" And the angel answered and said that the four angelic chariots were the four spirits of heaven, who are stationed in the throne room before the Lord of all the earth. In other words these four chariots live and operate out of the of the throne room of the living God. These four angelic companies were the cherubims of glory that live in the presence of the living God that the prophet Isaiah also alludes to in the 6th chapter of the book of Isaiah.

In the year that king Uzziah died I saw also the LORD sitting upon a throne, high and lifted up, and his train filled the temple. Above it stood the seraphims: each one had six wings; with twain he covered his face, and with twain he covered his feet, and with twain he did fly. And one cried unto another, and said, Holy, holy, holy, is the LORD of hosts: the whole earth is full of his glory (Isaiah 6:1-3).

The angel then tells the prophet of the Lord that these companies of high-ranking angelic beings are on a global Kingdom assignment to transfer the wealth of the wicked to the righteous. In Zechariah chapter 6 verse 9 the prophet is instructed by the word of the Lord to receive a gift from the captives who had come out of Babylon. This gift was a monetary gift and the prophet is then instructed by the Lord to take this monetary gift of silver and gold that came out of Babylon and carry it into the house of Josiah the son of Zephaniah. What is of note here is that prophetically speaking Babylon in the Bible always represents the world system and the demonic technologies that run the system thereof. Babylon is the anti-kingdom. We will quickly take a rabbit trail and see what the Apostle John in the apocalypse has to say about the mystery of Babylon.

MYSTERY BABYLON REVEALED

And after these things I saw another angel come down from heaven, having great power; and the earth was lightened with his glory. And he cried mightily with a strong voice, saying, Babylon the great is fallen, is fallen, and is become the habitation of devils, and the hold of every foul spirit, and a cage of

*every unclean and hateful bird. For all nations have drunk of
the wine of the wrath of her fornication, and the kings of the
earth have committed fornication with her, and the merchants
of the earth are waxed rich through the abundance of her deli-
cacies* (Rev 18:1-3).

The eighteenth chapter of the book of Revelation unmasks the mystery of
the demonic structure called Babylon through the apostolic revelation of the
apostle John. Several key things are revealed about this Babylonian system that
governs the nations of the earth today.

1. Babylon is in a fallen spiritual state

2. Babylon is the dwelling place of demons and every foul spirit.

3. All the nations feed into this demonic structure.

4. Babylon is full of corrupt business practices.

5. The Babylonian system is a system that worships wealth and fame.

6. The righteous judgment of God is set against the Babylonian
system, which governs the affairs of many nations.

7. Babylon and the system thereof is set for conquest by the
advancement of the Kingdom of God through citizens of the
Kingdom here on earth.

8. All financial systems and business practices connected to Babylon
is set for total collapse.

9. The most prized assets of the Babylonian financial system is gold
and silver and other precious stones.

10. This demonic Babylonian structure also trades in in the selling of
the bodies and souls of men.

Just by observing the bullet points above about this demonic structure
called Babylon, what the angel of the Lord revealed to the Prophet Zechariah
becomes that much more interesting. We will now go back to the sixth chapter
of the book of Zechariah to finish mining this amazing revelation that contains
the answer to the fulfillment of the promise of the supernatural transfer of
wealth from the hands of the wicked to the hands of the righteous.

CHANGING OF THE GUARDS

The Prophet Zechariah was then instructed by the word of the Lord to receive a gift of gold and silver taken out of Babylon by some of the children of Israel who had been held captive in Babylon. The prophet is then instructed to enter the house of Josiah. Josiah was from the tribe of Levi. Once he was inside the house of Josiah, the prophet is then instructed by God to make a crown of silver and gold. After he created an elaborate crown of gold and silver, the Lord told him to place it on the head of Joshua the son of Jehozadak, the high priest. What is interesting here is that Jehozadak was a Levitical high priest. This means that his son Joshua was also a Levite and next in line for the position of High Priest. What is also interesting prophetically is that the name Joshua is the Hebrew derivative of the name Jesus. So what the prophet of God is being used by the Lord to do is to demonstrate through a prophetic act the coming of a new and higher order of priesthood that would be led by a man by the name of Jesus or Joshua in the Hebrew.

When I saw this, my heart began to palpitate with unrestrained excitement, in anticipation of the explosive revelation about the priesthood of Jesus Christ for the New Testament church. Orthodox Jewish believers would be the first ones to tell you that the tribe of Levi, even though it was a priestly tribe, did not have a royal lineage running through it. But through this one prophetic act that the Prophet Zechariah was divinely instructed to construct, the tribe of Levi was being forewarned that there would soon be a radical change in the nature of the priesthood. Below is what the Lord had the Prophet Zechariah prophesy over Joshua as he laid the crown of gold and silver on his head.

> And say to him, Thus says the Lord of hosts: [You, Joshua] behold (look at, keep in sight, watch) the Man [the Messiah] whose name is the Branch, for He shall grow up in His place and He shall build the [true] temple of the Lord. Yes, [you are building a temple of the Lord, but] it is He Who shall build the [true] temple of the Lord, and He shall bear the honor and glory [as of the only begotten of the Father] and shall sit and rule upon His throne. And He shall be a [a]Priest upon His throne, and the counsel of peace shall be between the two [offices—Priest and King] (Zechariah 6:12-13, Amplified).

The prophet Zechariah prophesies over Joshua the son of Jehozadak, the High Priest. The prophet tells Joshua that there was a man coming in the future whose name would be the "Branch". We know from Scripture that Christ Jesus is the righteous "Branch" and we are the branches. This man called the "Branch" would be the one responsible for building the temple of the Lord. The book of Corinthians makes it very clear that members of the body of Christ are now the temples of the Lord. What is interesting is that the Lord Jesus Christ in the sixteenth chapter of the book of Matthew actually acknowledges that it is His responsibility to build the Church or the Temple of the Lord. So without a shadow of doubt the prophecy of Zechariah the prophet about Joshua is about the coming priesthood of Jesus Christ.

> *And Simon Peter answered and said, Thou art the Christ, the Son of the living God. And Jesus answered and said unto him, Blessed art thou, Simon Barjona: for flesh and blood hath not revealed it unto thee, but my Father which is in heaven. And I say also unto thee, That thou art Peter, and upon this rock I will build my church; and the gates of hell shall not prevail against it* (Matthew 16:16-18).

A Priest With a Throne

> *Now of the things which we have spoken this is the sum: We have such an high priest, who is set on the right hand of the throne of the Majesty in the heavens;* Hebrews 8:1

> *Yes, [you are building a temple of the Lord, but] it is He Who shall build the [true] temple of the Lord, and He shall bear the honor and glory [as of the only begotten of the Father] and shall sit and rule upon His throne. And He shall be a [a]Priest upon His throne, and the counsel of peace shall be between the two [offices—Priest and King].* (Zechariah 6:13, Amplified).

But what is most interesting about the prophecy of the prophet Zechariah is that in the prophecy the prophet mentions a unique characteristic of this new priesthood that was not available to the Levites. This unique characteristic would become the distinguishing factor between the two priestly orders making one higher than the other by the same unique characteristic. This unique characteristic was contained and captured in the elaborate royal crown made of silver and gold that came with the captives from Babylon.

The moment the prophet Zechariah coroneted Joshua by laying the royal crown on his head, Joshua was completely transformed. His priestly ministry changed radically through the coronation. He went from being a mere priest under the Levitical priesthood and instead became a king-priest. The prophet then was instructed by God to set Joshua after the coronation onto a makeshift throne. As soon as Joshua with the royal crown on his head sat on the makeshift throne, the prophet made a startling announcement. *He said that the priestly ministry of the man called the "Branch" would combine the functions of a king to that of a priest.* The king will also be a priest. This is a powerful and dazzling combination. Just remember that this entire prophetic act and demonstration of the coming priesthood of Jesus Christ was happening in front of all the Levitical priests of that era. Through the wisdom of God the Levites were being told that they would soon be replaced by a higher and more powerful priestly order that will combine the functions of a king to that of a priest.

My dear friends, there is no man in human history that has ever been able to fulfill this prophetic picture from the book of Zechariah like the Lord Jesus Christ. From the time when Jesus Christ was born in the manger, magi from the East entered Jerusalem to come and worship the King who will be born. Guided by the rise of a powerful Eastern star, the magi found their way to the baby in swaddling clothes. They came bearing gifts of worth for a great king. God Almighty in his eternal genius used the Magi from the East to coronate the King of the universe when he entered into his own world through the virgin birth.

The prophet Zechariah declares that the man whose name is the "Branch" shall be a priest on His throne. As a priest on His throne he would bear rule on the nations. Since the priest has a throne in this prophetic analogy it follows that the priest is also a King over a kingdom. Only kingdoms have thrones. Since the high priest in this prophetic analogy is a king with a kingdom it follows that Kingdom principles and laws of governance drive the machinery of His priestly order. What is truly exciting here is that the only priestly order in Scripture that allows a king to be a priest, is the order of Melchizedek. Through this one prophetic act, the prophet Zechariah was foreshadowing the return of the Melchizedek priesthood to a greater body of believers than the Levitical priesthood would allow. Under the Levitical priesthood only male members of the tribe of Levi could be admitted into the priesthood. Every other believer in Israel was excluded from the priesthood. But God was about to change the rules of the game. An ancient and more powerful priestly order was coming to our planet that would include a greater body of believers into the priesthood. This ancient priestly order was a priesthood that would integrate the activities of kingdom citizens in the marketplace and in the temple seamlessly.

SUPERNATURAL WEALTH TRANSFER

A good man leaveth an inheritance to his children's children: and the wealth of the sinner is laid up for the just (Proverbs 13:22).

What is of critical importance here, is to notice that the emergence of this new priesthood would involve the plundering of all the gold and silver of the Babylonian financial system by citizens of the kingdom of God. The Angel who spoke to the prophet Zechariah told him that the four companies of high-ranking cherubim angels were given a kingdom assignment to plunder the nations of its gold and silver supply and use it to create royal crowns to coronate the children of the Kingdom. Notice here that the long anticipated supernatural wealth transfer is intricately connected to the coronation of the children of the kingdom as kings and priests unto God. Without this understanding, the church will remain stationed outside the golden gates of its God given spiritual inheritance.

For the most part, many churches function under a Levitical system of worship and ministry. This Levitical mindset that overemphasizes the importance of the temple at the expense of the church engaging the marketplace, thwarts the process of the much needed transition from an institutional local church based priestly ministry to a more broad based kingly and priestly ministry. But this transition must take place before the much-awaited supernatural wealth transfer. Without this divine coronation of the saints as kings and priests this proverbial promise will continue to elude the church's grip. In the institutional church, the majority of the members of the Body of Christ have been relegated to being mere members of the laity. This massive company of potential kings and priests are expected every Sunday to warm the pews of the church while the favored "few" perform for them. This technology of minis-try, which does not value the marketplace mantles of this massive company of Kingdom citizens, does not lend itself to the release of the end-time super-natural wealth transfer.

A BLOOD BOUGHT CORONATION

And from Jesus Christ, who is the faithful witness, and the first begotten of the dead, and the prince of the kings of the earth. Unto him that loved us, and washed us from our sins in his own blood, And hath made us kings and priests unto God and his Father; to him be glory and dominion for ever and ever. Amen (Revelation 1:5-6).

Many Christians around the world reverence the shed blood of Christ, as they should. But for the most part what the shed blood of Christ has pur-chased for the new creation is normally relegated to the cleansing from sin. Even though cleansing from sin is a vital part of the redeeming power of the blood of Jesus Christ, it's not the ultimate objective as to why the blood was shed. Cleansing from sin through the blood of Jesus Christ was merely a means to an end. The end that God sought in having His precious Son shed His blood for us, was to restore mankind to the position of stature in the economy of the Kingdom that Adam and Eve forfeited. It's only the sin consciousness church that fails to enter into all that the shed blood purchased for the new creation.

Recently a friend of mine, Dr. Jesse Bielby shared with me a scripture that I have read many times before but had failed to see its obvious connection to the Melchizedek Priesthood of Jesus Christ. The passage of scripture was Revelation 1:5-6. This passage makes a staggering connection between the shed blood of Jesus Christ and our ability as children of God to function in the earth as kings and priests. According to this passage in the book of Revelation, it is staggering clear that the primary reason why the blood of Christ was shed was to cleanse us from sin, ***so we can be made kings and priests unto God!*** Wow! The blood of Christ was shed to make it possible for sinners who are made righteous to instantly become a kingdom of kings and priests unto God. Stated in another way, the shed blood of Christ PAID for our supernatural cor-onation as kings and priests unto God in the earth realm. This is why I continue to insist that the promised supernatural transfer of wealth from the wicked to the righteous will never take place in its fullness until the Church enters into an accurate understanding of the Melchizedek Priesthood of Jesus Christ.

HEADS CROWNED WITH GOLD AND SILVER

Accept donations and offerings from these [as representatives of the] exiles, from Heldai, from Tobijah, and from Jedaiah, who have come from Babylon; and come the same day and go to the house of Josiah the son of Zephaniah. Yes, take from them silver and gold, and make crowns and set [one] upon the head of Joshua the son of Jehozadak, the high priest (Zechariah 6:10-11, Amplified).

In the sixth Chapter of the book of Zechariah, the angel of the Lord tells the prophet that the four companies of high-ranking cherubims from the throne room of God were on an assignment to crown the children of the Kingdom with crowns made of gold and silver that were taken from the world's Babylonian financial system. My dear friend these high-ranking angelic beings are still patrolling the earth today with an assignment to plunder the nations of their supply of gold and silver for the purpose of crowning the saints. This coronation is the crowning of the children of God, who are being made into kings and priests unto God within the earth realm. But here is a truth of critical importance. This divine crowning of the children of the Kingdom will not take place until the global Church understands and enters into the Order of Melchizedek. The Order of Melchizedek is the only divinely inspired priesthood in the bible that allows the kingly and priestly mantles to function together in one body seamlessly. The Melchizedek who intercepted Abram in the Valley of the Kings in Genesis 14 was a king-priest.

What is also interesting to note here is that the crown that the Melchizedek priesthood of Jesus Christ is bestowing upon the saints, is a crown made of gold and silver. It does not take a rocket scientist to figure out that gold and silver are two of the most precious metals on the global market. While the buying power of the US dollar continues to decline because of massive national deficits and rising inflation, gold and silver are at an all time in value. Those who are fortunate enough to have these two metals in their investment portfolios are smiling their way to the bank. Prophetically speaking a crown of gold and silver around our heads implies that God is going to crown His royal priesthood of believers with "wealth creating ideas." I am convinced that the best technologies (medical and scientific breakthroughs) have not yet been discovered. But those whom God will trust with these new technologies, medical and scientific breakthroughs are going to become multibillionaires, almost overnight. Some of the best sales and marketing ideas have not yet been harvested. The children of the Kingdom who will be given these breakthrough ideas will become major economic power brokers. *Some of the best books and movies have not yet been harvested and those whom the Holy Spirit will entrust with these assets will become extremely rich.* The wealth of the wicked will be transferred to the righteous through these Holy Spirit inspired, technologies, scientific breakthroughs and business ideas. Glory to God, Most High!!!

THE COUNSEL OF PEACE BETWEEN THE TWO OFFICES

Yes, [you are building a temple of the Lord, but] it is He Who shall build the [true] temple of the Lord, and He shall bear the honor and glory [as of the only begotten of the Father] and shall sit and rule upon His throne. And He shall be a [a]Priest upon His throne, and the counsel of peace shall be between the two [offices—Priest and King] (Zechariah 6:13, Amplified).

One of the casualties of the church's Levitical mindset is this sad and unnecessary division between the temple and the marketplace. This unfortunate and proverbial divide between the church and marketplace lies at the root of the rapid moral decline of the United States of America. The voices of secularism have trumpeted the proverbial divide between the church and the state, even though the founding fathers of the United States were men of faith in both private and public life. History books from the 1700s and 1800s on the United States clearly demonstrate that the founding fathers brought their private faith to their public service. No session of Congress would have started out without offering prayer to acknowledge divine providence, in the affairs of the United States government. But in today's culture of misguided political correctness, it's a taboo to bring matters of faith into public life. Consequently, there has been a deep and growing divide between the activities of the temple and that of the marketplace. This divide in American political life has actually become very hostile.

Sadly, most churches have accepted this state of affairs as the norm, because of bad theology that causes the church to become an end in itself. But to transform the culture with the gospel of the Kingdom, the church must enter into the marketplace. *The message and ministry of the church can no longer be quarantined with the four walls of our church buildings. But thank God, through the Melchizedek priesthood of Jesus Christ, the Holy Spirit is going to heal the proverbial divide between the church and the marketplace.* As the global church enters into an accurate understanding of the Melchizedek priesthood of Jesus Christ, which is a kingly and priestly ministry, the proverbial divide between the church and the state will collapse. The prophet Zechariah declares in Zechariah 6:13 that the priestly ministry of the Messiah (Jesus) shall bring the counsel of peace between the two offices of priest and king. The office of the priest allows the body of Christ to function effectively in temple ministry, while the kingly office allows the body of Christ to function effectively in marketplace ministry. It is clear that it has always been God's desire for these two offices, king and priest to function in divine harmony. As the church enters into the order of Melchizedek, the tension between the church and marketplace will come to an end. *The order of Melchizedek will bring about the counsel of peace between the two offices of priest and king.* As the counsel of peace between the offices of king and priest is restored, the church will become the greatest "change agent" in the affairs of nations.

LIFE APPLICATION SECTION

JOURNAL YOUR PERSONAL NOTES ON THIS CHAPTER

Endnotes

PREFACE

[1] From Bishop Tudor Bismark's teaching series on the "The Kingdom." Bishop Tudor Bismark is the founder of Jabula International Ministries.

CHAPTER 1

[1] Dr. Myles Munroe, *Kingdom Principles* (Shippensburg, PA: Destiny Image Publishers, 2006), 15.

[2] Dr. Tim Johns, *Paradigm Shift*, e-mail article.

[3] Encyclopedia on world religions

[4] Ibid.

[5] Munroe, 18-19.

[6] Johns, e-mail article.

CHAPTER 4

[1] J. Lee Grady, "Fire in My Bones: Jay Bakker's Big Blunder," *Charisma Online*, February 2007, accessed October 4, 2010, http://www.fireinmybones.com/columns/011207.html.

CHAPTER 7

[1] John Louis Muratori, *Rich Church Poor Church* (Plainfield, NJ: Gatekeeper Publishing, 2007), 20.

CHAPTER 9

1   Dr. Paula Price, *Eternity's Generals* (Tulsa, OK: Apostolic InterConnect, Inc, 2005), 146-147.

CHAPTER 10

1   Dr. Myles Munroe, *Kingdom Principles*, (Shippersburg, PA: Destiny Image Publishers, 2006) 209-213.

CHAPTER 11

1   T. Austin-Sparks, *The Cross, The Church and the Kingdom*, (Tulsa, OK: Emmanuel Church, 2008) 76.

2   Dr. Myles Munroe, *Kingdom Principles*, (Shippersburg, PA: Destiny Image Publishers, 2006) 31.

CHAPTER 12

1   Muratori, *Rich Church Poor Church*, (Plainfield, NJ: Gatekeeper Publishing, 2007) 20.

2   Ibid, 196.

"Sponsor a Pastor" Book Program

The author has a deep desire to mail FREE copies of this book to pastors and leaders in third world nations! Will you consider making a donation to help get these books into the hands of pastors and their leaders in underdeveloped countries?

To learn more about this program, please e-mail: drmyles@hotmail.com.

Interested in Scheduling Dr. Francis Myles?

The apostolic and prophetic ministry of Dr. Francis Myles is changing lives and transforming churches around the world. His life-changing messages on the Kingdom and the Order of Melchizedek are transforming the spiritual culture of churches and business corporations. As a successful businessman and spiritual mentor to heads of corporations, Dr. Francis Myles has a seasoned word which is helping activate many Kingdom business men and women into their God ordained ambassadorial assignments in the marketplace. If you are interested in having him at your church, business or conference, please e-mail us at the address below:

tdmyles@gmail.com or drmyles@hotmail.com

Are you Interested in using this material in your church's life groups?

If you are interested in incorporating Dr. Francis Myles's book in your church's life group program, please feel free to contact us at:

tdmyles@gmail.com or drmyles@hotmail.com

Are You an End-Time Joseph?

• Do you feel called to something FAR GREATER than what you are currently doing in the marketplace?

• Have you achieved mega personal and business success, and still feel like that there is something missing?

• Has God given you dreams for His Kingdom that are far greater than simply ushering people to their seat or serving on the deacon board in the local church?

• Has God given you dreams for His Kingdom that cannot be contained within the four walls of the church?

• Do you desire to be a great blessing to your church and the world once you come into the inheritance that God has for you in the marketplace?

• Do you desire to connect and network with other Kingdom minded Joseph's across the world who are also awakening to their Kingdom destiny to father the "Movers and Shakers" of this world?

God is raising an end-time company of Josephs across the nations of the world. This is a prophetic company of men and women who are bringing the fathering spirit to the marketplace. It is a "new breed" without greed. It is a network of ordinary men and women who are bringing the power of an extra ordinary God into corporate boardrooms and the corridors of government! It is a Kingdom network of Kingdom minded men and women who are using their God given favor with their "Pharaoh" (business associates) to transform world systems into the Kingdoms of God and of His Christ.

If the above questions describe you and what you are feeling inside, then we encourage you to visit us at www.kingdommarketplacecoalition.com or e-mail: drmyles@hotmail.com. WARNING: Our coalition of Kingdom businessmen and women will only cater to marketplace ministers who respect the role of the local church in their lives. We encourage members of our Kingdom Marketplace Coalition to be faithful members of a local church in the regions where God has planted them!

About the Author

Dr. Francis Myles is the Founder and Chairman of the Board of Kingdom Marketplace Coalition, Inc.

He is Founder and Chairman of the Board of The Joseph Project Global Foundation (Kingdom Philanthropic Society).

Network Websites: www.mykmcportal.com

Dr. Francis Myles is also the Senior Pastor of Breakthrough City Kingdom Embassy. Church website: www.breakthroughcity.com

Other books by the author

The Kingdom of God and the 7 Mountains of Babylon

The LORD'S PRAYER: Spiritual Technology for Manifesting the Kingdom of God on Earth

The Return of the Lost Key: Tithing under the Order of Melchizedek

For audio and MP3 versions of this book, as well as other great titles by Dr. Francis Myles, please visit:

www.FrancisMyles.com.

ABOUT THE UNIVERSITY

The Order of Melchizedek Leadership University is a first class, cutting edge "School of Ministry" with a Vision to educate Kingdom Citizens (Followers of Christ) in understanding "The Gospel of the Kingdom, The King-Priest Leadership Paradigm, Spirit led Marketplace Ministry, Kingdom Theonomics, Christology, Demonology and How to Influence the 7 Mountains of Culture."

University Objectives

- Transform ordinary believers into CMVP's = "Christ's Most Valuable Players."
- To create a Platform for "Total Transformation" for men and women who are called to be "Josephs and Daniels" in the Marketplace
- To "Train and raise" an End-time Dominion minded Company of men and women who have a ministry that is patterned after the "Order of Melchizedek" (King-priest paradigm)
- To Train Pastors who desire to "Introduce their Congregation to the Order of Melchizedek."

Request an Invitation: OMLU is a by "Invitation ONLY" school of ministry to request an invitation please go to www.theomlu.com

Launch a Satellite School: Find out how you can launch a satellite campus of the Order of Melchizedek Leadership University in your City or Church by going to www.theomlu.com

| Home | My Page | Members Page | Directory | Mall | Blog | Chapters | FAQ | Resources | Forum | Events | News |

Members

See More Members

About

Welcome to the Kingdom Marketplace Coalition Community Page. On this part of the Portal we offer a place for all of our members to connect, see our community's groups, businesses, spheres and areas of interest. Take time to connect with others, find groups that share your like interests and make yourself at home!

Click Here Join Now

University Courses

Groups

KMC Affiliate
1 member

Trade Ambassadors
1 member

Kingdom Master's Mind Group #1 Fayetteville AR
1 member

The Order of Melchizedek Alumni Association
1 member

See More Groups

Blog Posts

Welcome to our Community Page!
Congratulations on joining our Tribe and utilizing our powerful Portal. Our blog is one of our key tools in staying in touch with you and keeping you updated on our Tribe and Community.

Make sure you update your Profile so other Tribe members can connect with you.

Enjoy the Portal!

Posted August 25 at 4.40pm

See All Blog Entries

Directory

Looking for recent KMC & AMI workshop...

Helen Elizabeth Couture

An appointment with Ardyss will chang...

Publishing in Excellence

See More Businesses

Latest Activity

Nicole Mobley and Abraham Sahad are now friends.
13 hours ago

Nicole Mobley and William Winship are now friends.
13 hours ago

Photos

Hurry Up! Join the fastest growing faith based social, business, e-commerce and educational Networking Portal in the world today. How would you like to create real wealth $$$$ doing the same things you're doing on…Facebook, Twitter, LinkedIN and MySpace for FREE!

To SIGN UP and launch your own social networking business: visit www.mykmcportal.com

Join thousands of Kingdom Citizens who have already signed up for this God-given portal of blessing and join with other Melchizedeks around the world.

Made in the USA
Monee, IL
22 February 2021

60682676R00223